FRENCH-LANGUAGE ROAD CINEMA

Traditions in World Cinema

edinburghuniversitypress.com/series/tiwc

FRENCH-LANGUAGE ROAD CINEMA

Borders, Diasporas, Migration and 'New Europe'

Michael Gott

EDINBURGH
University Press

Edinburgh University Press is one of the leading university presses in the UK. We publish academic books and journals in our selected subject areas across the humanities and social sciences, combining cutting-edge scholarship with high editorial and production values to produce academic works of lasting importance. For more information visit our website: www.edinburghuniversitypress.com

Edinburgh University Press Ltd
The Tun – Holyrood Road
12 (2f) Jackson's Entry
Edinburgh EH8 8PJ

First published in hardback by Edinburgh University Press 2016

Typeset in 10/12.5 pt Sabon by
Servis Filmsetting Ltd, Stockport, Cheshire
and printed and bound in Great Britain by
CPI Group (UK) Ltd, Croydon CR0 4YY

A CIP record for this book is available from the British Library

ISBN 978 0 7486 9867 7 (hardback)
ISBN 978 1 4744 2601 5 (paperback)
ISBN 978 0 7486 9868 4 (webready PDF)
ISBN 978 1 4744 1397 8 (epub)

CONTENTS

ACKNOWLEDGEMENTS

I would like to thank the staff at Edinburgh University Press, particularly Gillian Leslie and Richard Strachan, for their interest in and support of this project from its early stages. The same appreciation is due to series editors Linda Badley and R. Barton Palmer, who offered invaluable insight and support. Joe Mai, Thérèse Migraine-George, Denis Provencher and Thibaut Schilt all generously offered constructive input on the initial proposal and/or individual chapters. I am grateful for their advice, insights and close readings. The University Research Council and the Charles Phelps Taft Research Center at the University of Cincinnati provided research funding and the Center for Film and Media studies at the University of Cincinnati provided a very helpful course release while I was at a critical stage of writing.

This book is part of a long and winding detour from what began as a single chapter on road movies in my doctoral dissertation at the University of Texas at Austin. As such, it is the product of many conversations with my committee members Hélène Tissières, Dina Sherzer, Michael Johnson and Madhavi Mallapragada. Although *French-language Road Cinema* deals with an entirely different corpus and is its own project, it grew from the seed of that dissertation topic. Another building block for this book was furnished by the collection of similar if not precisely identical scope that I co-edited with Thibaut Schilt, and everything in the following pages is part of an extended dialogue on French-language road cinema and its parameters that I have undertaken with Thibaut and the contributors to that volume. In the meantime, I have refined by thoughts on French-language road cinema in the course of numerous discussions with students in my classes on the topic at the University of Pennsylvania and the University of Cincinnati. Each group brought new perspectives and insights to the films that would make up my corpus. Rebecca Deaton, who was a MA student in one of those courses, later provided editorial assistance. Lastly, Chapter 3 first appeared in modified form in *Transfers: Interdisciplinary Journal of Mobility Studies* and a different iteration of Chapter 4 first made it to print as an article in *Contemporary French Civilization*. The anonymous input of referees for each of those journals and the support of the editors has played no small part in the final shape of my arguments.

ILLUSTRATIONS

TRADITIONS IN WORLD CINEMA

General editors: **Linda Badley and R. Barton Palmer**
Founding editor: **Steven Jay Schneider**

Traditions in World Cinema is a series of textbooks and monographs devoted to the analysis of currently popular and previously underexamined or under-valued film movements from around the globe. Also intended for general inter-est readers, the textbooks in this series offer undergraduate- and graduate-level film students accessible and comprehensive introductions to diverse traditions in world cinema. The monographs open up for advanced academic study more specialised groups of films, including those that require theoretically oriented approaches. Both textbooks and monographs provide thorough examinations of the industrial, cultural, and socio-historical conditions of production and reception.

The flagship textbook for the series includes chapters by noted scholars on traditions of acknowledged importance (the French New Wave, German Expressionism), recent and emergent traditions (New Iranian, post-Cinema Novo), and those whose rightful claim to recognition has yet to be established (the Israeli persecution film, global found footage cinema). Other volumes concentrate on individual national, regional or global cinema traditions. As the introductory chapter to each volume makes clear, the films under discussion form a coherent group on the basis of substantive and relatively transparent, if not always obvious, commonalities. These commonalities may be formal, stylistic or thematic, and the groupings may, although they need not, be popularly identified as genres, cycles or movements (Japanese horror, Chinese martial arts cinema, Italian Neorealism). Indeed, in cases in which a group of films is not already commonly identified as a tradition, one purpose of the volume is to establish its claim to importance and make it visible (East Central European Magical Realist cinema, Palestinian cinema).

Textbooks and monographs include:

- An introduction that clarifies the rationale for the grouping of films under examination
- A concise history of the regional, national, or transnational cinema in question
- A summary of previous published work on the tradition
- Contextual analysis of industrial, cultural and socio-historical conditions of production and reception
- Textual analysis of specific and notable films, with clear and judicious application of relevant film theoretical approaches
- Bibliograph(ies)/filmograph(ies)

Monographs may additionally include:

- Discussion of the dynamics of cross-cultural exchange in light of current research and thinking about cultural imperialism and globalisation, as well as issues of regional/national cinema or political/aesthetic movements (such as new waves, postmodernism, or identity politics)
- Interview(s) with key filmmakers working within the tradition.

INTRODUCTION

Somewhere in the Balkans a father-and-son travelling duo scrutinise a map and argue over the former's preference for back roads and the latter's predilection towards highways. A French man studies a map of Sweden as he exits a ferry in his car; unsure of which route to take he decides to pull over and pick up a young Swedish hitchhiker to help navigate. A Belgian man and his young son arrive in the purported birthplace of the man's father, a hamlet in Ukraine, only to learn from the hand gestures of a local that the place they seek is actually an indeterminate distance down the road. A francophone Belgian woman meets a Flemish man on the road in France; he unsuccessfully attempts to draw a map that will lead her home down a complex series of one-way streets.[1] Getting lost is a virtually unavoidable aspect of cinematic travel. The inevitable failure by travellers to negotiate space – at least on their first attempt – is a necessary narrative ingredient. Voyagers squinting over dishevelled maps or struggling to comprehend directions given by locals are ubiquitous tropes in road movies. Yet within a contemporary European context such wayward travellers are more than a cliché. The voyagers from the aforementioned cases are all literally lost and also, to varying degrees, lost in life. In his influential work *Cartographic Cinema*, which theorises a number of links between mapmaking and cinema, Tom Conley has identified an ontological function in maps within films that encourages consideration of 'where we come from and where we may be going' (2007: 3). In her work on European cinematic mapping, Rosalind Galt observes that 'in the early 1990s, Europe became, as if it had not been so before, a question of space' (2006: 1). Various radical upheavals 'made a collective demand on an idea of Europe as a psychic, cultural, or geopolitical location' (2006: 1). It is increasingly clear that this renegotiation of space is an ongoing process that affects not only how Europeans experience mobility but also the ways in which travellers from beyond the continent experience roads to and through Europe. From tourist to migrant, voyagers are faced with new routes to map and new ways of relating to space and to the people they travel with and encounter along the way.

Road cinema has increasingly become a privileged form of expression for European directors attempting to answer crucial questions about space and to pose ontological queries such as 'where are we?', 'who are we?' and 'where are we going?' Filmmakers have hit the road in order to come to terms with a protean landscape marked by shifting conceptions of identity and citizenship in the wake of the collapse of communism in Eastern Europe and the Soviet Union, European Union (EU) expansion, the Schengen Agreements, population shifts from south to north and east to west, evolving outlooks on sexual citizenship, continuing debates over postcolonial national identity, and a renewed focus on regional identities that often transcend national boundaries. Within these new parameters of contemporary Europe a diverse range of recent road films made since 2000 narrate quests of discovery, returns to origins, economic migrations, and the movement of goods and jobs. French-language productions from France, Belgium and to a smaller degree Switzerland account for dozens of road movies over the past fifteen years. Despite the popularity of the road format and the recent publication of two books in English focusing on French or French-language road movies, dozens of French films remain unexplored.

French-language Road Cinema aims to delineate the unique formal and thematic qualities of the contemporary French-language European road movie, which I argue should be situated in a space between traditional definitions of American and European road iterations. At the same time it explores the ways in which this cinematic form both serves as a barometer for, and contributes to, the process of remapping of French, Belgian and Swiss spaces and identities within the parameters of New Europe. Europe is changing (Ballesteros 2015: 4–7) and road movies furnish an ideal template for the discovery of new outlooks on self and citizenship.

Road movies are presently flourishing in Europe because they articulate a desire to come to terms with updated identity formations. However, as a cinematic format they have been more traditionally associated with the vast open spaces of the United States and other terrains that might be considered more 'uncertain' (Boer 2006). An example of this common conception is provided by Brazilian director Walter Salles, who is well known as the director of road movies such as *Diarios de motocicleta/Motorcycle Diaries* (2004) and *On the Road* (2012), set in South America and the United States, respectively. In an interview for the 2006 documentary *Wanderlust* (Shari Springer Berman and Robert Pulcini), Salles contrasted road movie nations – those whose identities have not yet 'crystallised' – such as Brazil, with nations that he argues do not make road movies, such as Switzerland. In subsequent chapters I will in fact address two road films from Switzerland. More broadly, however, I would like to emphasise that it is no longer accurate to classify road movies as an inherently American endeavour. Nor is the notion, until quite recently very prevalent, that French and European directors do not make road movies.

Steven Cohan and Ina Rae Hark suggested in the introduction to their 1997 collection on the road movie that American road movies 'form part of a potent cultural myth far more powerful than in Europe where all possible routes were mapped before their nation-states consolidated' (1997: 18). It is becoming increasingly clear, however, that Europeans feel the need to (re)map their post-Schengen and post-EU unification spaces and identities, a process that has led to the recent proliferation of road movies blazing new pathways on the 'old continent'. As Wendy Everett points out, 'European cinema is fundamentally concerned with questions of identity, and one fascinating aspect of the current road movie boom is the genre's ability to represent postmodern identity as essentially fluid and migratory' (2009: 166). In her study on diasporic cinema Daniela Berghahn makes a similar point about European road movies' critique of 'hegemonic and territorialised conceptions of identity and belonging' and 'emphasis on borders and border crossings – political, cultural, social and linguistic . . . [which draw] attention to the barriers that a territorialised understanding of nation and national belonging entails' (2013: 66). The popularity of European road movies as observed by Everett and others in recent scholarship (Mazierska and Rascaroli 2006; Archer 2013; Gott and Schilt 2013; Ballesteros 2015) is certainly not limited to French-language cinema industries. A diverse range of recent European road films narrate quests of discovery, returns to origins or economic migrations within the new parameters of contemporary Europe. Examples of this trend include *Pusinky/Dolls* (Karin Babinská, 2007, Czech Republic), *Vivere* (Angelina Maccarone, 2007, Germany/Netherlands), *Handlarz cudów/The Miracle Seller* (Boleslaw Pawica and Jaroslaw Szoda, 2009, Poland), *Avé* (Konstantin Bojanov, 2011, Bulgaria), *Italy: Love It, or Leave It* (Gustav Hofer and Luca Ragazzi, 2011, Germany/Italy), *Tatăl Fantomă/The Phantom Father* (Lucian Georgescu, 2011, Romania), *Rabat* (Victor Ponten and Jim Taihuttu, 2011, Netherlands), *Vivir es fácil con los ojos cerrados/Living Is Easy with Eyes Closed* (David Trueba, 2013, Spain), *The Trip to Italy* (Michael Winterbottom, 2014, UK) and *Xenia* (Panos H. Koutras, 2014, Greece/France/Belgium).[2]

France and Belgium in particular are ideal starting points for an exploration of this European phenomenon because they – sometimes for different reasons – are European microcosms. Each nation exemplifies Wendy Everett's observation that it is impossible 'to drive far in Europe without crossing borders', be they political, linguistic, cultural or social (2009: 168). Belgium has been a 'melting pot' of various cultural and linguistic influences. Factors such as the recognition of French, Dutch and German as official languages; the creation of a federal state in 1993; the presence of large numbers of civil servants from the wider EU; and postcolonial and Jewish diasporas and other post-war migrations have resulted in what film scholar Lieve Spaas terms 'a mosaic of different groups of people' (2000: 8). Belgian filmmakers are fond of citing this diversity as a creative influence. Actor–director Bouli Lanners, for example, has pointed to an instinctively diverse Belgian 'cultural subconscious' behind his work (Van Hoeij 2010: 88). Ursula Meier, who was born in Switzerland and studied film in Brussels, also points to a unique creative environment that inspired her to maintain a base in Belgium after completing her studies. While Belgian road movies are derivative of and tend to celebrate that nation's diversity, for French directors the road format offers the possibility of elaborating flexible, transnational and multicultural alternatives to a monolithic vision of France. Put differently, those who see French identity as 'crystallised' are not likely to make a road movie. France's history of immigration and internal diversity have provided the material for dozens of cinematic journeys to points of family origin abroad in addition to explorations of the borders within that have gained renewed resonance with the renaissance of regional identities within the EU. While the focus of this book is on French and Belgian cinema, films from Switzerland will also be covered. Given the small size of the French-language film industry in that nation, in pure numerical terms its road movie output is limited. Yet despite Salles' comments on the irreconcilability of Swiss outlooks with road movie production, Switzerland's French-language industry has experienced a minor 'boom' of sorts in road cinema. At the forefront of this tendency is director Lionel Baier, who is halfway through a proposed tetralogy of films (see Chapter 4) that venture in the four cardinal directions from Switzerland and in the process help 'align his native Switzerland more visibly and palpably with the geopolitical and sociocultural changes taking place in post-Wall Europe' (Van Heuckelom 2014: 49).

OBJECTIVES AND APPROACHES

This book has three primary aims. The first is to assess the impulse to remap European space through the vantage point of French-language European cinemas. Secondly, I aim to delineate the parameters of the European French-language road format and identify a number of its narrative, technical and formal particularities. The third objective of the project is to expand the discursive parameters of 'French' cinema to encompass a wider realm of inter-related spaces of narrative, film production and reception that I label 'French-language Europe'.

The first goal of *French-language Road Cinema*, to attempt to understand the ways in which contemporary Europe is being remapped, requires an interdisciplinary approach to our topic. In subsequent chapters film analysis is combined with cultural studies approaches because the contemporary French-language road movie's formal characteristics respond to specific cultural, political or economic contexts. Each chapter will analyse key formal characteristics of three to six films through the optic of a particular cultural issue related to cinematic the reshaping of contemporary European space and identities. Étienne Balibar suggests that 'borders' frame our notions of citizenship (2009: 190). My focus will be on how travel narratives reformulate borders within France and between France and bordering francophone nations as well as between those nations and Europe and the postcolonial world. Klaus Eder's distinction between hard and soft borders offers a conceptual starting point for my discussion of cinematic voyages in contemporary Europe. While hard borders are inscribed in law, the soft borders of Europe are 'encoded' in culture and indicate 'the reality of images of what Europe is and who are Europeans and who are not' (2006: 256). Building on Eder's definitions, Laura Rascaroli has argued that films can both represent and produce soft borders by creating 'images of what Europe is and is not' (2013: 23).

My theoretical exploration of borders expands on a fundamental division outlined in the collection that I co-edited with Thibaut Schilt, *Open Roads, Closed Borders: The Contemporary French-language Road Movie* (2013). Exploring an entirely new corpus of films, this project aligns 'positive' road movies with soft borders and, more provisionally, 'negative' road movies with hard borders. Positive films are more closely associated with open roads and by extension mobility, while those on the negative side are primarily concerned with the implications of closed borders and institutionalised restrictions on movement. These categories, while infrequently overlapping within a single narrative, do not represent contradictory impulses. As hard borders lose some of their consequence for European citizens, some of the road movies I address participate in the task of formulating 'soft borders', exploring the significance of national boundaries and cultural porosity in a unified Europe and postcolonial world. Yet as Balibar suggests, European borders are no longer situated at the frontier but have been dispersed within the nations of Europe in places of transit and cities, 'wherever the movement of information, people and things is happening and is controlled' (2004: 1). This shift comes into focus in negative road movies that map the dispersion of hard borders by tracking migrants as they cross Europe or following their restless quest for solid footing in European cities, societies and economies.

While I devote the final chapter of this book to negative films, the prevalence of positive voyages in European road cinema compels us to rethink the common association of (cinematic) border-crossing with dispossession, discomfort and the loss of home due to (im)migration. Elizabeth Ezra and Terry Rowden observe, with Hamid Naficy's concept of 'accented cinema' (2001) in mind, that

> more often than not, transnational cinema's narrative dynamic is generated by a sense of loss. The lingering appeal of notions of cultural authenticity and normative ideas of 'home' prompts filmmakers to explore the ways in which physical mobility across national borders necessarily entails significant emotional conflict and psychological adjustment. (2006: 7)

The case studies in subsequent chapters often problematise this assessment because they generally involve voyages that construct new, more flexible ways of thinking of home. Rather than refuting the assessments of Nacify, Ezra and Rowden, and others, these films provide a generational update that certainly does not exclude depictions of the losses and costs associated with migration. The protagonists in many contemporary films of the positive variety are able to hold positive outlooks on travel precisely because their forebears struggled, while others react against imagined, totalising notions of home and homeland as immutable and immune to or endangered by outside contamination. Building on Rascaroli's theorisation of spaces such as ports, bodies of water and even trucks as 'borderlands' (2013), *French-language Road Cinema* considers the potential of road cinema as a conduit for 'borderland' exchanges in a variety of settings that promote what Balibar terms 'overlapping' spaces and 'multiple citizenship' (2009: 210). This belies the suggestion by Andrew Nestingen, in his reading of Aki Kaurismäki's road cinema, that 'travellers are by definition outsiders in the area through which they travel' (2013: 39). This is arguably not the case in all, or even most, contemporary European road movies, at least if we equate an 'outsider' with a foreigner. Nestingen's point is, however, valid if we apply a wider interpretation of 'outsider'; indeed much of the interest in exploring spaces stems from the novelty the landscapes and cultures represent to the voyaging protagonists. As David Laderman puts it in his influential study of road movies, 'borders' crossed in road movies can be more than official lines drawn to separate spaces but also the 'status quo conventions' of any society (2002: 2).

The second key goal of *French-language Road Cinema* is to delineate the parameters of the European French-language road format and identify a number of its narrative, technical and formal particularities. Continental films often have much in common with what is perceived to be the 'classic' American road template, from the tracking shot to recurring narrative tropes of mapping, the random 'road event' and often parodic references to outlaws. However, French-language directors harness these elements in ways that are adapted to the European social and political context and indeed to distinctively different and varied landscapes found in each nation. The ways in which these films are embedded cinematographically in diverse European landscapes that encompass the industrial and the pastoral, the non-places of circulation and transit, public spaces and cities reveals a great deal about the social and political contexts of each nation. My intent is to take into account the different types of mobilities that have an impact on contemporary Europe (migration, flight, tourism, business and commerce) as well as the typical techniques (see below) and tropes of the road movie. In subsequent chapters I ask what happens when often well-worn road conventions are applied to narratives which engage with key issues facing Europe, from boundless and fluid identity quests within the Schengen zone to less overtly celebratory modes of voyage.

As a protean form with border-hopping inclinations, the French-language road movie is resistant to sweeping categorisations. I will argue that the films analysed do not conform strictly to a particular model or belong to a definable, univocal genre but rather start with a road movie template that is moulded to fit a particular type of exploration of self, space and community. Chapter 1 sketches out a brief history of European road cinema, starting in 1962 and touching on every decade through to the 1990s. Each of the following chapters reveals how the formal and thematic characteristics of the European road movie are adapted to the extremely diverse range of geographic, economic and social displacements that are part and parcel of the contemporary European experience characterised by new possibilities but also, potentially, by disorientation. Beyond the cinematic (notably transnational cinema and road cinema) contexts and theories and political backdrops that inform my readings of road movies, this book is also informed in a variety of ways by mobility studies and cultural geography. In the analysis of particular films I will draw on theorists such as Doreen Massey, John Urry and the French sociologist Jean Viard. Mobility studies not only sheds some light on the social, economic and political forces behind the voyages narrated in the films I consider, it also illuminates issues related to practical production choices and the forms of mobility represented in each film.

Massey's (1994) conception of place as a dynamic, unbounded concept is behind my third and final overarching objective: to expand the discussion beyond 'French' (that is to say 'French national cinema') to a wider realm of inter-related spaces of narrative, production and reception that are best, if imperfectly, classified as 'French-language Europe'. If places are fundamentally 'open' for many theorists of geography and mobility (Moores 2012: 76), so too are contemporary road movies. National cinema, to paraphrase Andrew Higson, suffers from limitations of imagination while 'borders are always leaky and there is a considerable degree of movement across them' (2006: 19). Contemporary European cinematic production is characterised by 'fuzzy and flexible border crossings' (Iordanova 2010: 68–9) that have unmoored French cinema from its national context and cast it out into the 'transnational margins of filmmaking', as Catherine Portuges puts it (2009: 48). For these reasons I have sought to avoid geographic containment in the selection of my corpus. Road cinema is about crossing lines and forging (or at least attempting to forge) connections across boundaries whilst resisting binaries, so I have sought out examples of European French-language road cinema from beyond the Hexagon. Unlike Neal Archer, who intentionally limited his recent study of French road cinema, *The French Road Movie: Space, Mobility, Identity* (2013) – the only previous monograph on the subject – to French productions, I contend that road movies cannot be adequately studied within a purely national context.[3] It is within this context that I hope to redress the scholarly imbalance that has neglected the Belgian cinema, particularly the so-called post-Dardenne generation of directors that has emerged over the past decade (a list that includes Bouli Lanners, Olivier Masset-Depasse, Ursula Meier, Micha Wald, and Dominique Abel and Fiona Gordon, to cite directors that have made what could be classified as road movies or their close relatives). English-language scholars have generally overlooked contemporary Belgian cinema with the notable exception of the Dardenne brothers and Chantal Akerman. However, the work of the above directors and others account for more than twenty francophone Belgian road movies – often, though certainly not exclusively, co-productions with France – from the past ten years The latter figure is significant considering that on average only eleven Francophone feature films are made each year in Belgium as majority productions.

Both as an actor and a director Lanners has been at the forefront of a Belgian road movie 'boom'. In early 2015 he began filming his fourth feature – all of which are road movies – entitled *Les premiers, les derniers*. He has also acted in a number of road films, including *Louise-Michel* (2006) by French directing duo Gustave de Kervern and Benoît Delépine, whose 2004 film *Aaltra* (France/Belgium) is considered in Chapter 3. Lanners also stars in a film released in 2015, Guillaume and Stéphane Malandrin's *Je suis mort mais j'ai des amis* (France/Belgium), which follows a rock band on tour through North America (including Quebec) with the ashes of a deceased bandmate. Yolande Moreau is another Belgian actor–director who has both made and played in multiple road movies, including *Louise-Michel*, *Quand la mer monte* (Moreau and Gilles Porte, 2004, Belgium/France; see Chapter 3) and the recent *Voyage en Chine* (Zoltan Mayer, 2015, France). While Belgian cinema certainly merits consideration in its own right, due to the intersections and 'overlappings' (to borrow from Balibar) of the two national cinema industries evident in the above examples and to increasingly transnational trends in European cinema in general,

Belgian films are best explored in relationship to the French industry. At the same time this book does not relegate to the margins of French cinema studies the cinema of the smaller nations bordering France. Indeed it also holds true that French road films should also be considered in relationship to productions from beyond the boundaries of the Hexagon.

As one might imagine given its limited size, the most common trajectory in Belgian road movies leads beyond the borders of that nation. If Lanners' 2008 road film *Eldorado* (discussed in Chapter 3) is an exception to this, at least in purely narrative terms, in other ways it demonstrates the numerous points of contact and imbrication between the film industries of France and Belgium. To start with, Belgian francophone films take advantage of the much larger French market and many actors and directors such as Lanners and Moreau constantly cross the border. French-language cinema is itself a travelling commodity, with each nation's cinema traversing frontiers and to a large degree reaching common audiences. Indeed parts of *Eldorado* that were set in Belgium were filmed in France, just a few kilometres across an official national border that in many ways – though certainly not all – has lost its significance as a boundary. Yet many Belgian films do retain a certain specificity and this book will assess both the national particularities and transnational affinities in French, Belgian and also Swiss road cinema. French-language European cinema is a multilateral entity; while francophone Belgian films benefit from access to the larger French and global French-language audience, Kervern and Delépine – who have collaborated on five feature films – note a preference for what they describe as a 'Belgian approach' to filmmaking. Whether their films travel through Belgium en route to Finland or crisscross France, they have a distinctive, quirky feel that connects them to many Belgian productions. That such an eccentric approach to cinematic travel is both readily identifiable to some element of the public is demonstrated by the catchphrase used to market Jérôme Le Maire's 2011 Belgian production *Le grand'tour*: 'un very Belge trip'. Following the various threads in these films allows us to consider how the specificity of a small national cinema (Hjort and Petrie 2007) is retained and absorbed within a broader French-language category.

While the border-hopping inclinations of French-language road cinema and the cross-border, European continuity of the themes I address led me to avoid organising chapters solely around national film industries, I made an exception for Belgium. Several factors supported the choice to devote Chapter 3 to the Belgian cinema industry: that nation's prolific road movie output, the aforementioned lack of attention granted so far in English-language scholarship (and indeed in French-language scholarship) to Belgian filmmakers beyond the Dardenne brothers and the Belgian particularity identified by Kervern and Delépine. In keeping with my self-imposed charge to avoid discursive containment, however, I have included a those directors' 2004 film *Aaltra* in the

Belgian category. While it is officially a majority Belgian and minority French co-production, the directors – who also star in the film – are French and widely recognised as such. In short the film demonstrates that the 'Belgian' tag, like that of any national label, conceals a certain amount of ambiguity.

CATEGORISING EUROPEAN FRENCH-LANGUAGE ROAD CINEMA: THE ROAD MOVIE TEMPLATE

When it comes to road cinema, geographic parameters are inevitably flexible, as the above discussion of the intertwined Belgian and French industries' productions demonstrates. Likewise any categorical definitions of the extremely adaptable road movie model are destined to remain somewhat slippery. Nonetheless certain key tenets of European French-language road cinema can be outlined. Scholars have proffered a number of characteristics that typically mark road movies, from cars and tracking shots to wide open spaces and rebellious and (often troubled) masculinity. While the road movie form is protean and malleable, Jason Wood provides a good starting point for a basic categorical definition: 'In archetypal terms, road movies commonly entail the undertaking of a journey by one or more protagonists as they seek out adventures, redemption or escape from the constricting norms of society and its laws' (2007: xv). Road narratives are frequently driven by the 'road event', seemingly unexpected happenings that slow down and/or change the course of the journey. As Timothy Corrigan explains, 'unlike other genres, such as the detective film where characters initiate events, in the road movie events act upon the characters' (Corrigan 1991: 145). As for the makeup of those characters, road movies travel has traditionally been the purview of men (Cohan and Hark 1997: 11; Wood 2007: xix). In keeping with a highly gender-coded notion of the aforementioned 'adventure', those men might be on the road to escape the perceived constraints of domestic space associated with females or perhaps to meet, seduce and ultimately cast aside women encountered en route (Mazierska and Rascaroli 2006: 166–8).

Honing in on geographically based distinctions, David Laderman argues that while the classic American strain of the road movie espouses rebellion against cultural norms, the European variety tends to be concerned with travelling 'into the national culture, tracing the meaning of citizenship as a journey' (2002: 15). Mazierska and Rascaroli forward a similar distinction while maintaining some distance from what they consider oversimplified binaries between European and American road templates: American protagonists 'tend to be outcasts and rebels looking for freedom or escape' whereas European voyagers are more commonly 'ordinary citizens' (2006: 5). I will assert that French-language European road movies represent a hybrid of the two strains. As a group, the films I address follow the European model as defined by Laderman by staging travel 'into culture'. At the same time these films do incorporate elements associated with the American strain of road movie: crossing boundaries and reacting against 'constricting norms', as Wood puts it. I argue that revolt in these movies, however, should not be seen as an attempt to travel outside of culture and society per se, but as symptomatic of a desire to evade certain dominant and restrictive conceptions of national or communitarian culture and identity. Citizenship in contemporary Belgium, France, Switzerland and Europe is reframed as inherently linked to mobility, a stance that rejects fixed, monolithic identity formulations and the closed spaces associated with national identities and conceptions of Fortress Europe. The contemporary European movies explored here are also much more likely to be driven by female protagonists and/or directors than in the traditional road movie model. Thibaut Schilt points out that in contrast to the rebellious, and often white, male protagonist that is the staple of American road cinema, French-language films have often featured characters with diverse national and ethnic origins as well as female travellers. In films such as *Drôle de Félix/The Adventures of Félix* (Olivier Ducastel and Jacques Martineau, 2000, France), *Le grand voyage* (addressed in Chapter 2), *Sans toit ni loi/Vagabond* (Agnès Varda, 1985, France) and *Western* (Manuel Poirier, 1997, France) the 'road leads to an exploration of the travellers' own sense of otherness (be it gender-related, religious, cultural or sexual)' (2007).

I propose a basic technical criterion for the French-language road cinema template that will be tested on the films addressed in the subsequent chapters: the 'travelling shot'. While it might seem self-evident that road movies would require images of movement, this particular criterion is useful for two primary reasons. First, it helps furnish a line of demarcation between films about 'leaving and arriving' and 'true road cinema' (Mazierska and Rascarli 2006: 25). Secondly, an expanded conception of travelling shots allows us to better account for the types of travel commonly seen in European road cinema. The 'travelling shot' has been theorised by David Laderman as a tracking shot intended to convey 'a visceral sense of traveling at a hyper-human, modernized speed' (2002: 15). Travelling shots might be from the driver's or riders' perspective, from a camera mounted on a vehicle looking inside or towards the landscape, mounted on another vehicle or even a helicopter. The many variations on these shots will be considered in the following chapters. First, however, it is worth pausing on the 'modernized speed' element of Laderman's definition, which would seem to limit such shots to motorised vehicles. Timothy Corrigan, in a relatively early piece of scholarship on road movies, argued that they are defined by the engines that propel their voyagers: 'road movies are, by definition, movies about cars, trucks, motorcycles, or some other motoring soul-descendant of the nineteenth-century train' (1991: 144). In a rare scholarly commentary published in French on the subject, Walter Moser suggests that 'images of a vehicle in movement . . . preferably a private automobile' and the accompanying iconography of roadside infrastructure are crucial ingredients of road movies (2008: 21). While automobile travel in particular holds an important place in European road cinema, it is only part of the picture. Archer proposes the neologism 'autopia' to describe the road movie, synthesising 'auto' and Foucault's heterotopia to account for, among other things, a 'retreat behind the cinematic, hermetic space of the automobile's windscreen and dashboard' (2013: 34). Indeed most of Archer's corpus is auto-driven, running counter to the prevalent conception that European road directors generally prefer alternative modes of travel. As Mazierska and Rascaroli put it, the North American model tends to embrace automobile journeys, preferably in a convertible or on a Harley Davidson motorbike, in contrast to the European films that often stage movement by foot or public transport (2006: 5). The other only other book focused on French-language road cinema, *Open Roads, Closed Borders: The Contemporary French-language Road Movie* (Gott and Schilt 2013), considers a roster of films that are much less auto-centric. My project falls somewhere in-between, with approximately two-thirds of the films under consideration involving automotive conveyance to some significant extent. This encompasses different degrees of reliance on vehicles and my analysis will account for different ways of driving – Urry's distinction between 'inhabiting the car' and 'inhabiting the road', for example (2007: 125–6) – and discuss differences between driving in a car and riding in a motor home.

Although my selection of films acknowledges the importance of the automobile to the road movie template, I argue that the typical preference in European road movies for slower modes of conveyance such as walking or public transit demands a new and broader conception of Laderman's travelling shot as a tracking shot that captures at any speed, and depending on the film's positive or negative outlook, either the spirit or the disorientation involved in travel. In subsequent chapters I will analyse travelling shots that track movement in cars but also on foot, by bicycle, in trains and public transport, and by boat. Chapters 1–4 will consider the employment of travelling shots in a variety of films that could be classified as positive. Chapter 5 focuses on the disorientation and lack of vision typically involved in clandestine trajectories, whether towards points in Europe or within metropolitan areas after the initial trek is complete.

Although I will delve further into a number of examples in the following chapters, because the travelling shot is of fundamental importance to the analysis in each chapter I will first attempt to briefly illustrate my point here with a couple of pertinent examples not included in my subsequent case studies. In *Drôle de Félix* the titular protagonist sets off to cross France by foot. While he does at times hitch rides, he prefers back roads and aims to avoid fast trains, clearly the most rapid and efficient way of getting from one side of France to

Figure I.1   The protagonist walks joyfully across France in *Drôle de Félix/The Adventures of Félix* (Olivier Ducastel and Jacques Martineau, 2000).

another. Part way through his trek a sequence of three travelling shots track Félix as he walks joyfully through the French countryside (Figure I.1). The hand-held camera frames him in medium and medium-long shots at an angle that offers a clear vantage point on the verdant terrain that surrounds him. The sequence marks his movement as an act of pleasure; this is not a beleaguered trudge but a merry promenade. As he advances, Félix's pace quickens and he trots and skips to a soundtrack of his own creation (a song he conceived about his voyage to Marseille). With each cut the camera gradually changes perspective to reveal more of the road and the scenery behind him. Although it lacks the variety of perspectives and distances one often sees in auto montages, this sequence fulfils the role that Laderman ascribes to driving montage by sublimating 'travel to an idea or sensibility, in contrast with the linear, destination-oriented concept of travel' (2002: 16).

Another archetypal European travelling montage – in this case assembled from a more varied series of travelling shots – is found in Tony Gatlif's 2004 film *Exils* (France/Japan).[4] This sequence begins as the Algeria-bound protagonists Zano and Naïma hide the keys to their Parisian apartment by sealing them in a stone wall. They then set off to the unmistakable background sounds of unseen cars flying past on what is apparently a busy motorway. The first of numerous travelling montages starts with a high angle, aerial extreme long shot of the couple walking down a road that cuts through green fields. From this silent shot, the film cuts to a series of travelling shots that fuse music and movement. The next take looks upon moving tracks from the perspective of a train driver (Figure I.2), the rhythmic sound of the rails joined with the whishing of the windscreen wipers. The beat of the rails continues as the camera cuts to a close-up of Zano in headphones, bobbing his head rhythmically, and then to a close-up of Naïma's feet propped against the train window. She taps her foot against the glass as we see the beige hues of the Spanish

Figure I.2   One perspective from a particularly European travelling montage in *Exils* (Tony Gatlif, 2004).

countryside race by, still to the sound of train moving over rails. Before cutting to a medium shot of the travellers facing each other while looking out the window, the camera zooms in for a close-up of their music player, propped between them with a cable extending to each person's headphone. During the ensuing medium two-shot, the techno beat they are listening to takes the place of the rhythmic hum of the rails, which it resembles closely. This sequence demonstrates the dual purpose of travelling montages. It both, as Laderman describes, 'sublimates' travel into a process and exhibits a good deal of linear geographic progress; in ninety seconds their odyssey advances from the green fields of central France to the earth-toned olive groves of Andalusia. Both of the above examples represent characteristically more European forms of travelling shots and montages. Each also provides its own version of the 'vigorous music soundtrack' so common in American road films (Laderman 2002: 16). As I plan to demonstrate in later case studies, travelling shots are a fundamental component of road cinema and also a highly versatile element that can be adapted to a number of social and geographic contexts.

The above examples suggest that what Dimitris Eleftheriotis calls 'mobile vision' and 'panoramic perception' (2010: 15–16), crucial ingredients in road cinema, need not be solely the purview of automotive travel. Panoramic perception, which will be discussed in more detail in Chapter 2 for its presence and in Chapter 5 for its relative absence, often plays a key role in the 'knowledge acquisition' that transpires in road narratives (2010: 78). If panoramic perception implies a certain privileged, or at least open and unobstructed, vantage point, 'mobile vision' need not be limited to positive road cinema: 'the dizzying experiences of mobile vision challenge established and traditional certainties as they push travellers out of the stability of home and into unknown and uncertain territories' (2010: 77). Limited mobile vision is a key element in the films that will be addressed in Chapter 5, which considers what negative iterations of travelling shots and montages look like. Often less visually appealing, they are generally limited to dreary points of transit and dark urban passageways, settings representative of the struggles of migrants to reach and find solid footing in Europe.

European and American Road Cinemas: Intertwined Traditions and Mutual Influences

Until relatively recently, the road movie format has primarily been linked in popular imagination and in scholarly literature to the geographic, cultural, political, historical and economic particularities of North America. Writing in 2001 and approaching the topic from a French perspective, Carrie Tarr and Brigitte Rollet note that the road movie is 'generally considered an archetypal American genre' (2001: 228), which they consider 'a relatively rare phenomenon' in France (2001: 229). In *Driving Visions*, published in 2002, Laderman proposes that European road films offer a means of better understanding the American road cinema, for the former seem to be a 'reaction to, or reformulation of, the American genre' (2001: 247). In their edited volume simply entitled *The Road Movie Book* (1997), Cohan and Hark define the object of their study as a 'Hollywood genre that catches peculiarly American dreams, tensions and anxieties, even when imported by the motion picture industries of other nations' (1997: 2).

Such conceptions of the road movie as a 'peculiarly American genre' was widespread before being challenged in more recent scholarship by Mazierska and Rascaroli (2006: 2), Wood (2007), Archer (2013: 10) and Devin Orgeron (2007). For example, Orgeron's book seeks to re-evaluate the previous scholarly tendency to assume the 'inherent *Americanness* of the road movie' (2007: 6; original emphasis). Mazierska and Rascaroli argue that travel and road narratives have been made in Europe since the start of the cinema industry, perhaps even before catching on in Hollywood (2006: 4). In his *100 Road Movies*, which combines a succinct but highly informative introduction to the genre (or subgenre) with carefully selected short case studies, Jason Wood affirms that 'the road movie is by no means an exclusively American domain and has been historically embraced by filmmakers from across the globe' (2007: xix). His earliest European example is Jean Cocteau's *Orphée* (1950), a film that predates the American road films commonly viewed as foundational. As the films addressed in Chapter 1 demonstrate, it is more accurate, then, to see American and European road movies as part of a continuum of shared inspiration.

A handful of examples should suffice to demonstrate the interconnected nature of US and continental road movie currents. Wood supports his assertion on the global nature of road cinema by following a number of interconnected threads and mutual influences. For example, Nicholas Ray's 1948 US production *They Live by Night* (1948) was informed by Italian Neorealism, marking it as 'one of the earliest examples of the European influence on the genre' (2007: xvii). Wood traces the lineage of Greg Araki's 1992 American film *The Living End*, which is produced more than forty years later, back to Godard's 1965 *Pierrot le fou* (2007: xix). Shifting influential directions, Archer points out in his study of French road movies that *Bonnie and Clyde* (Arthur Penn, 1967), a film that Laderman identifies as foundational to the crystallisation of an identifiable US road movie genre in the late 1960s and 1970s (2002: 4, 43) bears strong traces of imprints from Godard and Truffaut (Archer 2013: 13). Despite the fact that he situates road movies within a distinctly American context that relegates European films to a derivative category to be addressed primarily at the end of his book, Laderman's study at times also sketches a more complex and multidirectional conception of generic influences. An example of this is the inclusion of German director Wim Wenders' 1984 film *Paris, Texas* in an earlier chapter on postmodern road movies from the 1980s. For Laderman, however, this film set in California and Texas and written by American playwright Sam Shepard is less an example of a European road movie than a foreign inflection of the American road genre (2002: 142). Laderman draws a number of parallels between Wenders' film and American director Jim Jarmusch's *Stranger than Paradise*, released the same year. The latter film both descends form the '1970s existential road movie' and brings a 'European perspective to the American landscape' (Laderman 2002: 144). Meanwhile an earlier chapter on 1970s existential films draws on Thomas Elsaesser's observation that the films of this era were characterised by numerous 'European qualities' (2002: 85).

On one level, it is tempting to conclude that following all of such strands to find their true 'origins' would be both a complex and ultimately unproductive undertaking. After all, the related question that is of primary concern to the following chapters is what, precisely, is the significance of traditional road movie tropes and iconography – be they American or European – when applied to the contemporary European landscape and political-social context. Yet in order to respond to this query it seems productive to begin with a cursory introduction to the roads already travelled by directors of European road movies. This in turn makes the task of understanding how the road movie format has itself 'travelled' between the two continents a necessary undertaking even if it does not require settling on a precise (and likely elusive) theory of the history of origins and influences. Because the issue of origins has been extensively discussed within the scope of existing scholarship on the European road movies, I will not devote significant attention to this debate. Instead, I will take as a starting point the general theses of Mazierska and Rascaroli, Wood, Orgeron and Archer that the origins are intertwined and mutually influential.

The above outlines of the classification and history of road cinema establish some basic starting points that the subsequent chapters will return to. The origins of road cinema will be central to Chapter 1, which provides an introduction to European road cinema from 1962 through the 1990s. The films addressed, all of which have some connection to France or the French language, are *Il Sorpasso* (Dino Risi, 1962, Italy), *Le corniaud/The Sucker* (Gérard Oury, 1965, France/Italy), *Les petits matins/Hitch-Hike* (Jacqueline Audry, 1962, France), *Im Lauf der Zeit/Kings of the Road* (Wim Wenders, 1977, West Germany), *Leningrad Cowboys Go America* (Aki Kaurismäki, 1989, Finland/Sweden) and *Lisbon Story* (Wim Wenders, 1994, Germany/Portugal).

The following chapters will be more concerned with how the criteria for road cinema laid out above, particularly the travelling shot, are applied to a number of contemporary European contexts. In selecting the corpus of contemporary films, I aimed for films that should be readily available on DVD or video-on-demand (VOD), often although not always with English subtitles. I also sought to avoid movies that were already covered in *Open Roads, Closed Borders* and generally eschewed those already well represented in English-language scholarship. Exceptions to the above ground rules were made in a couple of cases when I thought that a particular film was an ideal fit for this book. Chapter 2 assesses five diverse contemporary films from three different nations that respond to the Europeanisation of economies and identity formulations with a particular eye on how the passages through diverse landscapes are filmed: *Le grand voyage, Rendez-vous à Kiruna* (Anna Novion, 2012, France), *Saint-Jacques . . . la Mecque* (Colline Serreau, 2005, France), *Torpedo* (Matthieu Donck, 2012, Belgium/France) and *La vraie vie est ailleurs* (Frédéric Choffat, 2006, Switzerland). The parameters of Belgian road cinema, an issue already broached above, will be the topic of Chapter 3. In that chapter I consider *Eldorado* (Bouli Lanners, 2008, Belgium/France), *L'iceberg* (Dominique Abel, Fiona Gordon and Bruno Romy, 2005, Belgium), *Quand la mer monte, Les folles aventures de Simon Konianski/Simon Konianski* (Micha Wald, 2008, Belgium/France/Canada) and *Aaltra*. Chapter 4 examines what is likely the most common type of positive road films, the 'return to origins' movie. I begin with a discussion of how mobile and layered outlooks on citizenship fit into the conception of French republicanism and European identity frameworks before moving on to examples from France and Switzerland. *Voyage en Arménie/Armenia* (Robert Guédiguian, 2006, France), *Ten'ja/Testament* (Hassan Legzouli, 2004, France/Morocco) and *Comme des voleurs (à l'est)/Stealth* (Lionel Baier, 2005, Switzerland) furnish the examples. Chapter 5 changes directions to consider the flip side of the European mobility boom. In that chapter I analyse three films whose protagonists are migrants from beyond the EU: *Hope* (Boris Lojkine, 2014, France), *Illégal* (Olivier Masset-Depasse, 2010, Belgium/France/Luxembourg) and *Marussia* (Eva Pervolovici, 2013, France/Russia). In the conclusion I take the question of migrant travel a bit further and ask if migrant films and indeed European anxieties over the issue of migration might lead to the end of the road for ready mobility and by extension the road movie boom.

NOTES

1. The following examples, which will be analysed in greater detail in subsequent chapters are, respectively: *Le grand voyage* (Ismael Ferroukhi, 2004, France/Morocco/Bulgaria/Turkey), *Rendez-vous à Kiruna* (Anna Novion, 2012, France), *Les folles aventures de Simon Konianski/Simon Konianski* (Micha Wald, 2008, Begium/France/Canada) and *Quand la mer monte* (Yolande Moreau and Gilles Porte, 2004, France/Belgium).
2. For more on European road cinema from beyond the French-language sphere, see Rascaroli (2003), Mazierska and Rascaroli (2006), Petek (2010), Georgescu (2012), Gott (2012) and Ward (2012).
3. Archer explains that his choice to focus on French films and to devote limited attention to transnational voyages is derived from the desire to consider the 'possibility of re-configuring space, rather than the relationship between two places (in terms, say, of the "adoptive" nation and the "home")' (2013: 7). Elsewhere he does admit that 'the road movie complicates received or essentialised notions of nation and national cinema' (2013: 13).
4. While both of the films that provided these examples would have fit nicely within my corpus, I set out to avoid any films that were already covered in the 2013 collection I co-edited with Thibaut Schilt, *Open Roads, Closed Borders: The Contemporary French-language Road Movie*. That volume features a chapter on *Drôle de Félix* by Florian Grandena and another on music in Gatlif's oeuvre by Sylvie Blum-Reid. *Drôle de Félix* in particular has already been the focus of numerous scholarly works in English. It is addressed in Archer's *The French Road Movie* (2013) and in articles by Joseph McGonagle (2007b), Thibaut Schilt (2007), and Vinay Swamy (2006).

1. MAPPING THE HYBRID EUROPEAN ROAD: FRENCH CONNECTIONS, EUROPEAN TRADITIONS AND AMERICAN INFLUENCE?

Films covered: *Il Sorpasso* (Dino Risi, 1962, Italy), *Le corniaud/The Sucker* (Gérard Oury, 1965, France/Italy) *Les petits matins/Hitch-Hike* (Jacqueline Audry, 1962, France), *Im Lauf der Zeit/Kings of the Road* (Wim Wenders, 1977, West Germany), *Leningrad Cowboys Go America* (Aki Kaurismäki,1989, Finland/Sweden) and *Lisbon Story* (1994, Germany/Portugal)

Open spaces – perhaps deserts – and boundless horizons. Long roads redolent of burnt rubber and rock music that meet the sky at the horizon and then pursue their trajectories through landscapes peppered with wayside filling stations, scruffy diners and smoke-filled havens for road-weary lorry drivers. Assorted social outcasts, rebels and fugitives wreaking havoc, robbing, scheming and shooting their way through the country, or else fleeing the long arm of the law or evading other crooks. Adventurers in search of a better place. Iconic, high-powered automobiles from the post-war era like those that furnished what Laderman calls the road movie's 'modernist engine' (2002). Men in search of woman as well as escape or adventure and often – although not always – behind the wheel. Flight from the oppression of society, or at least away from the constraints of everyday domestic life and the drudgery of the workplace. For many European viewers, critics and filmmakers alike, road movies invariably evoke such images and sensations. All of the seemingly 'American' elements enumerated above are to be found in the European films analysed in this book. Also evident are a number of more distinctively European elements, spaces, outlooks and characters. This chapter aims to set the stage for an exploration of contemporary French-language European road movies by tracing the inter-woven lines of the tradition in its American and European iterations back to the 1960s, the period during which the template for contemporary road cinema crystallised. In the process it becomes evident that the contours of the road movie tradition sketched out in the above lines are not strictly the product of a direct lineage from seminal American films from the late 1960s such as *Easy Rider* (Dennis Hopper, 1969, USA) or *Bonnie and Clyde* (Arthur Penn, 1967, USA), but the result of complex transnational interactions within European cinemas and between European and American cultures.

I will focus on five examples that span the period from the 1960s to the 1990s, selected to provide background for the subsequent chapters focused on more contemporary productions. While in my choices I have aimed to provide cinematic context that stretches beyond the boundaries of French-speaking Europe – from Finland to France via Germany – for the sake of continuity and in order to limit my corpus I have selected films and directors that share some connection to France or the French language. Three are individual films: *Il Sorpasso* (Dino Risi, 1962, Italy), *Les petits matins/Hitch-Hike* (Jacqueline Audry, 1962, France) and *Le corniaud/The Sucker* (Gérard Oury, 1965, France/Italy). The other two case studies look more broadly at the filmographies of notable road movie directors Aki Kaurismäki, with a focus on *Leningrad Cowboys Go America* (1989, Finland/Sweden) and *Leningrad Cowboys Meet Moses* (1994, Finland/Germany/France), and Wim Wenders, with his films *Lisbon Story* (1994, Germany/Portugal) and *Im Lauf der Zeit/ Kings of the Road* (1977, West Germany) at the centre of attention.

The corpus of any chapter of this sort will unavoidably omit certain films. My primary objective was to select films that seemed to represent the best points of comparison and contrast with subsequent contemporary case studies. Some of those that I chose to address also made the cut because they have yet to receive significant scholarly attention, whether in general or as road movies in particular. Others, from quintessential European road directors, have been included for precisely the opposite reason. Indeed, it seems impossible to discuss contemporary road movies made in Europe without first taking a detour through the work of Wenders and Kaurismäki. Moreover, in keeping with the purview of this book, both directors speak French and have ties to France and the French cinema industry, having set films there or worked in cooperation with French institutions or companies.[1] In addition to the productive and narrative links to the Hexagon, their work has informed and interacted with French-language road cinema, as have the other European productions discussed here. Their films, like the others considered in this chapter, exemplify how the road movie, as Orgeron observes, is the result of a long 'cinematic conversation' between directors whose works have moved back and forth across continents in a process of 'cinematic reference and borrowing' (2007: 76).

Beyond the question of influence and cinematic intertextuality, each of the European films discussed here shares some point of contact with France, be it in the physical itinerary or via the presence of an actor. The French-language films covered, all dating from the formative decade of the 1960s, were selected according to three criteria that will be foundational to the case studies examined in the following chapters. First, these films are notable for their genre-bending and border-crossing inclinations. As I have already noted in the introduction, scholars have pointed out the malleability of the road movie category. On the iconic Criterion Collection's thematic web page devoted to the road films in their library, road movies are defined as a subgenre that 'can be comedies, romances, thrillers, psychological dramas, or broader social commentaries' (Criterion Collection, nd). The corpus of this chapter was chosen to highlight this diversity and generic permeability. However, as I contended in the introduction, I would prefer to think of European road cinema not as a genre or subgenre but as a template or tool kit upon which a variety of approaches can be superimposed. Secondly, all of the films covered in this chapter involve travel by car in some form, although the protagonist in *Les petits matins* sets off on foot and must rely on hitchhiking to traverse France. While this is not necessarily representative of a preference for auto-driven narratives in French-language road films, it does demonstrate that French-language cinema does have its own tradition of automobile road films. This belies a distinction commonly drawn between American and European modes of transit and outlooks in general that the former privilege automobility while the latter more typically opt for public transportation, walking or hitchhiking (Laderman 2002; Mazierska and Rascaroli 2006: 5).[2] Because the majority of films addressed in later chapters involve automobile voyages, car travel is a road cinema norm against which – even in the European context, as I argue – other methods of transit are to be compared. For this and indeed for other reasons I have therefore opted not to consider in this chapter films centred on walking voyages such as Jacques Brel's surrealist fantasy road trip *Le Far-West/Far West* (1973, France/Belgium) or on train travel as is the case in Chantal Akerman's *Les rendez-vous d'Anna/The Meetings of Anna* (1978, France/Belgium/West Germany). As in this chapter, though, subsequent analysis will consider what transpires when travellers turn to other modes of travel in the course of their voyage or when their vehicle serves as a 'home' as much as a mode of transit.

Finally, tracing this transnational current in European road cinema allows us to see that while the mapping impulses discussed in the introduction account for the current boom in European road cinema, border-crossing is in itself certainly not a new cinematic phenomenon. The appeal of transnational travel in road cinema predates 'New Europe'; indeed it is a natural inclination in continental road movies even if all 'possible routes were mapped before their nation-states consolidated' (Cohan and Hark 1997: 18). However, as we shall see in the following examples, borders in pre-Schengen era cinema present roadblocks to full enjoyment of travel and represent calls to law, order and regulation that counter the escapist reflexes of itinerant protagonists. That said, aside from the policing of national frontiers, with the effect of slowing down or at times impeding progress, in the films under consideration here the act of crossing a border represents an opportunity to expand one's horizons and possibilities. Many European road films set in the 1960s can be read as reactions to dramatic economic growth and concomitant expansion of mobility as an economic and social imperative.[3] Mazierska and Rascaroli rightly suggest that the 'open spaces of North America, with their straight, boundless highways and the sense of freedom and opportunity to invent one's life, are in clear contrast with the European reality of a mosaic of nations, cultures, languages and roads' (2006: 5). However the road need not be boundless in the (mythic) American sense to allow for escape from quotidian drudgery, societal constraints, or to otherwise inspire what Tarr and Rollet, in their chapter in *Cinema and the Second Sex* on female-directed French road movies from the 1980s and 1990s, term an 'imaginative space for exploring freedom, friendship and power' (2001: 234). Put differently, while globalisation and European unity opened many new doors for the exploration of complex transnational identities, earlier directors still found the roads to be sufficiently open in both geographic and narratives terms to serve as a conduit for exploration and personal reinvention. These films also chart social and economic transformations, both through their panoramic perception of the spaces traversed (Eleftheriotis 2010: 15–16) and by means of narratives that engage with the particular tensions of the period. In this way they also serve as precursors to contemporary road movies' engagement with globalisation. Road narratives from the 1960s are particularly well-situated to chronicle the most evident fault lines that emerged from the first decades of post-war economic prosperity, expansion and 'Americanisation'. This includes new roads and suburban developments, the newly democratised practices of mobile leisure and holidaymaking and the culture clashes caused by differential mobilities and automobilities. One of the most important features of the road movie template is that it has commonly provided a vehicle for cultural critique (Laderman 2002: 1) and 'a ready space for exploration of the tensions and crises of the historical moment during which it is produced' (Cohan and Hark 1997: 2).

Before continuing to a closer reading of the films, it is worth reprising some other fundamental classifications and divisions that have informed scholarly approaches to road cinema. In *100 Road Movies* Jason Wood proffers a basic categorical definition that involves journeys in search of 'adventures, redemption or escape from the constricting norms of society and its laws' (2007: xv). Laderman further parses this in order to outline geographic and cultural distinctions. He argues that while the classic American strain of the road movie espouses rebellion against cultural norms, the European variety tends to be concerned with travelling 'into the national culture, tracing the meaning of citizenship as a journey' (2002: 248). I asserted in the introduction that European road movies represent a hybrid of these two conceptions. As a group, the European model stages travel 'into culture'. Although these voyages sometimes engage with national culture, it should be emphasised that even in the earliest examples I address the limits of the nation-state do not adequately and fully contain the cultures and spaces explored in road cinema. At the same time these films do incorporate elements commonly associated with the American strain of the road movie: crossing boundaries and reacting against the 'constricting norms' Wood cites. This rebellion against norms often takes a form that parodies or celebrates the typical iconography and thematic associations of the American road movie. As I hope to make clear in the subsequent discussion, we can acknowledge both the inescapable influence of the American side of the genre and the properly European traditions that continue to inform European road filmmaking. By tracing these interconnected threads back to 1962 – a date whose significance I will explain in due course – I aim to demonstrate that references to the speed-driven cinematic rebel in contemporary European road films do not necessarily belong uniquely to the lineage of the classic American counter-culture road cinema that emerged in the late 1960s. In other words, a recent continental film could be perceived to be under the influence of American cinema while also quoting the speed of *Il Sorpasso* rather than, for example, *Vanishing Point* (Richard C. Sarafian, 1971, USA/UK) or the rebellious impulse of *Easy Rider*.

THE 1960S: THE BIRTH OF CONTEMPORARY EUROPEAN ROAD CINEMA

Although I will selectively refer back to earlier examples, this chapter begins with case studies of three European road films from the 1960s. The reasons behind the choice to draw the inevitable yet always problematic line of demarcation with two films released in 1962 are twofold. First, these films follow a pair of events that were crucial to the way that Europe, and the maps of Europe, continue to be conceptualised: the 1957 Treaty of Rome that established the European Economic Community (EEC) and the 1961 construction of the Berlin Wall, a significant if primarily symbolic line of demarcation for the continent. Secondly, the 1960s was also the decade in which the road movie template that most evidently informs the contemporary films addressed in this and the following four chapters came into being. As already noted, that model claims both American and European origins and influences. In the 1960s numerous European directors started to make road films that engaged more 'overtly with the rules and trappings of the Hollywood genre', while at the same time other road films from that decade 'continued to be more resolutely European' (Mazierska and Rascaroli 2006: 3). Both the former and the latter are contrasted by Mazierska and Rascaroli with examples from the prior decade that they identify as 'peculiarly European cinema, with little connection to American forms of the genre', a list that includes *Viaggio in Italia* (Roberto Rossellini, 1954, Italy/France), *La strada* (Federico Fellini, 1954, Italy) and *Smultronstället/Wild Strawberries* (Ingmar Bergman, 1957, Sweden), among others. What sets apart the road cinema of the 1960s most dramatically from those films is advances in filming technology that allowed for mobile cinematography, notably the travelling shot, and through the greater possibility for location shooting in a more diverse and widespread array of settings. As Randalle Halle puts it, the 'dynamic exploration of space' in cinema has been made possible by advances in camera and support system technologies that have led to increasingly mobile filming (2014: 110).

The role of technology is crucial to the development of the road movie model in the 1960s. The automobile, as Neil Archer points out, was still a novelty in the 1960s, a luxury commodity and a symbol of superior mobility, but would become banal by the 1970s (see Jacques Tati's 1971 *Trafic*, which Archer offers as an example, and in a very different sense Brel's *Le Far-West*) and, after the end of *les trentes glorieuses* and the onset of the oil crisis, rather uneconomical (2013: 16). Many films from the 1960s feature automobile travel while remaining sensible to the technological novelty involved and to the striking contrasts and lingering imbalances of mobility. This is manifested in confrontations, sometimes literal, between horse-powered locomotion and mechanised vehicles and between vehicles inhabiting very different places on a technological and speed-based hierarchy of automobility. It is this tension that marks the 1960s as a particularly apt period from which to begin our exploration of road cinema. Laderman argues that American films of the 1960s 'infused the cinematic act of driving with a politically rebellious spirit' (2002: 3–4). Laderman locates the key examples of this movement in the latter part of the decade, with *Bonnie and Clyde* and *Easy Rider*, and contends that the road movie has flourished ever since having crystallised as a genre with *Easy Rider* (2002: 4, 71). Tracing European road cinema that is clearly in the same technological, auto-powered vein back to the beginning of the decade allows me to suggest in this chapter that European antecedents predate the American films that are often taken as the influence for contemporary road cinema.

Archer (2013: 15) cites Kristin Ross' *Fast Cars, Clean Bodies*, a brilliant cultural history of the post-war modernisation of France, as an influence in his study of French road movies, pointing to the white Cadillac in Jacques Demy's 1961 *Lola* as a fetish object that symbolises the desire for burgeoning consumer culture (Ross 1996: 30). Archer's book claims to pick 'up where Ross's leaves off and where the road movie as we commonly know it comes into being' (2013: 15). His case studies, however, were all made after 1968. This is in itself a perfectly logical choice in terms of socio-political framing, as the case could certainly be made that contemporary French-language road movies, which are less engaged with cars, are just as solidly positioned in the lineage of May 1968 as they are in the heritage of the modernist automobile culture that drove many American and European road movies during the previous two decades. Indeed lines must be drawn somewhere and that crucial year is an entirely reasonable place to do so. Ross reads the upheavals of 1968 as fundamentally derived from a refusal to remain within assigned places (2002: 25–6), certainly an impulse that could be convincingly interpreted as the spiritual forerunner of a good number of contemporary road movies. But of course European cultures have other rebellious or anti-authoritarian antecessors at their symbolic and ideological disposal, as shown by the references to nineteenth-century anarchists in the films of Benoît Delépine and Gustave Kervern (Chapter 3) or the Swiss pioneer-adventurer Johann Sutter in a film by his compatriot Lionel Baier (Chapter 4). Crucially, however, the choice to start where Archer does results in some very noteworthy road movies of the 1960s being overlooked. As I aim to demonstrate in the following case studies, films from the early part of the 1960s are essential to our understanding of the interconnected and multidirectional influences that inform latter-day road cinema. It is important to acknowledge that these predate the coalescence of the genre in the late 1960s to 1970s as described by Laderman. While this era clearly cannot be ignored as an intertextual reference point, it should be understood as only one of many influences rather than the foundational decade for road cinema.

IL SORPASSO: SPEED, MACHISMO AND THE EUROPEAN ROAD

The first film under consideration was a popular success in Italy when it was released in 1962 and has been described as the 'archetypal European road movie' of that decade (Porton 2014). In addition to its status as an 'iconic' (Atkinson 2014) road film, *Il Sorpasso* provides a valuable reminder that transnationalism is not a new force in European cinema. Entirely 'pure' national film industries and cultures are a myth (Galt 2006: 2). As Andrew Higson argues, 'since at least the 1920s, films have been made as co-productions, bringing together resources and experiences from different nation-states' (2006: 19). In this case it is an actor who crosses borders. Celebrated French actor Jean-Louis Tritignant is dubbed into Italian for his role in *Il Sorpasso*, one of a number of Italian films he played in during the 1960s with directors such as Valerio Zurlini and Ettore Scola. Dubbing, as with subtitles, is in itself a mark of transnational cinematic travel (Eleftheriotis 2010: 179), but what interests us most here is the film's deployment of road tropes and techniques that would later become staples of European road cinema. If, as Rascaroli contends (2003: 76), there is a distinctive Italian road tradition, this film is also representative of European cross-pollination.

Il Sorpasso leaves an imprint in a variety of ways: as a mismatched buddy comedy, an ambivalent portrait via travelling shots of a landscape and society in the midst of exciting and rapid social change that generated a good deal of unease, and a foundational early European example of a road movie that thrives on speed-driven thrills. Both the fiery denouement and petroleum-fuelled tagline of the 1971 American film *Vanishing Point*, 'watch carefully because everything happens fast', would seem to apply equally well to this film made across the ocean and almost a decade earlier. While some commentators consider *Il Sorpasso* to contain the essence of an American road film, it also provides an example of how road conventions can be applied to very specific non-American cultural contexts and use travel as a lens through which to explore the possibilities and tribulations of a volatile period. Cinema in general both contributes to and records changing perceptions (Orgeron 2007: 13) and the 'dreams, tensions and anxieties', as Cohan and Hark would put it, on display here are intrinsically Italian – and in a broader sense European – rather than simply imported from America.

The film opens in Rome closed during a holiday. The carefree and loquacious Bruno (Vittorio Gassman), who brims with verve and machismo to spare, finds himself dressed up so to speak with a speedy roadster – a Lancia Aurelia equipped with a horn that matches its driver's shrill braggadocio – but with nowhere particular to drive. The meandering journey lacks any set destination or specific aim, recalling what Laderman describes as the meandering or circular trajectories of the early 1970s American road film (2002: 83). On the pretext that he needs to use a telephone, what will become a prototype cinematic odd couple is formed when Bruno catches the attention of the demure Roberto (Tritignant), a law student and the audacious Bruno's apparent opposite, who had intended to shut himself in for the weekend to study for an important exam. Michael Atkinson credits Risi with creating 'the mismatched-buddies road-comedy footprint that a thousand spoofs have stepped into since' (2014). Indeed, Wim Wenders so admired the film and the dynamics between the travelling partners that he chose to name the protagonists of his 1976 *Kings of the Road* – a film typically seen as primarily derivative of American road cinema – after Roberto and Bruno (Figure 1.1).

Bruno's phone call goes unanswered, leaving him without aim or destination. He invites his unwitting host for a ride through the abandoned and eerily silent streets of the Italian capital. The drive turns into an invitation for drinks that in turn becomes the suggestion of a shared lunch. These suggestions are mere pretexts, however, and driving is revealed to be Bruno's primary motivation. The first restaurant is closed for the holiday, leading Bruno to suggest – overriding

Figure 1.1   The legendary odd couple in *Il Sorpasso* (Dino Risi, 1962) takes on the road.

the objections of Roberto, who can hardly get a word in – another eatery further outside of town. There Bruno brashly manoeuvres his car through the outdoor dining area of the purported destination before the heroes rapidly change their minds and return to the road in order to pursue a car with two blonde German women inside. Tellingly, this is the only occasion that Bruno is content not to pass someone. Instead he lets the women overtake the Lancia so that he can 'chase' them. The film's title translates simply as 'the pass', but also conjures a number of socio-cultural and gender connotations. In an essay entitled 'Sex and the Italian Driver', originally published in 1970 and republished online in 2014 by the Criterion Collection to coincide with the DVD rerelease of *Il Sorpasso*, Jackson Burgess underscores the cultural significance of the term:

> The paramount feature of Italian highway driving is *il sorpasso*. The word *sorpassare* means both 'to pass with an automobile' and 'to surpass or excel'. To *sorpassare* someone is to excel him socially, morally, sexually, and politically . . . When an Italian driver sees the car ahead of him on the highway slow up or stop, he knows there can be but two causes. The driver ahead has died at the wheel or else he has suddenly and mysteriously become a Person of No Consequence, which is roughly the same thing as a fate and which, in Italy, hangs over every head. (2014)

The link between machismo and speed is revisited countless times in road cinema, even the European variety (notably in our next case study, *Les petits matins*). Bruno's interest in the two German women proves to be limited and the men set their sights on another improvised short-term goal that involves more driving. Such an aimless quest for women and speed-driven thrills also belies Laderman's reading of European road cinema as more cerebral than American strains (2002: 248). Initially at least the only goal of their voyage is the sometimes overlapping search for women and an open restaurant, preferably one that Bruno deems to have good fish soup and, ideally, rooms to rent in case he hits it off with a waitress. In this sense the film epitomises Ladermans's observation that 'car travel in road movies becomes not merely a means of transportation to a destination; rather the travelling itself becomes the narrative's primary focus' (2002: 13). It should be noted that Laderman ascribes this type of emphasis on 'the imagery and activity of the car (or motorcycle) as the foundation of the narrative' to a fundamentally American tendency and context (2002: 13). Risi's film provides a reminder that the iconography of the road and the technological and narrative need for speed is not solely the domain of American road movies. If the distinctive iconography of the road movie features, in Wood's words, 'recurring shots of a speeding vehicle heading towards distant vistas' (2007: xvi), *Il Sorpasso* certainly has the velocity, if not precisely the same wide-open vistas. In place of vast deserts and open skies, the film features landscape that is typical in European road strains: iconic cityscapes (notably a virtually empty Piazza San Pietro), newly constructed suburban developments dominated by apartment blocks, roads populated with what Bruno derides as 'old Italian' families, and the winding roads and beaches of the coast. The coast often marks the end of the road in American films but for geographic reasons tends to play a different role in European cinema where it can in some cases serve as the final, idealised destination or ultimate site of escape but in general is a more commonplace feature of the landscape.

What might be described as a more recognisably European imprint in *Il Sorpasso* can be seen when the narrative veers away from aimless wandering and towards a terrain that even by that time had already been well-traversed in road films from Europe. The men venture into their respective pasts, first via a stop at the country home of Roberto's aunt and uncle, a spot where he spent holidays as a child (a scene reminiscent of Bergman's *Wild Strawberries*). Later, after stumbling out of a bar decidedly worse for wear, Bruno leads them to a house belonging to his estranged wife and their daughter. In what is now archetypal road movie fashion, these stopovers are used to stage encounters that will change the protagonists' outlooks and frequently their itineraries. A monologue by Roberto's self-absorbed lawyer cousin instils the seed of doubt about his career path, while Bruno's misgivings about his daughter's much older boyfriend seems to cause him to question to a small extent his free-wheeling lifestyle and perhaps regret that he is not present in her life. However, only Roberto undergoes a clear transformation, as evidenced by the ultimate sequence, in which he encourages an ill-advised pass along a tortuous stretch of coastal road that leads to a spectacular accident and his ultimate demise. When the duo first hit the road, Roberto was particularly averse to speed and stiffened up whenever Bruno attempted what Roberto saw as imprudent road manoeuvres. His transformation over the course of a couple of days on the road from studious, timid future lawyer to self-assured daredevil is signalled earlier when he attempts to telephone a young neighbour for whom he has had eyes but to whom he had resisted speaking on the pretext that his studies left him no time for romance. Ironically, his metamorphosis into a man of the road par excellence is sealed with his death, which, let us recall, is according to Burgess the only acceptable reason for an Italian of the period to stop his car. The accident propels Roberto, in the car from which Bruno has somehow managed to escape, over the precipice and onto the rocks below. His highly dramatic downfall aligns Roberto with the eponymous female protagonists of *Thelma and Louise* (Ridley Scott, 1991, USA), for whom in a mobile – and supremely cinematic – death is viewed as a far better result than a return to the society from which they fled. In other words, in the logic of some road movies it is better to die than to stop moving. This gesture distils the fundamental escapist impulse at the heart of so many road movies into one dramatic and fiery crash. Perhaps having been transformed during the course of his time on the road, Roberto was unable to return to his old life in which he was doomed to live cloistered in his study and to follow a path prescribed by his social standing. However one opts to interpret the ending, Roberto's voyage typifies the perceived suitability of the road as a narrative and physical space for social critique, personal transformation and self-evaluation.

The demise of the initially unwitting and unwilling sidekick could also be read as a warning against social change and irrational economic exuberance, and the dark climax in which both Roberto and the car meet their end distinguishes *Il Sorpasso* from many European road movies. In the *commedia all'italiana* tradition, Bruno's superficially carefree, speed-infused machismo actually hides a more complex matrix of social and economic aspirations and misgivings. While Bruno would seem to possess the outward trappings of economic success and sexual conquest in the form of his speedy Lancia, on the road he encounters a number of people, notably the older rich man dating his daughter and his new friend Roberto, who have attained more economic success, or who at least seem poised to do so. The film subtly evokes on a number of occasions a gap between economic mobility and the shiny and showy automobility as modernity that Bruno embraces. The driving duo encounter a number of Italians enthusiastically partaking in the twist, a dance craze imported from America that becomes a symbol of unstoppable and sometimes incongruous social change. Aside from a few stops to chat up woman, the only occasion on which Bruno takes his foot off the pedal is when he and Roberto stop to gawk in amazement at a hamlet full of peasants doing the twist in a field. Just as their awkward new dance moves are unlikely to propel these rural residents into modernity, Bruno's fast car seems to be getting him nowhere fast in the realm of economic mobility.

I will conclude the discussion of *Il Sorpasso* with an analysis of the opening driving sequence, which illustrates some of the key techniques and images commonly employed in road cinema. The film begins with a speedy travelling montage that demonstrates Bruno's compulsive desire for excessive velocity, as manifested in both personality traits and driving technique. The opening twenty-four second take from a camera mounted on the back of the car sets the tone for the rest of the film. Bruno races through the empty streets of Rome, tires squealing as he frenetically searches for a telephone. The shot frames Bruno from behind against the car, the windscreen through which he sees the world, the city streets ahead (aligned with the perspective of the 'car itself', as Corrigan [1991: 144] describes such shots) and the rear-view mirror, which frames Bruno's face. A rear-view mirror often serves as a 'literal projection of the character onto the car' (Laderman 2002: 16). The first cut is to a static shot of an empty intersection where the car from the opening shot reappears. It makes an illegal turn onto a one-way street, signalling that the driver is not one to abide by the rules of the road or indeed society. After Bruno and Roberto meet and the road trip proper begins, the camera takes more distance from the car, capturing it in long-shot pans as it makes its way through Rome. It is on the open road beyond Rome where the car, and the film, find their preferred pace and a series of travelling shots structured around passing – suggested by the title to be the film's crucial element – ensue. These breath-taking sequences are filmed by cinematographer Alfio Contini, who would later shoot Michelangelo Antonioni's 1970 road movie *Zabriskie Point*, from another moving vehicle at a variety of angles and distances. Notable are those at long-shot distance, tracking the Lancia as it weaves through traffic or in medium frontal or rear two-shots that draw our attention to the shifting relationship between the two characters. The latter are interspersed with cuts to brief close-ups of telling details from the car's interior, such as the speedometer and the picture of French actress Brigitte Bardot with the caption 'drive carefully, I'm waiting at home for you', a reference to the traditional road movie alignment of females with the domestic space and males with itinerant adventure. At one juncture the car rapidly overtakes an overloaded motorcycle with a sidecar carrying what Bruno derides as an 'old Italian family' ('where is Grandpa?' he quips). This *sorpasso* demonstrates an encounter common in road movies between differential mobilities, which often stand in for symbols of broader social transformation (as in this case) or socio-economic standing. While Bruno has no trouble overtaking the overladen motorcycle, other passes involve duels with more modern vehicles, filmed from behind by a visibly shaky camera to a cacophony of horns and squealing tires, sounds that predominate throughout the narrative.

LES PETITS MATINS (1962): FAST CARS AND FEMALE EMPOWERMENT?

As *Il Sorpessa* aptly demonstrates, from the earliest crystallisation of the category road movies were considered to be masculine turf. Corrigan notes that road cinema is 'traditionally focused, almost exclusively, on men and the absence of women' (1991: 143). When women were present it was often to be the object of the male gaze from the passing car and evaluated for potential entry into the car as a (generally temporary) passenger. A goal, albeit generally of a secondary nature, of male cinematic road trips was frequently to encounter and seduce females (Mazierska and Rascaroli 2006: 166–9). Bertrand Blier's 1974 French road film *Les valseuses*, to cite just one example, was controversial for the mistreatment of women encountered in the course of a voyage by two rebellious male protagonists (Tarr and Rollet 2001: 229). Traditionally, female-driven or directed road films have been uncommon. The films that tend to receive attention as landmark exceptions to this rule include in French cinema Diane Kurys' 1980 *Cocktail Molotov* and 1983 *Coup de foudre/Entre nous* and the better-known and more commercially successful *Sans toit ni loi/ Vagabond* (Agnès Varda, 1985) and the American film *Thelma and Louise*, which Wood labels a 'rare example of a road movie with female protagonists in what is a traditionally male terrain' (2007: xix).

Les petits matins, a 1962 film by Jacqueline Audry, represents a stark contrast to the speed and testosterone-propelled itinerary of *Il Sorpasso* and stands out as a rare early incursion by a female director and female protagonist into the cinematic fiefdom of men. Audry, whose work has been critically overlooked before Brigite Rollet's 2015 *Jacqueline Audry: la femme à la camera*, was in 1949 the only female feature filmmaker working in France (Tarr and Rollet 2001: 1). *Les petits matins* is a clever contribution to the road movie corpus and a forerunner of other female-directed films that would take novel approaches to the road template by marking the road a space not for rebels and fugitives but rather as a template for the exploration of 'interpersonal relationships away from the constraints of the (patriarchal) domestic sphere' (Tarr and Rollet 2001: 229–30). Audry's film also represents an example of how the typical tropes of road cinema can be activated for narrative purposes while simultaneously falling under a lightly critical and sometimes parodic eye. *Les petits matins* maintains a lightness that was uncommon in road movies of the period (Rollet 2015: 73) as it turns a mildly critical eye to male-dominated society. As such, it also furnishes an early example of what Archer describes as the 'more positive possibilities at work' in 'feminine road movies' (2013: 119).

The film opens with its protagonist Agathe (Agathe Aëms), an eighteen-year-old Belgian, on the coast of Belgium, where she has won a beach vacation. The arrival of rain showers opens the door to her first of many encounters with men who hope to seduce her, this one yielding an umbrella and the suggestion that if Agathe pines for a sunny beach she should make her way to the Côte d'Azur. The trip, he adds, only takes one and a half hours by plane. When she asks how long the same voyage would take in a car, he responds that it depends on the variety of car, acknowledging a hierarchy of automobility that is socially constructed and a staple element in road films such as *Il Sorpasso*. The connections between sexuality, desire, social standing and vehicle horsepower and price will become the object of parody in the ensuing voyage.

This voyage across the Belgian border and through France to the Mediterranean port town of Cassis takes place almost exclusively by automobile, with a few intervals of walking and one carriage ride. Crucially, however, Agathe does not own a car and must rely on hitchhiking to make her way south. Hitchhiking has a fundamentally different ethos than driving oneself, and also offers different angles of vision. Agathe must walk a fine line between self-determination and reliance on others, in particular men. All of her lifts come from males of a variety of ages and social echelons and virtually all of whom seek unsuccessfully to sleep with her (Rollet 2015: 95). Behind her outwardly coquettish demeanour Agathe is a chameleon willing and able to selectively adapt – or at least pretend to do so – to male-dominated social conceptions and escapist fantasies about women when it helps keep her moving towards her geographic goal. She claims in turns to be on vacation, visiting family, a travelling actress and a bilingual secretary. Like the apparent initial impetus for her southward trek, many of these ideas reflect male preconceptions about a solitary young travelling woman and common encounters in road movies that are more typically viewed from the perspective of the mobile male protagonist. When a French border guard wonders what a young woman is doing on the road – not to mention crossing borders – without her family, Agathe announces that she is travelling in order to visit relatives. The first man to pick her up, a gentleman of a certain age, asks if she is a secretary – a role suggestive of the limited possibilities for women in the typical spaces of society at the time – and recounts his longstanding dream of absconding with just such a secretary. Agathe later adopts this identity when she tells another older man that she encounters at a café in Orly that she is a bilingual secretary. Beyond her desire to appeal to the businessman's sensibilities (she is hoping that he will fund her voyage), this particular choice of imagined profession also underscores her capacity to absorb and adapt to the world around her. As she sits in the airport we hear announcements for flights to points around Europe in Spanish, French and English. In this way, the road trip facilitates Agathe's creative approach to self-identification and foretells the flexible approach to identities espoused by 'postmodern' road movies (Mazierska and Rascaroli 2006) in which identity is presented as 'liquid' (Bauman 2000). In other words, well before it was common to find female protagonists on the road, Audry's film demonstrated that the road narrative could furnish what Tarr and Rollet describe as imaginative space outside of the patriarchal constraints of society (2001). For Agathe, more than a geographical journey, her quest for sunshine is also an *apprentissage*. Being on the road equates to the opportunity to reinvent herself, to write her own story and to try at least to get outside of the traditional role of women in society.

Men are the only drivers in this film and Agathe accepts rides from a number of them, but she does not allow herself to be 'picked up' by them, at least until she finds a man she likes as her voyage nears its end. While hitchhikers are often subject to the vicissitudes of chance and the whims of passing drivers, on a number of levels Agathe's voyage is to a large extent the product of her choice. Added to her relative freedom of self-identification that arguably stretches the social limits placed upon her, Agathe mentally maps her own itinerary, which constantly changes (Capri and Marseille are both listed as possible destinations) and, most importantly, she is able to select the drivers who take her on this voyage. Rameau (Bernard Blier), the man who drives her on a segment leading to Valence, where she will be put up for the night in a café owned by his mistress Gabrielle (Arletty), announces that it was in fact Agathe who selected him rather than the other way around. The reversal of typical roles is announced early on when Agathe takes advantage of the line-up of cars at the border-crossing to size up the vehicles and their drivers. Where men are more commonly seen ogling (or deriding) women from the front seat and evaluating their appeal as temporary passengers or their desirability as sexual partners, here Agathe has a range of options that she scopes out while approaching from behind. This contrasts with a scene from Godard's *A bout de souffle/Breathless* (1960) in which Michel Poiccard jeers at two hitchhiking women he finds 'ugly' and refuses to stop for them after slowing down. In this case Agathe's angle of approach at least momentarily affords her to subvert the power of the male gaze. Her selection made, she simply crosses the border and waits for the car of her choice to pass by.

Agathe chooses to ride in an older vehicle driven by Belgians, passing up a Cadillac Eldorado described by its driver and passenger as 'une belle américaine', a formulation that demonstrates the conflation of masculine road fantasies of fast cars and accessible women. Not content to take 'no' for an answer, they 'chase' her as in *Il Sorpasso* by slowing down and letting the older car pass. This sets the stage for an ongoing duel between the vehicles and a running parody of socially ascribed notions of speed and their uses in cinema. Although she opts for the slower ride in this instance, Agathe later changes cars when the first stalls and needs to be manually started up again with a crank. The speedy Eldorado, however, soon runs out of gas and is overtaken by the now-functioning Belgian car, which Agathe climbs back into. A shot of the two cars stopped next to each other showcases the 'Belgium' and

'France' stickers that adorn the rear of each, playfully underlining the film's border-crossing spirit and Agathe's otherwise unremarkable and generally unremarked Belgian identity. Audry also light-heartedly quotes Godard with a scene that, coming just two years later, inevitably would have again recalled the early road portion of *Breathless*. When the out-of-service bus she is riding on (piloted by Lino Ventura) is stopped by two policemen on motorcycles, Agathe is to be taken to the station. She gives them the slip and runs down a path into the woods, an escape that resembles the scene in which Jean-Paul Belmondo's Michel Poiccard shoots two *motards* on the way to Paris. This nod to the early outlaw connotations of the road film and to the merging of road narratives with *noir* sensibilities and anxieties in films such as Edgar Ulmer's 1945 *Detour* (Corrigan 1991: 144–5; Laderman 2002: 26) ends when Agathe (non-violently in this case) evades the officers in the forest and hitches another ride from an older gentleman. This man, however, is not behind the wheel but at the reins of a horse-drawn carriage, completing the circle of various modes of 'driven' transport used by Agathe on her passage towards the coast. Beyond engaging in a certain parody of road movie speed, the different forms of transit featured in the film also serve to highlight the stark social contrast of mobility and velocity brought on by rapid post-war modernisation. This is emphasised when the man leads his cart up to a petrol pump at a Mobil station, where the horse is fed by the attendant who refers to the driver by his noble title, baron. The shiny modern station is emblazoned with that corporation's iconic Pegasus logo, and the winged horse serves as an ironic symbol given the fact that flight is rejected as a mode of transit in the film. Earlier in the narrative Agathe turned down money offered for her passage on a plane to Nice by the pilot, with whom she drove to the airport on the mistaken idea that he was driving his car to Nice rather than flying there. She rejects his offer – and insinuated romantic overture – on the pretext that he was an unsafe driver, calling attention to her desire to use the road as a mode of transit and exploration rather than a space for achieving dangerous velocity and adventure as an end unto itself. In keeping with this, the travelling shots by cinematographer Robert Lefebvre do not have the same concern for speed on display as in *Il Sorpasso*. Instead frontal two-shots (with an occasional three-shot) predominate, turning our attention to the interactions between passenger and driver rather than espousing the panoramic perspective of the driver or focusing on automotive speed.[4] More importantly in the narrative economy of road cinema, the fastest route does not generally represent the most interesting cinematic possibility and the film's rejection of flight and embrace of a series of less efficient modes of transport are both gestures that will be frequently repeated in later road movies examined in this book.

Another prominent feature of European road cinema evident in *Les petits matins* is the circular nature of the voyage. A change of final destination over the course of the voyage has become a cliché in road films, but Agathe does ultimately reach her rather vague objective: somewhere on the Mediterranean coast. A circular twist is added when the man she selects en route, Jean-Claude, who rather conveniently lives in an apartment with a view of the sea in Cassis, learns after they have spent the night together that he has been promoted to be head of sales for his company's northern office in Lille, just a handful of kilometres from the Belgian border and less than an hour away from where Agathe initially crossed into France on her way south to escape the weather. The film closes with this suggestion that Agathe's voyage will likely follow a pattern that is common in European road films. Rather than setting off for a new destination, Agathe seems likely to retrace her steps towards the north, albeit after having undergone an *apprentissage* in the ways of the world and, particularly, of men (Rollet 2015: 73).

Le Corniaud: Cops, Robbers, Tourists and a Tati-esque Innocent Abroad

Le corniaud (1965) is part vaudeville farce, part chase caper and part transformative quest (albeit hidden in a tourist package), as signalled by the closing exclamation 'quel voyage!' uttered by protagonist Antoine (Bourvil). Indeed despite its popular success (11.7 million spectators saw it in theatres) the film was critically panned and critiqued for its penchant for excess. A *Cahiers du cinema* review charged that the director tried to 'throw everything in', including American cars, striking landscapes and a police element (Vincendeau 2000: 141, 143). While its comedic bent would certainly set it apart from *Pierrot le fou*, which was released the same year, and other films by Godard that are closely aligned with the road movie, *Le corniaud* does confirm the suggestion that cinema could be distilled to a gun and a girl, as Godard put it, and as Orgeron adds particularly in relation to the 1960s, a car (2007: 77). Director Gérard Oury and comic pairing Louis de Funès[5] and Bourvil are best known for *La grande vadrouille/The Big Runaround* (1966), the extraordinarily successful follow-up to *Le corniaud* that would retain its spot at the top of French box-office records for forty years. As one British reviewer of *Le corniaud* put it, '[t]he formula is as unpretentious as it could be: pretty girls, tourist attractions (including the leaning Tower of Pisa) and situations that allow Bourvil and Louis de Funès to squeeze the last drop out of every joke' (Anonymous 1966).

The film stands out in the road movie lineage for its combination of tourism, the common road movie penchant for framing masculine quests in terms of sexual conquest over women met along the way and the comedic chase that pits a seemingly bumbling protagonist against a gaggle of inept gangsters and international criminals. By tracing the literal voyage of naïve middle-class tourist Antoine Maréchal as a symbolic passage from pushover (the 'sucker' of the title, which is more aptly translated as 'nitwit') to schemer who hoodwinks the criminals who set him up as well as a second different band who followed along to pilfer the loot, *Le corniaud* demonstrates the generic crossing-over often at work between standard road narratives and other categories of cinema. The road narrative serves as a canvas for the transformation of a protagonist and the conduit for a cinematic comedy and a humorous rendition of the post-war gangster film. Antoine ends the trip as a very different person, or at least perceived very differently by the crooks whose paths crossed with his. An innocent Tati-esque bumbler at the start, Antoine eventually catches on as the voyage continues and undertakes no small amount of scheming himself.

The voyage in question turns out to be very different from the one on which Antoine set off and the initial destination for his road trip becomes the starting point of a voyage that makes up most of the film's narrative. Antoine departs from Paris for an Italian holiday, but does not get very far before a comically rendered accident leads to a change of plans. In what would become a legendary scene, Antoine's overloaded Citroën *deux chevaux* is struck in an intersection by a bigger, faster Bentley driven by Leopold Saroyan (de Funès). While this now familiar confrontation between different grades of mobility does not result in injury to either party or any significant damage to Saroyan's car, Antoine's breaks apart at the seams, leaving him standing in the street with a pile of luggage. This initial road event leads Saroyan to propose a mission that will replace Antoine's ruined holiday: to drive a new Cadillac that will be unloaded at the port of Naples all the way to Bordeaux, on the pretext that it is a favour for a friend. In fact the Cadillac has been modified to allow Saroyan to stash in it and smuggle a variety of stolen riches, from gold to a legendary diamond, and the naïve Antoine would seem to be the last person who would arouse suspicion. The loot is seamlessly integrated into functioning parts of the car – the diamond is embedded in the horn, causing it to malfunction and the gold crafted into a fender – placing the vehicle at the literal and symbolic centre of the narrative. The car also does double duty as the means of transit and – unbeknownst to Antoine – the very object of the quest itself for Saroyan and the rival band who are following him from Naples. The chase to keep up with, yet remain undetected by, the unknowing protagonist is the source of much of the film's humour and of various gags. After the car is damaged in a scrum between the two gangs vying for its possession while Antoine loafs in his hotel room, a choreographed scene in a repair shop begins with Saroyan miming the repairs that he wants done before ultimately doing them himself much more rapidly than realistically possible and to the amazement of the Italian garage owner and son.

Antoine's leisure trip remains narratively self-enclosed as long as he is unaware of the gangsters after his car. This self-contained bubble of a voyage, a road movie within the greater film, offers Oury the opportunity to satirise post-war tourism, which reached previously unknown heights in France over the course of the 1950s (Viard 2011: 112–13). The scene in which Antoine, a camera dangling around his neck marking him distinctively as a tourist, takes delivery of the car at the docks in Naples is particularly reminiscent of Jacques Tati's Monsieur Hulot. Overwhelmed by the technology represented by gadgets in the new car, Antoine promptly smashes both bumpers (one made of gold) and seems to cause a horn malfunction that we later learn is attributed to the diamond stashed in the steering column. Despite the strong dose of comedy that ensues, the film does frame Antoine's interactions with the spaces and cultures he traverses in a way that allows for a critique of how humans see the world through the 'screen' of automobility. These images also provide a record of a rapidly changing European landscape. The scene of the arriving car on the docks and a subsequent slow tracking shot down crowded Neapolitan streets from the driver's perspective thrust the modernity of the Cadillac into sharp contrast with local culture and economy. As in *Il Sorpasso*, the landscape witnessed here is in a state of constant transformation, exemplified by marquees and billboards advertising for multinational corporations and international banks.

Unlike in *Il Sorpasso* and another notable French road film, Henri-Georges Clouzot's 1953 *Le salaire de la peur/The Wages of Fear*, danger in *Le corniaud* lies not in the (winding) road itself, or even with the rather ineffectual gangsters, but in tourism. In this way this popular comedy also formulates a critique of automotive and tourist gaze. Antoine cruises nonchalantly down the road with his nose buried in a guidebook to Italy. At other times, his vantage point is refracted through the lens of his camera, and the quest for a perfect vacation image almost leads to his demise at one point. Tourism has been the object of regular critique and derision (Mazierska 2013: 122) and tourist guides, while informing the tourist about the cultural sights, also decontextualise, simplify and homogenise the places visited by tourists (Urry 1990: 3). Antoine's travelling vantage point can be aligned with what John Urry has theorised as the 'tourist gaze', a product of the culture of the second half of the twentieth century (Urry 1990). Even if Oury does not consciously set out to chronicle socio-economic transformation or to parse the contrast between his protagonist's contrived vantage point and the more complex realities of the world that is traversed, the shifting Italian landscape of the 1960s is tracked, albeit superficially, along with Antoine's trek. Road cinema presents an opportunity for discovery for spectators as well as within the narrative logic, and enjoying beautiful landscape, and less commonly cityscape, is often part of the expected viewing experience and even an expectation. The narrative in *Le corniaud* is interspersed with slow perspective shots showing Rome, Pisa and the coastline, sharing with viewers the pleasure of discovery Antoine experiences.

It should be noted that the aforementioned car, girl and gun cinematic trinity is again fulfilled here. Antoine enjoys apparently chaste romantic encounters with young women who join his voyage temporarily: an Italian hairdresser's assistant (closely followed by her fiancé, a mercurial Sicilian) and a young German student and self-described naturist touring Italy. The latter transcends the typical female road movie role of passive passenger when she saves Antoine from one of the gangsters. This positive female intervention in the crime caper element of the narrative could be contrasted with the depiction of women as *femmes fatales* in earlier American *noir* tradition, exemplified by émigré director Edward G. Ulmer's cult 1945 film *Detour*. That film 'imagines a world spinning toward chaos precisely because women have suddenly gained access to mobility' (Orgeron 2007: 59).[6]

Le corniaud exemplifies the porous generic boundaries that distinguish road films from comedies or crime capers, and Ursula, the young German woman picked up by the side of the road, serves primarily to call attention to the ways in which the film ultimately ridicules the hodgepodge cinematic conventions in which it also simultaneously revels. Romance is foiled when Antoine abashedly declines to join her for a naked swim in the Mediterranean; the gangster's plot to kill Antoine and make off with the car is thwarted when she demonstrates the mechanical savvy to disable the vehicle, and her choice to leave Antoine and his Cadillac dismantles the typical speed-and-flash-based hierarchy of automobility. There is more to a holiday than a stylish and fast car, she suggests, when she trades the convertible for a lorry filled with mooing cows and driven by a farmer much like those mocked in *Il Sorpasso*. 'I prefer a calmer vehicle to a pretty car', she explains while embarking. In the above gestures *Le corniaud* exemplifies road cinema's intertextual web, reflexive propensity to quote and/or parody itself, and capacity to bend genre distinctions, all of which will be on display in subsequent chapters. Ursula also represents the emergence of a more significant role for women in the road narrative. While the film is not primarily about Ursula, like Agathe in *Les petits matins* she is travelling Europe on her own and wields a not insignificant degree of authority in her brief time on the road with Antoine, which ends by her own choosing and not because he has grown tired of her presence. This stands in contrast to the hitchhiking Vera in the aforementioned *Detour*, who can be read as 'the unlikely poster child for the threat of auto-mobility' (Orgeron 2007: 59), and Linda, the only woman with a significant role in *Le salaire de la peur*, who is relegated to the home base where she first begs Mario not to undertake the treacherous voyage and then helplessly await news of his fate.

While the (1940s) American-inspired gun, girl(s) and car element of *Le corniaud* demonstrates the interconnectedness of 1960s European and American road movie templates (with American noir, and B movies as forbears; see Orgeron 2007: 77), it also demonstrates some distinctly European characteristics. The voyage from Naples to Bordeaux faces an extended pause when the cars are stopped at the Menton border post between Italy and France. That Mediterranean city is highly symbolic in a road movie context as not only a key international border crossing, but also as the culminating point of the iconic French *Nationale 7*, a roadway connecting Paris to the Côte d'Azur. As Agathe's voyage in *Les petits matins* demonstrates, the southward route become quite popular during the 1950s and 1960s with the massive expansion of free time and by extension mobility (Viard 2011: 85). The roadway was a principle route south from the capital until the 1970s and now holds a mythic status as part of the national *patrimoine* (Turel 2012). In stark contrast to the myth of the speedy American road, the *Nationale 7* is perhaps best remembered for its more leisurely pace of travel, often due to circulation bottlenecks on the narrow portions of the road that bisected towns and villages. The *bouchons* (traffic jams) that become regular occurrences are fondly remembered and annually re-enacted in Lapalisse, a town in the Auvergne region.

As in *Les petits matins* the pauses at border crossings in *Le corniaud* show the dramatic change in European travel since the Schengen Zone went into effect in most of Western Europe. Each of the cars in Oury's film is virtually disassembled by a suspicious police detachment, resulting in delay and literally placing mobility at risk. By contrast a similar scene in the 2008 film *Les folles aventures de Simon Konianski* (Micha Wald, Belgium/France/Canada; analysed in Chapter 3) serves to highlight the fact that the travellers have reached the political and symbolic border of Europe beyond which travel is constrained. Other distinctively French touches are added by the motorcycle police duo, a seemingly ubiquitous sight in the cinematic imaginary of French roads (*A bout de souffle*, *Les petits matins*, a larger group in Billy Wilder's 1934 French production *Mauvaise graine*), who here thwart a settling of score between gangsters, the coastline, also much more prevalent in European films, and stopovers at sights such as the Cité de Carcassonne, a medieval fortress that is distinctive from anything found in the American landscape. Lastly, *Le corniaud* ends with a gesture of narrative (if not geographic) circularity when the car in which Antoine and Saroyan are riding, this time driven by the police, is involved in an accident in a roundabout resembling the site of the two protagonists' initial encounter in Paris.

The elements common in 1960s European road films – circularity, slowness, crime (real or parodied) – will continue to inform contemporary films. This brief voyage through the decade in which the road movie as we now commonly recognise it crystallised does not suffice to disprove Laderman's contention that 'many European road movies seem a reaction to, or reformulation of, the American genre' (2002: 247). As I have already argued, however, the question of ultimate origins is not as pertinent to the objects of this study as the idea that both European and American traditions inform contemporary road movie makers. With this in mind, the preceding analysis should suffice to demonstrate that European road films that predate iconic American contributions to the category such as *Easy Rider* do contain many of the seeds of more recent continental road movie inspiration. The following contemporary films should most accurately be seen, then, as belonging firmly to a European road movie tradition that has interacted with and borrowed from American cinema at various junctures of cinematic history.

Contemporary European Routes: Aki Kaurismäki and Wim Wenders

The remainder of the chapter will focus on more recent European road films that represent overlapping American and European connections as well as inter-European points of contact. The focus will be auteur-centric, with our discussion of a *Leningrad Cowboys go America* (1989) and its sequel *Leningrad Cowboys Meet Moses* (1994) by Aki Kaurismäki and Wim Wenders' *Lisbon Story* (1994) integrated into the wider contexts of the directors' respective oeuvres, especially the latter's 1977 *Kings of the Road*. Both authors have made films in the US and in Europe, including some produced, set or at least partially filmed in France, as is the case with those under consideration here. Both are also widely associated with road movies (Romney 2003: 43; Nestingen 2013: 36). Wenders' *Alice in den Städten/Alice in the Cities* (1974, West Germany), *Kings of the Road* and *Paris, Texas* (1984, West Germany/France/UK/USA) are road classics and at least four of Kaurismäki's films stage journeys (Nestingen 2013: 36). The two directors also share what Andrew Nestingen describes in Kaurismäki's work as a 'nostalgia for a bygone film culture' (2013: 7). These elements combine to fuse both directors into the DNA of road cinema; their work is part of an active intertextual dialogue with tradition and has in turn become significant sources of influence for contemporary road directors.

In contrast to the first three case studies, the work of Kaurismäki and Wenders has been the object of significant critical attention. For this reason I will focus on reading their work through a perspective that will be particularly important as a prelude to subsequent chapters: that of cross-border mobility in contemporary Europe. The films analysed in the following pages are examples of post-Berlin Wall travels, and the two directors have very different perspectives on an ostensibly 'borderless' Europe. Where Kaurismäki sees the risk of dissipation and loss, Wenders sees possibility. Whereas *Le corniaud*, *Les petits matins* and *Il Sorpasso* each represent combinations of various degrees of quest and escape tendencies, these directors are firmly in different camps. Wenders' *Lisbon Story* is a positive quest while Kaurismäki's duology is more closely aligned with flight and the negative side of open borders. Despite their distinctively different outlooks on post-1989 Europe, both directors nonetheless share a vision of identity as a flexible, border-crossing construction.

Together *Leningrad Cowboys Go America* and *Leningrad Cowboys Meet Moses* tell the story of a voyage to America – and ultimately back – by a quixotic Soviet rock band with extravagant pompadour hairstyles. Two elements immediately stand out in the first film. One is Kaurismäki's offbeat, darkly comical vantage point of the world, which manifests itself in his unmistakably unique signature cinematic universe that Nestingen labels 'bohemian' (2013) and often veers towards the Tati-esque (Romney 2003: 44). Second is the lugubrious tone that seeps into almost every shot, even in the many humorous scenes, a wider tendency in the director's work that lead Jonathan Romney to liken his films to 'country and western songs of the old school' (2003: 43).

In the first film the titular Cowboys are travelling with the body of their bandmate Peka, who died while rehearsing on the eve of their voyage. Their trek across the US to Mexico via America's most seedy and/or downtrodden roadside spaces begins in New York City and takes them through Memphis, New Orleans and various outposts in Texas. The voyage is recorded in melancholy (often night-time) travelling shots along roadways replete with strip malls and chain hotels. The sense of freedom and camaraderie common in road movies (if generally punctuated by the occasional dispute) is nowhere to be seen. Their autocratic and parsimonious manager Vladimir yells out commands, doles out small change to buy refreshments and bags of onions for dinner, and hoards a stash of beer for himself. The bottles are hidden in the coffin, which has been iced down to preserve the body, a touch that furnishes a fitting example of Kaurismäki's brand of dark comedy. Likewise the penury faced by the travellers in *Cowboys* is exaggerated to the extent that it becomes comical, but also serves to convey the hardship experienced by many migrants (Mazierska and Rascaroli 2006: 23). In this sense, the film offers a cogent reminder that all is not rosy on the road, and that not all travellers are seeking metaphysical adventures or the attainment of spiritual understanding. With this in mind, it is also notable that these voyagers do not grow closer, 'find themselves' or undergo visible or dramatic transformations of their socio-economic standing in the course of the journey, as the generic prescription would typically dictate (Mazierska and Rascaroli 2006: 25).

That said, the group are musical chameleons of sorts and demonstrate some capacity to adapt progressively – if awkwardly – to their environment. Among the fiats handed down by Vladimir is that the musicians familiarise themselves with rock 'n' roll in order to transition from a polka repertoire to something more marketable in the US. They test their musical apprenticeship at a biker bar, where the punk-style song they open with is not well received. The same crowd appreciates their rendition of the American band Steppenwolf's classic song 'Born to be Wild', however. This could be due to the fact that the lyrics are performed by the cowboys' long-lost American cousin in southern-accented American English, suggesting that despite their efforts these Russians cannot truly 'translate' in the US or at the very least they still lack the cultural competency to 'read' the crowd and the setting and select an appropriate tune. Of course 'Born to be Wild' is also strongly symbolic within the road movie context, having been featured in the soundtrack to *Easy Rider*. The same interest in road cinema history is evident in a cameo by American director Jim Jarmusch as the stereotypically unscrupulous used-car salesman who outfits the group with the Cadillac that they will drive across the continent. If road trips and border-crossing are not always wholesome for individuals, Kaurismäki suggests that they can at least provide cinematic nourishment.

Returning to the narrative, when the troupe arrives in Mexico, where their manager has booked them to perform at a wedding, they again mould themselves to the space they are traversing and competently play mariachi standards with the help of a Mexican singer. In the next film the Cowboys have mastered the art of that musical form and have learned enough Spanish to take over singing duties. Perhaps even more absurdist than *Go America*, *Leningrad Cowboys Meet Moses* picks up the storyline five years after the first film and adds some new twists – most notable is the Statue of Liberty's missing nose – to the saga of the Cowboys, who are still living in Mexico when their narrative resumes. Less appreciated by critics – Romney refers to the second film as the 'crashing hangover' from the 'boozy road trip' of the first (Romney 2003: 45) – *Meet Moses* is nonetheless of interest here for its geographic trajectory. The film follows the band's return voyage to Russia, via Coney Island, Brittany (incorrectly labelled as the 'Westernmost point' of Europe), Amiens, Leipzig, Dresden, the Czech countryside and Warsaw. This route closes the narrative circle by bringing the group back to their initial starting point. As in *Go America*, it is again difficult to identify any significant transformation that has taken place. While the musicians have expanded their repertoire and diversified their wardrobe, their ultimate desire is to return home and to do so they reverse what was perhaps the most significant act in the first film: firing and casting off their exploitative manager. Vladimir reappears in the second instalment and is accepted as the Cowboys' 'Moses', the one who will lead them on the way back home.

While the two films do not conform to the expectation of the road as a space for meaningful growth and transformation, they nonetheless confirm the prevalent tendency in post-1989 European road cinema to map identities in a fluid fashion. The significance of open borders in Kaurismäki's cinema demands some further parsing. Despite their setting in a period in which a narrative of borderless, East-to-West 'progress' was broadly interpreted in positive and even euphoric terms, as we will see in *Lisbon Story*, Kaurismäki sees post-Berlin Wall developments under a decidedly pessimistic light. Sanna Peden (2013: 115) has appropriated Thomas Elsaesser's term 'double occupancy' (2005) in relation to two other films by the director in an attempt to account for an approach to filmmaking that fully accepts a post-national reality without embracing the sometimes emancipatory discourses that accompany transnationalism. As Peden explains: '[d]ouble occupancy is a flexible term, but at its core is the idea that cultures and identities are in constant flux, characterized by overlaps and contradictions, and the history of one nation is entwined with that of another' (2013: 115). Kaurismäki was on record as opposing Finland's EU accession during the 1995 enlargement phase (Peden 2013: 116). Thus on the one hand the director opposes the political consequences of open European borders, on the other hand it could be argued that national borders in films such as both *Leningrad Cowboys* tend to be largely inconsequential (Mazierska and Rascaroli 2006: 17). These 'cowboys' are neither cowboys nor from Leningrad and are thus, by their very name, examples – for better or for worse – of the possibility of postmodern 'liquid' identity (Mazierska and Rascaroli 2006: 17).

The actual and symbolic crossings in Kaurismäki's cinema of this period might be read as 'reflections on the possibilities as well as the precariousness of the geopolitical shifts of the late 1980s and early 1990s' (Peden 2013: 119). Kaurismäki's approach to borders represents an acknowledgement of the fundamental structural paradox of ostensibly borderless Europe. A traveller might aspire to a borderless life, and the physical act of traversing borders between nations has become easier, but policies, economics and crass human nature consistently render this impossible. Nestingen sums up the premise of the director's journey narratives as a clash between the desire to identify with the world being traversed and the inability to enter it (Nestingen 2013: 40). In Kaurismäki's vision of a post-1989 world, the obstacle to belonging is not borders demarcated by actual walls but by seemingly infinite symbolic barriers. This 'open borders' paradox will inform my reading of the migrant films covered in Chapter 5, all of which share thematic connections with Kaurismäki's 2011 *Le Havre*, a film that focuses on a Frenchman's attempt to help a young African who hopes to travel clandestinely to rejoin family in the UK.

The voyages of the Leningrad Cowboys problematise the very mobility that makes them possible, and in this way the two films offer a valuable reminder of the perils and limits of open borders. What travel looks and sounds like in the two films is informed by the director's ambivalence towards the very act of travelling. While the voyages traverse long stretches of American highway that bisect a wide array of landscapes, we as spectators are not presented with the beautiful panoramic shots or glorious montages that are considered a hallmark of road cinema. Instead, the journeys hop from one 'non-place' (as theorised by Marc Augé [1992]) to another (Peden 2013: 117). The voyage is signposted by a series of location intertitles with black backgrounds, the first of which reads 'International Airport'. It is difficult to imagine a more suggestive symbol of a 'placeless' world than a geographically anonymous 'international airport' announced on an empty black backdrop. When terrestrial travel is involved, the voyage is recounted with travelling montages, but as suggested above, these tend to be characterised by a particularly morose feel and display a bleak slice of America, the pieces of roadways between the dive bars, used auto lots and downmarket convenience stores frequented by the Cowboys. Moreover, unlike in many auto-centric road films, the camera does not privilege the driver's perspective (Mazierska and Rascaroli 2006: 21).

In Nestingen's assessment of Kaurismäki's road movies he suggests that 'travellers are by definition outsiders in the area through which they travel' (2013: 39). While this would be characteristic of what I have identified as a 'negative' road film (see the Introduction and Chapter 5 for further discussion of this term), it is, however, certainly not the case in all or even most European road movies. Rather there is a division between films in which travellers are outsiders ('negative') and the more common brand of 'positive' film in which travel facilitates connections and underscores porosity of frontiers and identities. The final film under consideration here exhibits the contrast between positive and negative by espousing a radically different perspective on mobility. Wender's *Lisbon Story* (1994, Germany/Portugal) starts with a similar premise – the possibility of borderless travel – but demonstrates a very different outlook on the post-1989 European landscape. Rüdiger Vogler reprises his role as Phillip Winter in *Bis ans Ende der Welt/Until the End of the World* (1991, Germany/France/Australia/USA), *In weiter Ferne, so nah!/Faraway, so close!* (1993, Germany) and as 'Philip' Winter in Wender's early road movie *Alice in the Cities* and Bruno Winter in *Kings of the Road*. The following discussion will draw out some comparisons and contrasts between *Lisbon Story* as an example of post-1989 European mobility and *Kings of the Road*, a quintessential example of Wender's hybrid Euro-American road cinema. *Lisbon Story* differs from many road films in that it only contains approximately thirteen minutes of travel between destinations – Frankfurt and Lisbon in this case – at the very start of the narrative. Yet *Lisbon Story* manages to distil the basic essence of road cinema into that time. Moreover, upon closer examination, the thirteen minutes of travel represents thirteen per cent of the film's total running time, which is slightly more than the percentage of actual driving sequences in *Kings of the Road*, which is entirely set on the road (Geist 1988: 53).

In *Lisbon Story* Philip Winter, a movie sound man and self-proclaimed citizen of a newly open and united Europe, is on the road at the behest of a director friend who needs him to record sound for a film about that city. The first portion of the narrative is comprised of Winter's eminently borderless voyage across the continent, a marked change from the geographic parameters of Wenders' first road films. Those films must be considered in order to fully grasp the significance of the boundless continental jaunt in *Lisbon Story*. As Nick Roddick argues, Wender's early work imported the 'spirit of the American road movie' into a European format (2008) while Derek Malcolm calls *Kings of the Road* 'Europe's most telling example of the American road movie' (Malcolm 2002). An example of the distinctively European qualities of these films would be how, in Wenders' Europe-set films, from *Kings of the Road* to *Wings of Desire* (1987), filmed in Berlin just two years before the Wall would fall, 'the sense of being hemmed in by a border is still crucial' (Roddick 2008). *Kings of the Road*, set on the East German border, 'pushes the aimless, nomadic road narrative to new extremes' (Laderman 2002: 259). It is therefore both enclosed and wide open. As one critic observed, what Wenders borrowed from American road films 'is the sense of movement only possible in a country with huge, empty open spaces of a kind we don't really have in Europe' (Roddick 2008). In other words, Wenders filmed Europe, and Germany in this case, in a way that makes it feel vast but his landscape remains awash in reminders of spatial limitations. British filmmaker Chris Petit addresses the same issue in somewhat contradictory terms, suggesting that European space can feel 'cramped' but admitting that he 'saw no reason why contemporary England could not be a cinematic landscape' (Wood 2007: xii). A similar approach will be found in some of the contemporary films addressed later, particularly in Chapter 3 on Belgian road films and the territorial limitations presented in them.

Kings of the Road opens with Bruno Winter (Vogler), who earns a mobile living maintaining movie projectors in sleepy towns along the East/West German border, taking a break from his route when Robert (Hanns Zischler) comes zipping along in his car on a crash course for a pond next to Bruno's truck. Robert drives into the water but walks out unharmed, if clearly psychologically frail, and is taken in by the other man. The duo (Figure 1.2) then rides together on the cinema circuit, forging a friendship along a meandering path that includes detours from Bruno's repair route to visit the places they grew up, including the summer home of Bruno's family. Such voyages into a past are a common ingredient of the road movie itinerary, as demonstrated by a diverse array of films such as *Il Sorpasso*, Bergman's *Wild Strawberries* (1957) and more recently *Nebraska* (Alexander Payne, 2013) as well as a number of the films discussed in the following chapters, including another 'mobile home' film, *Torpedo* (Matthieu Donck, 2012, Belgium/France; see Chapter 2). These often unplanned deviations from the initial route add an introspective and retrospective dimension to the road movie's symbolic and metaphysical exploration of where the travellers are headed. Bruno and Robert often drive to the backdrop of rock music, another hallmark of road cinema that frequently lends a 'liberating lilt' to the isolation of the voyage (Laderman 2002: 262). The upbeat soundtrack that accompanies travelling sequences stands in sharp contrast to

Figure 1.2   The travelling duo in *Kings of the Road* (Wim Wenders, 1977)

the more melancholy tunes, often plaintive blues melodies, complementing the travelling shots in *Go America*. Most of the films in subsequent chapters will feature soundtracks that are either (more commonly) liberating or melancholy in tone, with the exception of the migrant films in Chapter 5, which tend to pair images of travel with the ambient, realist sounds of movement.

The truck, which is both a mobile home and an 'office' on the road and thus suggests a parallel between road and life itself – versus purely an escape from it – travels by day (sometimes seemingly without aim) and pulls off the road at night. Pauses in the journey are as important to the road narrative as the road itself, and are often employed to facilitate introspection and reflection (Laderman 2002: 262). A final element worthy of attention is the now familiar duelling mobilities represented in two sequences in which Bruno's truck is framed against a train. This distinguishes the 'more creative and free' variety of automobility from 'controlled, destination-oriented travel' (Laderman 2002: 262) on the tracks and guided by schedules. This comparison and similar visual staging is employed in various European films, perhaps most notably in Laurent Cantet's *L'emploi du temps/Time Out* (2001, France), in which a man who lost his job spends his days on the road, occasionally 'racing' a passing train that is presumably full of commuters headed to work.[7] The narrative in *Kings of the Road* comes to a close after the pair drive up to a symbolically charged barrier with East Germany, an abandoned American military station, which Laderman calls the 'end of the road, on many levels' (2002: 264). This ending of their travelling pairing is not the literal ending of the voyage, however. In *Kings of the Road* that road seems to go on forever, closing with both characters still in motion, albeit now separately, in a sequence that cross-cuts between Robert on a train and Bruno in his truck. This ending and the gesture of constant motion is a recurring one in road movies (Moser 2008: 22).

A close examination of the initial travel sequence in *Lisbon Story* also reveals a combination of common road movie traditions. The montage that delivers Winter to the Portuguese border is comprised of mainly frontal travelling shots, a recurring angle in *Kings of the Road*, that unlike in the *Leningrad Cowboys* films take the vantage point of the driver. The landscape that he – and the viewer – initially sees is largely limited to the motorway and the familiar extensions of the road, with the exception of a centre-city detour through Paris. Winter's car races past now abandoned border stations, roadside petrol stations, truck parks and restaurants, bridges, with occasional vistas of fields and mountains framing the road. In contrast to the circular and cyclical itinerary and 'unhurried attitude' of *Kings of the Road* (Geist 1988: 52–4), the route in *Lisbon Story* is linear and the pace precipitous due to Winter's haste to arrive. The vehicle is symbolically ushered onward by a recurring image of forward directional arrows painted on the roadway. At the same time post-Schengen Europe is compressed into a montage of jump cuts and sonic fragments indicating the national language at times when the rock music soundtrack is replaced with radio news reports. While Winters marvels at the open borders and the fluidity of movement and extols the possibilities of an ostensibly borderless continent in a series of monologues (which recall travelling scenes from Vogler's traversal of the US as 'Philip' Winter in *Alice in the Cities*), he seems oblivious to news on the radio of massacres in Algeria recounted as he drives through France as well as to the ongoing wars and strife within the continent that risk troubling his idealised notions of Europe (Mazierska and Rascaroli 2006: 204). In short, the film seems to embrace only the positive aspects of open borders, and does so from a perspective of those privileged with mobility and Western passports (Gott 2013c: 139).

Such condensed montages are not unusual and are indeed exemplary of a technique common in road cinema. However, what seems completely normal in an American film involving the passage of 'empty space', when applied to Europe has the effect of compressing into a jumble cultures whose differences are more readily obvious. As he drives Winter claims that he is a 'citizen of Europe' and marvels that borders have disappeared. There is also another possible interpretation beyond such overly simplified and perhaps naïve 'one Europe' thinking: to some extent, the national borders have always been somewhat arbitrary and Winter as a cinema artist is now free to enjoy boundary-free politics in addition to a borderless artistic vision. Winter's hasty and carefree course across the continent's open roads comes to an end more than six minutes into the film when a road event intervenes. He suffers a flat tyre near the Portuguese border, followed by a series of mishaps that virtually stalls his mobility and ultimately lead him to trade his disabled car in exchange for a ride to his final destination. First the spare tyre falls off a bridge and the patched car hobbles into a final abandoned border outpost visibly more desolate than those through which he sped en route. The water there has been turned off and the phone line disconnected, symbols of the obsolescence of border posts within the EU. Road events often fundamentally alter the course of the trip by putting travellers in touch with new people or sending them along unplanned routes, but this event only slows down the voyage. It might be read then as a nod to road cinema convention, or perhaps Winter's enthusiasm for rapidly crossing through space without pausing to engage with it is punished, for the derelict border post offers neither the water he needs to hydrate his dying radiator nor – paradoxically in an ostensibly connected Europe – the possibility of communicating with the outside world to get assistance. All this renders him lost on several levels, and he rues his decision to leave the fast lane for the more scenic and desolate routes that recall the American West. 'I shouldn't have left the motorway, I'm an idiot', he mutters to himself while looking at a map, the quintessential road movie prop. The setting, presumably in the Spanish province of Extremadura – etymologically linked to the Latin words 'end' and 'border' – based on the landscape and the eventual route into Lisbon, is also highly symbolic. After thousands of kilometres of borderless travel, Winter finds himself marooned at a border. He patches his car only to see it break down yet again, forcing him to continue to the nearest town on the back of a horse-driven cart with his large pile of luggage. Protagonists forced to give up on malfunctioning vehicles in favour of rides via slower modes of conveyance is a recurring trope in road cinema that calls into question the importance of the vehicle and parodies the need for speed central to so many films. Winter barters the car for a ride to Lisbon in a truck, a voyage that is not filmed until the destination in the Alfama quarter is tantalisingly close but ultimately resistant to his attempts to locate it. The truck arrives in Lisbon, crossing the iconic 25th of April Bridge, only to get lost in a warren of streets, demonstrated by another montage with a time-lapse effect that humorously encapsulates the search. Such navigational difficulties are another recurrent feature of road cinema that plays on the notion that the intended destination in question is often not truly the true end of the route.

Fittingly, neither the voyage nor the quest truly ends in Lisbon. Winter finds his friend Friedrich's apartment empty and must search for him in the city – an endeavour that recalls the hunt for the home of Alice's grandmother in *Alice in the Cities*. He simultaneously begins recording the sound for Friedrich's film, a task that involves walks through the neighbourhood in search of the sonic matches for his friend's black and white images as well as rides on the trams that rumble down the narrow streets of the Alfama, captured in more travelling shots. *Lisbon Story* is both a road trip to Lisbon and a voyage through the enchantingly worn streets of the Portuguese capital. The time-warp setting of the village-like Alfama scouted out by Wenders, a place resistant to speed and which appears 'frozen in time' (Mazierska and Rascaroli 2006: 205–6) is the fitting site for a third mode of 'travel', a voyage into cinematic history.[8] The Alfama quarter is also significant because it was the old Moorish heart of the city and therefore like the Extremadura border post represents another prior zone of contact between cultures. Friedrich employs a hand-cranked camera to shoot the city and Wenders conjures the silent era with iris out transitions. As he awaits his friend, Philip demonstrates to some neighbourhood children his talent for producing sound effects that postdate the silent era but had long since gone out of style. The first sound he tests is a horse, which he prods the children to associate with cowboys. Winters proceeds to produce a play using sounds based on the cowboy, nodding to the cinematic traditions that Wenders is mining with this road trip to the Western frontier of Europe. After they are finally reunited, Friedrich takes Winter to an abandoned movie house 'The Paris', announcing in French 'voilà ma cinémathèque'. The gesture recalls Wenders' own cinematic initiation at the Cinémathèque française in Paris and underscores the borderless nature of cinematic inspiration. Orgeron has described Wenders' earlier road movies as the result of a 'cinematic conversation' taking place with Godard and Hopper (2007: 10), reference points that leave traces in *Lisbon Story* as well. Ultimately, although *Lisbon Story* is among other things a cinematic ode to the city, some of Lisbon's vitality has been lost in Wenders' portrayal of it, much like, it seems, the less-pleasant realities of contemporary Europe are lost to Winter in the course of his voyage. Mazierska and Rascaroli contend that while the film is concerned with Winter's renegotiation of his identity, and revels visually in images of water suggestive of fluidity, Portugal's colonial past and its capital's diverse postcolonial present are nowhere to be found (2006: 208). In this sense while it encompasses everything that might be said to be the essence of post-1989 road travel, including the possibility of fluid and self-defined identity stances, *Lisbon Story* ultimately fails to forge true connections with the spaces it traverses or stops in.

THE ROAD FORWARD

We can draw some important points from the examples of European road films addressed in this chapter. First, in road movies the concept of nation or national language is often a blurry and fluid notion due to the border-crossing proclivities of film production, of cinema talent (from actors to production teams) and of the narratives themselves. Secondly, while it very difficult to view contemporary European road cinema without spotting references to Hollywood cinema, notably the highly influential road films of the 1960s and 1970s, and the American open spaces that now seem synonymous with boundless road travel, European road cinema from the 1960s and 1970s and beyond is also itself a rich source of influence. Distinctively European imprints can be found in numerous films addressed in the following chapters. *Aaltra* (Chapter 3) wears the influence of Kaurismäki on its sleeve and that director even has a cameo in that film. The northward routes traced in other films such as *Rendez-vous à Kiruna* (Chapter 2) also pay tribute in varying degrees to that director's work. As we will also see in Chapter 3, Belgian director Bouli Lanners' filmography owes much to American cinema, but also bears the marks of Wenders and other European road forerunners. Many films, both those covered in this book as well as others that are not, perhaps most memorably *Western* (Manuel Poirier, 1997, France), have followed in the footsteps of *Il Sorpasso*'s model of an odd pairing drawn to hit the road together by a chance encounter. The following chapter will further consider the characteristics of European road cinema within a more narrowly defined focus on contemporary films produced in the three major French-language film industries in Europe.

NOTES

1. The capability of the director to speak French 'correctly' is one of the criteria for inclusion of a film in the *Trophées Franophones du Cinéma* awards.
2. Moreover despite the popular association of the automobile with American life-styles, statistics have shown that Europeans also undertake the vast majority of their travel by car. A 1995 study indicated that 80 per cent of leisure travel in Europe was undertaken by car (Urry 1995: 168).
3. In *Éloge de la mobilité* French sociologist Jean Viard cites several statistical meas-ures of the rapid increase in mobility that took place in Europe of the 1950s: in 1950 the average French person travelled an average of 5 kilometres a day, a figure that expanded ninefold by 2005 (2006: 112). Holiday travel accounts for some of this increase. Only 15 per cent of French people left home for vacation in 1950, a figure that increased to 64 per cent by 2005. The largest percentage growth came in the 1950s, part of a trend of increasing tourism across Europe that is visible in *Il Sorpasso* and *Le corniaud*.
4. There is no special focus on the driver except in the rear projection travelling shots through the woods to Edouard's chateau, where we have a shot-reverse-shot series between driver and passenger.
5. Louis de Funès was born in suburban Paris to a poor Spanish family and would become the post popular star of post-war French cinema (Vincendeau 2000: 136–7). This popular success was not matched by critical acclaim, however.
6. Born in Olomouc, Moravia, when it was part of the Austrian Empire, Ulmer injected a European vantage point into his films.
7. For a reading of this film in a road cinema context, see Martin O'Shaughnessy (2013).
8. The voyage as trek into cinema history connects this film to Theodoros Angelopoulos' *Ulysses' Gaze*, made the following year. The multinational co-production narrates a voyage to the Balkans by a director searching for traces of the early filmmakers, the Manakia brothers.

2. REMAPPING THE EUROPEAN ROAD

Films covered: *Le grand voyage* (Ismael Ferroukhi, 2004, France/Morocco/Bulgaria/Turkey), *Rendez-vous à Kiruna* (Anna Novion, 2012, France), *Saint-Jacques . . . la Mecque* (Colline Serreau, 2005, France), *Torpedo* (Matthieu Donck, 2012, Belgium/France) and *La vraie vie est ailleurs* (Frédéric Choffat, 2006, Switzerland)

This chapter moves on to contemporary cinema to examine a representative sample of films made since 2004 that introduce the geographic range, key thematic and cultural issues, and most typical modes of transport employed in French-language European road cinema. As I argued in the introduction, road movies – a breed of travel cinema more traditionally associated with the vast open spaces of North America – are presently flourishing in Europe because they articulate a desire to come to terms with new relationships to space and identity. In this chapter I will return once again to the question of the road movie's geographic particularities. Unlike in Chapter 1, which explored interconnected points of influence and exchange, this chapter will aim to delineate the cultural and artistic specificity of contemporary European road cinema. This exploration of the characteristics of French-language European road films encompasses two overlapping angles of approach: one that considers a number of key thematic issues and the other that investigates the rich variety of modes of conveyance or travel harnessed in European road cinema. In other words, I will use the following case studies to examine the primary motivations for being on the road in French-language Europe (and Europe in general) and the ways in which the various modes of transit involved are represented and how the techniques and practicalities affect the issue of representation.

In the following I will assess five diverse films that employ the road format to respond to the Europeanisation of economies and identity formulations: *Rendez-vous à Kiruna* (Anna Novion, 2012, France), *Le grand voyage* (Ismael Ferroukhi, 2004, France/Morocco/Bulgaria/Turkey), *Torpedo* (Matthieu Donck, 2012, Belgium/France), *Saint-Jacques . . . la Mecque* (Colline Serreau, 2005, France) and *La vraie vie est ailleurs* (Frédéric Choffat, 2006, Switzerland). The process that Randall Halle calls 'Europeanization' (2014) has led to new ways of conceiving of identities outside and in complement to the nation. This has resulted in renewed interest in sub-national, regional identity formulations and in transnational affinities encouraged by tourism and cultural exchanges. Each film under consideration seeks to outline the new 'soft borders' of Europe by crossing a variety of national, regional and social boundaries. These films narrate voyages by tourists, businesspeople, religious pilgrims and residents of *banlieues* (the term applied to often economically disadvantaged housing projects on the outskirts of large cities) for whom travel offers the possibility to escape the constraints of their everyday existence and/or identity category. The most common modes of transit in European road movies are introduced here: walking, travel by train and driving.

The films considered in this chapter present a representative sample of recent European road cinema. They are all fundamentally concerned with remapping projects that bring people together within and across national lines, which are often less important than natural features of the landscape that sometimes mark national and cultural borders but also frequently transcend them. By comparing and juxtaposing films produced in three different nations with French-language film industries, I hope to see what sort of distinctions, or connections, are made between the component parts, nations, regions, highways and back roads that make up today's Europe. Scholars have suggested that due to the outsized cultural prominence of Paris in the French imagination and film industry, landscape does not feature prominently French cinema (Williams 2013: 24). As a general rule, by contrast, French road movies have avoided the capital (and in particular its core), even as a starting or ending point (Gott and Schilt 2013: 9). While only three of the films I examine are majority French productions, all five of them travel through France. Moreover these films are also representative of how the geographic marginality of European road movies extends to my corpus in general – with the notable exception of two films addressed in Chapter 5, which focus on migrants and post-migration urban trajectories – and is central to the project of redefining identities because the spaces beyond the city allow characters (as groups) to remake themselves against the backdrop of 'unmapped' or as Deleuze and Guattari (1987) theorise it, 'smooth' space (which is opposed to 'striated' space, something I will discuss later). Thus in all of these films, landscape features are more important than the cities that serve as starting points or as destinations.

James Williams' recent study on *Space and Being* in French cinema aims to 'determine to what extent film can project the world anew' (2013: xv). Williams explores a variety of films, which are primarily not travel films, by directors who, as he puts it, are concerned with 'the relationship between space, place and subjectivity', the relation between local, national and global, and the 'design and mapping of geophysical space by the agents of power and ideology' (2013: 29). The starting premise of this chapter is that the road movie format appeals to contemporary directors precisely because it is well suited to remap the pre-existing conceptions of space and identity, which have forwarded closed, binary, limiting and otherwise 'congealed' as Williams puts it in relationship to the French context – and for all these reasons fundamentally flawed – conceptions of belonging and not belonging. In a gesture that nods towards the association of the road film (like its precursor, the western) with 'conquering space', the empty spaces of landscape connote but do not dictate, allowing for the sense of liberty, the chance to (re)define one's identity. In European road cinema this process of remapping tends to bring people together, both within a particular culture or across national boundaries. This tendency conforms to the theory forwarded by Laderman that European films are about travel into culture as opposed to the dominant American strain of road cinema, which has at its core a fundamental impulse towards rebellion (2002: 15).

This chapter pays particular attention to the ways in which different modes of conveyance affects the connection between the characters and the landscapes they traverse. Road movies have most commonly been associated with motorised mobility. As I suggest in the introduction, the travelling shot is a key component – and arguably the crucial element – of road films, and has been theorised by Laderman as a tracking shot intended to convey 'a visceral sense of traveling at a hyper-human, modernized speed' (2002: 12). Likewise the travelling montage combines these shots in order to encapsulate forward progress while often emphasising the pleasure of travelling at high speed. Such montages commonly 'sublimate[s] car travel to an idea or sensibility, in contrast with the linear, destination-oriented concept of travel' (2002: 18). As I will discuss in the context of the individual films, the road movie's formal toolkit is particularly well suited for the cinematic exploration of self in changing spaces and across borders. Mirrors, reflections and framing devices using windows are incorporated into montages in order to highlight the shifting relationship of the protagonists to the spaces traversed, framing and visually narrate the (re)discovery of places (Gott 2013b: 78–9). The confined interior spaces of cars often encourage or even impose rapprochement and/or conflict (Wood 2007: xvi). Train travel theoretically situates more people together within a confined space but is less likely to engender meaningful contacts and, for this reason and others that I will address in greater detail below, has generally furnished a less fitting template for road films. The framing of inside spaces in car or train films is always juxtaposed (literally and symbolically) in travelling montages with the spaces outside, in the process highlighting the landscapes that are so crucial to the films explored here. One of the case studies in this chapter will also allow for a more detailed consideration of travelling shots at human speed, without the motorised power of the auto. As I argued in the introduction, the typical preference in European road movies for slower modes of conveyance such as walking or public transit demands a broader understanding of the travelling shot as a tracking shot that captures at any speed and, depending on the film's positive or negative outlook, either the spirit or the disorientation involved in travel.

Auto Films: Inhabiting European Roads

I will begin with two car-centred road films, in order to demonstrate how the fundamentally different ways that automobile travellers approach the world around them are translated into cinematic representations. John Urry has described the evolution of automotive travel in Western cultures as a movement from 'inhabiting the paved road' to 'inhabiting the car' (2007: 125–6). Early drivers and riders inhabited the road, meaning that they were in more direct contact with the world through which they travelled. In contrast, 'inhabiting the car' refers to a driving experience in which the car windows come to resemble a television (2007: 125–6). In this way of moving across space, the car fills the role of a veritable dwelling, resulting in an experience of travel that limits interactions with the people, places and indeed cultures traversed. A 'two-dimensional view' is generated by high-speed car travel that reduces the sights, sounds (be it music or language), tastes, and scents to something seen through the windscreen or mirror (2007: 129). As Urry contends, '[C]ar-drivers, while moving at speed, lose the ability to perceive local detail beyond the car, let alone to talk to strangers, to learn local ways of life, to sense each place' (2007: 129).

We have already observed that the European road movie template often avoids this pitfall of automobile travel. European road films are more frequently associated with public transit and walking in comparison to the heavily auto-driven North American road movie template. Many European films that do stage travel by car regularly evoke a number of the trappings of the American model, and automobile travel may – through choice of vehicle, for example – quote the car-centric American road movie. Films such as the 'return' road movies analysed in Chapter 4 commonly place their protagonists behind the wheel, at least in part, in order to exploit the possibilities of framing self-assessment and transformation that accompanies travel through spaces imbued with particular family and/or cultural significance. In the following pages I will consider the other motivations/possibilities involved in the use of automobile travel in road films.

European road movies generally lean more towards a stance that is much closer to 'inhabiting the road' than to 'inhabiting the car'. This frequently places travellers into contact with the myriad of cultures and languages that are characteristic of European spaces. I will consider two films that support this argument while also demonstrating different degrees of both forms of automobile travel. *Rendez-vous à Kiruna* portrays a transformation from inhabiting the car to inhabiting the road. The second example, *Le grand voyage*, is fundamentally concerned with the interactions within the sealed confines and enforced proximity of the car. However, while landscape does not have an immediately evident significance to the filmic narrative, the spaces traversed serve a crucial symbolic role. Coming to terms with the cultures that the father–son travelling duo crosses through is an essential part of the transformation that occurs within the space of the vehicle. These films also offer an opportunity to consider the particular significance of the 'road event' in driving films. In both cases, any intended insularity is thwarted by the 'road event', which thrusts the travellers into contact with the spaces they traverse. These events fulfil the purpose of putting characters into contact with people, cultures and places they would otherwise zip by, thus facilitating transformation (even when this transformation operates primarily as an internal process within the car). In the European road movie, the road event has the purpose of circumventing the impervious seal between inside and outside; space, culture, language – in short difference – can rarely be kept at bay on the European road.

Rendez-vous à Kiruna: Self-discovery and Family Building on the Road to the 'Great Wild North'

Rendez-vous à Kiruna (henceforth *Rendez-vous*), by Anna Novion, is a conventional road movie in terms of the personal growth and transformation it maps and interweaves with issues of family and romantic relationships. This driving road movie involves a solitary traveller joined for a significant portion of his voyage by a hitchhiker whose presence fundamentally alters the voyage. Ernest Toussaint is a highly successful Parisian architect who has been hiding a secret from a past relationship. Despite its familiar element of personal growth, the film reverses a typical theme in road movies that charts the voyages of younger protagonists into the cultures and places of familial significance or purported sites of family 'origins', where a common trope involves the desire of a father to be buried by his son in his homeland. In this case Ernest undertakes this voyage that will take him some 3,000 kilometres – almost as far as one can venture from Paris while remaining within the EU – to the far north of Sweden in order to identify the body of his son. The unique twist is that he did not know his son and indeed had never even laid eyes on him. The unknown progeny was conceived in France and born his mother's native Sweden after she and Ernest split due to a fundamental disagreement on the direction of their lives. She wanted children and he categorically did not, and after she left Ernest never sought out his son. As is common in personal quest narratives, the ultimate goal of the protagonist changes en route, although the intended destination does not, thanks in large part to influential encounters on the road. Ernest initially resists when he is asked to identify the body of his son, but ultimately decides to abruptly leave his busy job as an architect in Paris to make the trek by car and ferry to Kiruna, the northernmost town in Sweden. He leaves precipitously without having revealed the true motivation for his flight to anyone and without so much as having packed a bag.

Ernest is an elite brand of international traveller, endowed with what Vincente Rodríguez Ortega calls the 'circulatory privileges and cultural advantages' of European citizenship (2011: 23). Economically well-off, he is able to keep in touch with his work from virtually anywhere and to travel lightly, if not quickly. The long car and ferry voyage, necessitated by Ernest's fear of flying, proves to be transformative. He visits his son's apartment and 'meets' him at the morgue for the first time. As his course through Sweden begins, Ernest encounters a 'new' son in Magnus, a young man hitchhiking towards his home in the same region. Magnus speaks French and studied archaeology for two years in France. It is highly symbolic that Ernest meets a young would-have-been archaeologist while he is digging through and attempting to make sense of his own past by putting the various fragments together. The character also invites us to think back to Novion's first film, the 2008 French–Swedish co-production *Les grandes personnes/Grown-ups*, which too involves a trip to Sweden. In that film a tourist also played by Jean-Pierre Daroussin digs into the past in the form of Viking history. Magnus, the hitchhiker in *Rendez-vous*, is played by Anastasios Soulis, who also appears in the earlier film in the role of a French-speaking minor character with the same name. The reliance on the same troupe of in some cases transnational actors (Judith Henri and Swedish actress Lia Boysen also appear in both films, with the latter playing the role of a francophone Swede in the first) reinforces the impression of circular networks of transnational connections and incessant mobility over porous national borders that defines the contemporary European experience for those with the correct passports and adequate funds. Indeed most of the significant and common forms for inter-European mobility are represented in these two films: students, tourists, business travel and 'VFR' or 'visiting friends and relatives' (Urry 2007: 10). Ginette Verstraete's argument that the tourist is essential to the propagation of the European myth of unity-in-diversity because 'he or she combines freedom, cross-border mobility and openness to different cultures' (2010: 43), relates to several of the films covered in this chapter.

The auto-centric format is used in *Rendez-vous* to convey and frame the transformation of Ernest as he travels through space, in which a rather conventional road movie template provides the basis for the cinematice exploration of self-evaluation and the projection of self through space. The use of windows, windscreens and mirrors as framing devices charts the forward progress of Ernest's identity quest and suggests a process of self-reflection that, as Everett puts it, rephrasing Roland Barthes, becomes an 'effective metaphor for someone riding on the edge of self-identity' (2009: 172). My analysis of the ways by which travel is represented in this film will focus on two particular aspects of Ernest's voyage: the experience and significance of travelling long distances and the role of the particular spaces traversed, particularly Sweden.

As I have already noted, the film narrates a rather unique European road trip, encompassing over thirty hours of travel time towards the northern limits of the continent. This type of long-distance travel has been more typically associated with the American strain of road films, and such a venture would have provided a very different experience in pre-Schengen Europe when crossing borders necessitated a stop. In *Les grandes personnes*, Daroussin's Albert expresses an outlook linking him to the gleefully border-hopping Philip Winter in Wender's 1994 *Lisbon Story* (discussed in Chapter 1). Albert cites the fall of the Berlin Wall and European unification as the inspiration for an annual series of educational and initiatic voyages to different European nations he takes with his daughter, a tradition they began a few years prior with a trip to Berlin (Gott 2015a: 10). The attempt in that film to undertake a mental mapping of New Europe through tourism and to a smaller degree through potentially more meaningful encounters makes way in *Rendez-vous* to a related impulse of borderless post-Wall European travel.

The initial travelling montage in *Rendez-vous* closely resembles the voyage in *Lisbon Story*: Ernest races across nearly 1,000 kilometres of borderless Europe in a two-minute montage that features a rather drab slice of what Augé would term the continent's 'non-places', or to use Urry's vocabulary, 'transfer points' and 'places of in-between-ness' (2007: 42). Replete with images of power lines, tunnels, petrol stations and countless lorries that serve as a backdrop to all stops and announce the global flows of goods, the montage associates speed with a 'placeless' reading of contemporary Europe. In this way the film also meets Moser's criterion that road movies show vehicles in motion and the iconography of the road (2008: 21). Ernest stays connected to work by phone throughout this portion of the voyage, and in order to hide his past tells his partner Victoire that he is on emergency business trip related to the construction of a bridge in Sweden. His vantage point on work and on life begins to change after Ernest crosses the Baltic Sea and begins to inhabit the road instead of his car. The landscape of Sweden receives significantly more attention and the starkly beautiful forests, lakes and hills frame Ernest's personal transformation that begins with a move from obsession with job and being overly busy to silence, reflection and escape in the wide open spaces of northern Sweden. The empty space is not, however, a 'void', but a site of personal connection. Over the course of this journey and concomitant with the evolution of Ernest's relationship to the landscape, Magnus gradually becomes his symbolic 'Swedish son'. Being of a similar age to the deceased son and from the same region, Magnus is able to serve as a local guide and as a replacement son of sorts, and is even mistaken for his biological child by a roadside restaurant server. The stopover at this Swedish 'diner' is another nod to the iconography of the road, albeit one that portends the start of a new interaction with the culture of the places driven through.

The way that Ernest 'inhabits' his car plays a significant role in how this relationship is mediated. As exemplified in films such as *Le grand voyage*, the car is often a space that fosters or even imposes coming together or rapprochement (Wood 2007: xvi). Back in Paris Ernest was chastised by Victoire for his selfishness and proclivity to closing himself off from others. On the road the car permits the continuation of this tendency, and Ernest initially inhabits the vehicle in a fashion that insulates him from the world. The vehicle is his 'home away from home' (Urry 2007: 128), within the confines of which Ernest caries on his habitual business and personal life. At the onset of the voyage his only contact with others is furnished by his regular phone conversation with his assistant, who mediates his management at a distance from quotidian operations at his firm. Thus the car begins as a secure, personal space, hermeneutically sealed from others but constantly linked to work, marking it as a space of what Martin O'Shaughnessy terms the 'unfreedom and alienations of networked mobility' (O'Shaughnessy 2011: 439). Much like Vincent in Cantet's *L'emploi du temps*, as a man of networks the road resembles home for Ernest and he can therefore never be free or be transformed as long as he remains in constant contact with the world and the lifestyle left behind (O'Shaughnessy 2013). The 'road event' that changes this is a seemingly banal encounter in the ferry cafeteria over breakfast – a floating version of the roadside café that commonly serves as an important space in road films – with Magnus. The latter's remark about the destination indicated by Ernest's open map does not elicit a response from the architect, who is immersed in a telephone call. Outside his car and thrust into contact with other passengers, his mobile phone is Ernest's primary means of maintaining 'social distance' (Urry 2007: 106), something that I will discuss further in relation to road films set on trains.

The significance of Ernest's ferry crossing as a symbolic passage from old to new outlooks is underscored by a sequence of shots that represent his exit from the vessel. A series of characteristic frame compositions draw our attention to the role of travel in personal development and the ways by which cinematic automobile travel is particularly suited to capture the process. First a frontal shot frames Ernest in a virtual bubble created by the vehicle and various abstract reflections on the windscreen. Through this opacity Ernest's solemn expression reveals subtle yet unmistakable unease and doubt. The camera cuts to a short montage of shots that reinforce this impression by capturing Ernest's face in the rear-view mirror from behind his shoulder, connecting his doubtful countenance to the space he is facing and about to enter. The following shot reverses the angle again, this time framing the subject through the windscreen at medium close-up distance as he drives while casting seemingly frustrated glances at a map. The sequence, which leads to Ernest picking up Magnus from the roadside leading from the dock, concludes with a final reversal of perspective to again frame the driver's face in the mirror as the young man comes into view through the windscreen. The juxtaposition of the map and his expression suggest that Ernest is in uncharted terrain, outside his comfort zone and unable to navigate the landscape ahead of him. His desire for a point of entry into this world that is foreign to him but to which he is so closely connected to is demonstrated by the way he hails Magnus: 'Do you know Sweden?' This sequence suggests a correlation between Magnus and the map, a staple prop in road films that serves what Tom Conley has identified as an ontological function that encourages consideration of 'where we come from and where we may be going' (2007: 3).

Ernest initially interprets 'to know' in a very technical sense that involves the practical navigation of Sweden's roads. Ernest and Magnus initially establish a set of barriers within the shared confines of the car that serve to impede communication. After picking up the young man, Ernest insists that talking is not necessary. As for Magnus, either as a response to the parameters of travel outlined by Ernest or as a consequence of his own diffidence and insularity, he dons large headphones that preclude conversation. The silence is broken when Ernest needs directions and rousts the Swede from his private reverie. Topics of geographic navigation gradually leads to more profound conversations about routes both have followed in life. The conversation picks up even more after Ernest, contrite for having locked out Magnus from the car while he napped, causing the former to be soaked by passing rain showers, opens up even further, at least by his generally aloof standards. The developing rapport and Ernest's shifting attitude will track with a change in the terrain and the fashion in which travel is filmed.

A series of travelling montages are employed to further explore Ernest's interactions with and reactions to the space he traverses to reach Kiruna. The association of travel on Europe's recently borderless roads with American-style (cinematic) road trips is reinforced by references to images and stereotypes often associated with the American road and road movie. The film winks at familiar symbols of late-1960s American road movies, and indeed European films by directors such as Kaurismäki, with an outlaw incident, a motorcycle chase and country-tinged rock music played at a roadside locale by a band donning cowboy hats and 'Texas Longhorns' shirts as revellers dance happily in front of a token vintage American car. Such mapping of the iconography of the 'Wild West' road movie onto the vast 'great north' represented by Europe's Nordic region has become common in French-language cinema.[1] More generally, such 'extreme' spaces, the end of the world in a way, whether it be the *Finistère* in Brittany, the westernmost point of Spain or Portugal, or even the 'wild East' in films like *Simon Konianski* (Chapter 3) and *Comme des voleurs* (Chapter 4), stand in for the 'far west' of American cinema lore in a number of European films.

As Ernest nears his destination, he becomes more closely connected to the world and the world around him that includes charming locals, cosy villages, dramatic landscape and the Western stage set. As the landscape becomes wilder and more representative of the region, and by extension symbolic of Ernest's son, the Frenchman is placed in more direct contact with the world. This incremental process of 'inhabiting the road' is demonstrated by interactions within and beyond the car. Early in his trip Ernest talked regularly on his phone in his car or at various nondescript 'transfer points' that offered neither distraction from his communications nor any local particularity. In northern Sweden he is so immersed in nature that he crosses paths with an elk while conversing on the phone in a roadside forest. Later he will share drinks with locals, including the grandfather of Magnus, scenes that demonstrate Ernest's newfound ability to carry on a polite, if very rudimentary, exchange in Swedish, starting with 'thank you'.

In keeping with this process of opening up, the film's initial travelling sequences limit our vision of space to what can be seen within the car. The first shot of Ernest on the road frames the road from the back seat, offering no more than a partial vantage point on the concrete roadside barrier that suggests simultaneously a closed perspective on the outside world and, through a visually striking but unvaried pattern of shadows projected on the concrete, the geometric repetitiousness and oppressively ordered hierarchy of the life that Ernest is in the early stages of driving away from. The travelling montages that trace the final kilometres of road that Ernest and Magnus share demonstrate the former's stark adjustment of outlook by framing the travellers together in a series of two-shots that highlight their interactions and compositions that draw the camera out of the car. A series of static extreme long shots suggest a merging of vehicle and by extension driver into the rustic landscape. After they leave Kiruna, Ernest drives Magnus to a desolate bus stop (Figure 2.1), a segment of voyage represented by a series of jump cuts that look forward

Figure 2.1   Ernest and Magnus await a bus in the 'Wild North' of *Rendez-vous à Kiruna* (Anna Novion, 2012).

onto a starkly beautiful landscape bisected by a constantly curved roadway or towards the hills flanking the road, in both cases shot by an exterior-mounted camera that keeps the perspective outside the car's confined spaces. The tortuous route, in contrast with the rigid lines of the film's first travelling shot, provides a visual representation of Ernest's new outlook on life. The final image is another static shot, this time tracing the car driving off into the horizon and back to France, a place to which he will return a changed man. The film ends after Magnus promises to visit Ernest in Paris and climbs aboard a yellow and blue bus – the colours symbolising the younger man's return to his native Sweden and his role as Ernest's Swedish 'guide' – and after Ernest confides in Magnus that he regretted not having known his son. The closing situates both characters on the move again, closing a circle in the case of the older man and perhaps leading to new voyages for the younger one.

Le grand voyage: Pilgrimage, Generational Conflicts and New European Roads

The second private auto-based road film under consideration exemplifies a different approach to inhabiting the car and the road. For Ernest's voyage in *Rendez-vous* to be transformative, he needed to escape the car – which serves as an extension of his life and work in Paris – and inhabit the road. *Le grand voyage* is also premised on an escape from the normal parameters of life, but by contrast the characters must learn to inhabit the car in peaceful and accepting co-existence. The passing space plays a role in this, but only as an impetus for internal processes.

A rare film that depicts an even longer voyage than the one made by Ernest, *Le grand voyage* follows a Moroccan immigrant father and French-born son pair on the nearly 5,000 kilometre trek from the Bouches-du-Rhône department in southern France to Mecca. The father's intended pedagogical bent as well as the title of the film suggests comparisons to the Grand Tour practiced by many upper-echelon Europeans during the seventeenth to nineteenth centuries (Berghahn 2013: 76). The trip begins as a highly contentious undertaking for the son Réda, who was born and raised in France and does not share his working-class immigrant father's traditional religious views. Réda has no interest in the pilgrimage and the extended voyage is particularly inconvenient because it forces him to leave behind his French girlfriend Lisa as well as his studies.[2] Due to the focus on the father–son relationship, the interior spaces of the car are more visually significant than the landscape. In many ways this film is comparable to the 'return road films' that will be considered in Chapter 4. However, the homecoming (Berghahn 2013: 79) for the father is not geographic but cultural, and the initiation for the son does not involve the discovery of his ancestors' native soil but of their religious traditions. For the director as well, on a symbolic level the filmic voyage represents a cultural-religious revisiting of his past. Ferroukhi was born in Morocco and immigrated to France with his parents at the age of three.

Le grand voyage is notable for the way in which it harnesses the road narrative in order to escape the familiar tropes, settings and stereotypical representations of Franco-Maghrebi characters and milieus. The protagonists live in a working-class housing project in southern France and it is relatively difficult to find such films that do not contain what Rosello refers to as the 'list of classic ingredients' of *Beur* and *banlieue* cinema: high-rise apartments, stairways, basements, big brothers and the inescapable spectre of police brutality (2011: 259).[3] Higbee (2013: 169) suggests correctly that this is made possible by the quick exit from France, allowing for a voyage of escape from stereotypes, a twist on the road movie 'escape' element

Le grand voyage is on the surface an archetypal road movie, and some critics (such as Bertrand Loutte in *Les Inrockuptibles*) have called it too conventional. However, upon closer inspection *Le grand voyage* both leans on and resists classic road movie formulas. In the first instance, what is borrowed from the American strain of the genre is applied to the French and European context quite cleverly. For example, the roles of 'buddies of the classic American road movie', as Berghahn puts it, are filled in by the father and son (Berghahn 2013: 75), who are suitably mismatched to generate ample tension that will ultimately be resolved as the voyage progresses. Of course, as Chapter 1 sought to demonstrate, the popularity of that typical buddy road pairing likely originates with the 1962 French-Italian co-production *Il Sorpasso*. Meanwhile, Ferroukhi eschews certain standard tropes and expectations of road cinema.

To cite one example, the voyage begins not with a travelling shot on the open road but with a traffic jam. This brief image harnesses the viewers' pre-existing expectations of road movies to pithily encapsulate the utter lack of joy the young protagonist is feeling as he hits the road with his father. A little later, the father chides Réda for driving too fast, again reminding us that this is not a film that celebrates the exhilaration of travel. The elder man espouses slowness as a spiritual quality (Berghahn 2013: 77) and it is he, not Réda, who calls the shots and charts the course, even though the latter is behind the wheel. The reasoning behind the desire of the father to carry out his pilgrimage by car is only revealed later on, after the two antagonistic parties have gradually grown closer on the road: travel by foot is better than by horse, by horse better than by car, by car better than by boat, and by boat better than by plane.

Due to this proscription of joyful of travel or the exhilaration of speed, the process of growth and the spirit of possibility espoused in road cinema must be mined elsewhere. Ferroukhi opts to frame the gradual rapprochement of the characters and the way in which the two generations manage to co-inhabit the car is the director's primary concern (Jaafar 2005). Mireille Rosello has suggested that the travelling companions are incompatible to a point that they follow unique, individual itineraries defined by different experiences (2011: 258). A preoccupation with the interior spaces of the car translates into a lack of pro-longed attention to landscape, particularly as seen from the perspective of or in relationship to the moving vehicle. Most of the initial road segment takes place at night, leaving the outside world murky. The camera is almost always associated either with the vantage points of the characters or focused on the inside of the car; a relatively small number of extreme long landscape shots figure in the film's travelling montages. This is surely also due in part to budgetary limitations and indeed shots of terrain such as snow-capped peaks in Slovenia and Bulgaria and breath-taking desert expanses of Syria (though actually shot in Morocco), as well as urban sites in the Balkans and Istanbul, do provide the requisite establishing images that signpost the protagonists' geographic progression. As Berghahn sug-gests, the desert in particular is a crucially important space:

> Once father and son leave the narrow undulating roads of Europe behind, the landscapes change and resemble those of the American road movie, in which the desert features as a privileged landscape. Yet, significantly, the Saudi Arabian desert is not some kind of empty wasteland but, because of its proximity to Mecca, a realm of love and spirituality . . . The desert draws attention to the transcendental nature of the journey yet to come . . . (2013: 78)

Indeed the desert has traditionally served as a privileged space in road movies because it is a 'void where long established meaning vanishes' (Laderman

2002: 14–15). If the expansive desert leading to Mecca is clearly not represent-ative of a 'void' in a wider cultural sense, it does allow for a blank canvas upon which Réda and outside of their habitual spaces and differences (religious versus secular, education versus work, family traditions versus ethnic majority friends and love interests) at home. In other words, the sands of the Middle East are not entirely 'striated' (Deleuze and Guattari 1987) for the travelling pair. Towards the end of the trip, we witness a literal example of this in a scene in the desert where the father prays with other hajjis while Réda goes off on his own and writes the name of his girlfriend in large script in the desert sand. The moment symbolises the closing of a process of rapprochement between father and son and a process of accommodation by which Réda accepts his father's vantage point on religion but chooses not to participate, a desire that his father has come to accept over the course of their voyage. This familial and genera-tional rapprochement is connected to the physical voyage when the men spot the first convoy of fellow pilgrims. 'It seems that we are getting closer', Réda remarks with a smile ('il paraît qu'on se rapproche').[4] The observation applies to the distances involved in their physical and metaphorical voyages, both of which are nearing completion.

I would be hesitant, for two reasons, to locate too much transformative and liberatory significance solely in the desert – and the 'wide open spaces of the Middle East' in general – as Berghahn seems to (2013: 78–9). First, given the father's espousal of slowness, the entirety of the geographic space traversed in the film is significant, in contrast with *Rendez-vous*, in which the landscapes that Ernest flies past before his arrival on Swedish soil lack significance and are not granted much narrative attention. *Le grand voyage* employs space differ-ently, and overlooking the importance of the spaces between France and the deserts of the Middle East would also require that we cast aside the choice to stage this long, plodding voyage by land. A voyage from France directly to the Middle East, or one that compresses that voyage through ellipsis, would risk simply reproducing the binary generational opposition established in the opening scenes.

Secondly, while the early, Western European stages of the trip correspond to a limited visual economy of roads, borders and roadside waypoints very similar to what we initially see in *Rendez-vous*, the world begins to open up far before the duo arrives in the desert. Rosello situates the end of the 'systematic narrative choice' to not represent scenery outside the vehicle with the crossing into Turkey (2011: 264). I would trace the opening up of the car space to an earlier crossing: from Western Europe into the Balkans, a space of great sym-bolic significance in the relationship between traditional, religious father and secular son. Like in *Les petits matins* (Chapter 1), in which Agathe turns down the money for a flight that would take her directly and rapidly to her destina-tion, the trip by car is necessary because without it there would be a very different story to tell. The father's preference for slow travel on back roads begins in the Balkans borderlands between East and West and Islam and Christianity, demonstrating the significance of the particular spaces traversed on the development of the travellers. His interdiction of tourism, which he sees as antithetical to a pilgrimage and indeed a practice viewed with contempt since its very inception (Mazierska and Rascaroli 2006: 35–6), is set aside in Istanbul, a city that straddles the border between the Balkans (and by extension Europe) and Asia. There Mustafa, a French-speaking Turk who helped them cross the Turkish border guides Réda around that city's sights and introduces him to a more liberal view of Islam. Istanbul capture Réda's attention and interest and his tour of the Blue Mosque is part of an initiation into what he seems to perceive as a more 'cool' side of Islam. For Réda, the spaces of Islam in Europe play a role similar to Spain, and in particular Andalusia, in Tony Gatlif's road movie *Exils* (see Introduction), released the same year. In that film the historical borderland where Islam mixed with European cultures, on European soil, soften the passage of two young travellers with Algerian roots (one *Pied-noir*, the other of Maghrebi origins) from France to Algeria, the land of their parents where they had never previously set foot. In *Le grand voyage*, the result of staging a voyage by car to Mecca is that France and the Muslim Holy City are not presented in the sharp light or contrast and confrontation. Rather than the binary conflict that would be suggested, and furthered, by the extremes brought out by a rapid air passage or narrative elision, this voyage traverses an intermediary space. Slow progression smoothens over cultural differences as well as personal or generational ones between father and son.

The focus on interactions within the car, and to a lesser extent on culturally symbolic stopovers rather than the scenery that accompanies the actual voyage, means that *Le grand voyage* is filmed differently from many road films. There are no extended travel montage sequences that express the euphoria of car travel or the simple joy of movement through space in Katell Djian's cinematography. The travelling montage that best conveys the notion of speed and freedom is not motorised. Réda rides his bike in the opening sequence that demonstrates, as argued in the introduction, that any definition of European 'travelling shots' need not be limited to tracking shots involving car or other motorised transit. In a fleeting but exhilarating series of travelling shots, the road movie's archetypal expression of 'travel for travel's sake' (Laderman 2002: 16), the camera tracks Réda as a hilly tree-lined landscape whirs by. On the road, this shot announces, he is free. When he arrives at his destination, an auto junkyard where his older brother Khalid works, we see a brief encapsulation of the hierarchical family structure. Khalid pushes his younger brother around, ordering him to help piece together a car, until an annoyed Réda escapes on his bike. His freedom is short-lived, however, as we next see him entering the family apartment in a low-rise housing project. Door frames and closed windows doors dominate the subsequent interior shots and the restrictive, claustrophobic inside spaces are in sharp contrast to the freedom Réda enjoyed outside on his bicycle. Meanwhile his father stews silently in a corner. Réda proceeds to ask his mother what is going on, signalling that he and his father barely talk and that she must serve as mediator.

If the opening sequences of *Le grand voyage* suggests an intractable confrontation staged between inflexible binaries – namely religious father and traditional family versus integrated, secular son – escape is not immediately realised in the freedom of the open road. Rather, the binary structure of intergenerational conflict is transferred from the quotidian domestic space to the road, thematically and stylistically, where father and son are trapped in the close quarters of their automobile, which they often sleep inside. The title is displayed in French and Arabic, representative of Réda's communication with his father: each speaks in the language they are most comfortable with. On a formal level, this difference is represented by a dual colour scheme. Réda has a red French passport while his father carries a green Moroccan one. Even their car is multi-coloured: the body is blue but an orange replacement door has been added on the passenger side, where the father rides. As Will Higbee observes, this 'subverts the typical association of the road movie with freedom and self-discovery, in the process establishing an immediate tension between devotion to Islam and belonging to the (French) nation' (2013: 165–6). This initial continuity between home and road, however, contradicts the basic impulse of road cinema and conflict will ultimately make way for rapprochement.

The interior space of the car has provided a compelling space for character interaction in road movies, frequently staged as either romance or friendship but also on occasion as conflict (Laderman 2002: 13–17). *Le grand voyage* certainly takes advantage of this opportunity for framing the opposing parties, often offering windscreen shot compositions of the protagonists sizing each other up with what are initially furtive glances or more evidently hostile glares. Given the importance of interior space to the narrative, it is worth examining the *mise en scène* within the car as framed during the voyage. Two examples will suffice, both set early in the trip. Lost on Balkan back roads, the protagonists pause to consider a map, that seemingly ubiquitous road movie prop. That map is placed on the dashboard before the voyage continues and regularly features in subsequent shots, as in when the travellers hesitate at a fork in the road. In it a frontal frame composition captures father and son through the windscreen at medium-close distance. The various props included in the shot are telling as they represent the conflicts between the two men while simultaneously looking forward. In the background, curtains in the rear windscreen suggest a link between the vehicle and the home left behind while blankets visible in the back seat also remind us that the mobile vehicle is also a home away from home. In the foreground prayer beads hang from the rear-view mirror as a symbol of the final goal of this journey whilst the map remains prominent on Réda's side of the screen. He is associated with more typical mapping, whereas the father prefers to navigate by intuition, a difference derived from their fundamentally different outlooks on and experiences in life and levels of education. Réda glances at his father as he awaits the older man's decision on which route to take. After they spend the night at the crossroads, delaying the decision until the next day, a travelling shot frames the two within the car from behind as they pursue their voyage. As Réda reminds his father that they remain lost, a reflection of the map figures prominently on the windscreen, an inescapable symbol of navigation and of charting literal and symbolic courses. Yet it will not be used, at least on this portion of the road. Instead, the prayer beads at the centre of the frame seem to lead the way forward. This sequence is interrupted when they stop to ask a mysterious woman for directions. Her cryptic response and forward signal offer no reassurance save the impetus to keep going. The rear angle of this shot brings into play another staple road movie visual element, the rear-view mirror, which frames Réda. His face is juxtaposed with the reflected map and dangling beads, suggesting that even if the father controls the voyage, the road ahead is primarily about Réda and his construction of self. Despite the fact that the father maintains control over the route and the pace, Réda's position behind the wheel means that he is the only one featured in these mirror framing compositions. This underscores the process of self-reflection that Réda experiences; if his father knows himself and where he is going, Réda's position and direction in life are still unclear.

Ferroukhi's treatment of the travellers' ultimate destination marks a minor but significant point of divergence from the standard road movie template. Despite the transformative power instilled in the voyage itself, unlike in *Saint-Jacques . . . la Mecque*, the destination itself has a key role. A series of shots, both aerial and amidst the crowd, provide a rare glimpse into the Muslim holy city. *Le grand voyage* has the distinction of being the first fiction feature film allowed to shoot inside Mecca (Jaafar 2005). The road quite literally ends at the final destination for the father, who dies after entering the city, leaving Réda alone at their campsite on the outskirts. Our final view of him is a travelling shot representing an archetypal road movie ending, with the protagonist back in motion, in this case with the wind blowing into his face through an open window of a taxi that will take him to the airport after selling the car. In this way the film ends with a travelling image that evokes its opening, in which Réda moves through open space outside the confines of family structure or the vehicle. But if the itinerary is for him at least circular – he is headed home – he will return profoundly changed. Higbee has identified *Le grand voyage* as a rare example of a film that places the question of Islam's place in France at the heart of the narrative (2013: 164). My reading of the film suggests that the voyage will lead Réda to an ultimately more accepting but non-practicing outlook on Islam. Significantly, although distraught at the death of his father, Réda does not experience a religious epiphany. He manifests no interest in becoming a practicing Muslim, but has internalised some elements of the elder man's belief system. Immediately before embarking on his return voyage, he stops to give money to a beggar. The woman's black hijab and djellaba recall the woman to whom the father earlier gave money, provoking a confrontation with his son who was concerned by their dwindling funds. Crucially, Réda's participation in zakat, the third pillar of Islam known as 'compulsory charity', is purely the product of choice on his part. Thus Réda takes a lesson learned from the trip into the symbolic 'voyage of life' suggested by the closing scene of the film.

TORPEDO: LANDSCAPE, FAMILY AND THE 'MOBILE HOME' FILM

If less prevalent than driving films, movies set in motor homes or variations thereof nonetheless hold an important place in the road movie tradition. Mobile homes are similar to cars in terms of possibilities for mobility, framing and character interaction, but with a twist provided by the fact the vehicle in which the voyage is undertaken represents an extension of home. In this sense 'mobile home' films provide literal, or almost so, examples of the notion that road movies are fundamentally about home. *Kings of the Road*, discussed in Chapter 1, provides the inspiration for a number of recent cinematic treks that combine the spirit of the open road with some version of the comforts, and complexities, of the domestic context. These include *35 rhums*/*35 Shots of Rum* (Claire Denis, 2008, France/Germany), *Mobile Home* (2012, François Pirot, Belgium/Luxembourg/France) and *Voir la mer* (Patrice Leconte, 2011, France).

Torpedo (Matthieu Donck, 2012, Belgium/France) is an offbeat and occasionally dark comedy that typifies a dominant strain of Belgian filmmaking (which will be discussed in greater detail in Chapter 3). It recounts a trip by motor home to find/rebuild a family by Michel, a single man who earns a meagre and inconsistent living selling second-rate merchandise at outdoor markets. The voyage is undertaken in a dated and rather dilapidated camper van Michel uses to sell his latest product. The choice of mobile home as means of conveyance serves to blur the lines separating home, work and road. Michel's unfocused life already resembles a vacation of sorts to others, and his brother-in-law exhorts him to 'get a real job'. The object of the quest that draws him away from his quotidian is to build a family in a rather unconventional and rapid fashion. That process also implies a personal transformation for Michel from a failure in life, love and in his relations with his sister and elderly father to a well-functioning family man, if not quite a model citizen by most standards. The opening scene foregrounds the notion of identity games, something that will be central to the narrative. Scores of telemarketing employees hunch over screens at a phone bank, hiding behind the nom de marketing 'Pascal(e) Dumont'. The fake Pascal(e) Dumonts phone households to invite them to present themselves, with their family, at the nearest 'Sofa Life' furniture store for a chance to win a visit from Belgian cycling great Eddie Merckx, who the director has described as a symbol of Belgian unity that predates recent communitarian squabbles.[5] The hapless Michel is excited by what he sees as an opportunity to renew family ties. His elderly father, whose birthday is approaching, is a big fan of the cyclist. The phone call ends with a cut to Michel play-acting a meeting with Merckx in a grimy and tarnished mirror, a clear symbol of his unclear position in the world and self-doubt. Put in typical road movie terms, Michel is lost, a bit of symbolism that later becomes literal. Hitting the road will allow him to more concretely play out a similar fantasy in which is life is significantly improved.

If a visit with Eddie Merckx is the solution to at least some of his problems, Michel faces a significant obstacle – beyond the meagre odds of actually winning – being single and without children he does not qualify for the contest, in which the notion of a 'petite famille' is rather conservative: a wife and at least one child. It is fitting that he will seek to find a less traditional alternative to this vision on the road. By facilitating travel outside the typical social spaces, be they collective or domestic, road movies naturally lend themselves to the re-examination of the traditional, patriarchal family (Gott and Schilt 2015).[6] As opposed to the traditional American road template, 'escape' in continental road movies should not be seen as an attempt to simply revolt against dominant culture, but as symptomatic of an impulse to selectively evade certain restrictive elements within that culture. If the family drama in *Le grand voyage* is framed within the context of wider contestations over dominant conceptions of national or communitarian cultural identity, *Torpedo* sets its sights more clearly on detouring from societal notions of a nuclear family. Michel must assemble a 'false family' comprised of a neglected and mistreated young neighbour named Kevin and an ex-girlfriend Christine who is visibly displeased to see him appear but grudgingly acquiesces because she apparently owes him a favour. Unfortunately for Michel the improvised family shows up too late at Sofa Life and are turned away rather unceremoniously by the manager (one of apparently many live incarnations of 'Pascal Dumont'). The desperate Michel waits in the parking lot to plead his case. After revealing that the promotion is over in Belgium and that Eddie Merckx's next stop will be at the store in Brest, over the border with France and one thousand kilometres away, the manager slips while evading Michel and is knocked unconscious. Michel panics and absconds with the lifeless man tied up in the back of his camper. Brest, in Brittany, is about as far west as one can get in France, surely a nod to the road movie's American western strains as well as to Jacques Brel's notable Belgian road movie *Le Far West* (1973) and Poirier's Brittany-set *Western* (1997).

At this point all of the ingredients for a European road movie are in place: a quest, an accidental kidnapping – as Chapter 1 revealed, the criminal component associated with a certain strain of American road movie is a typical object of parody in European road films – and a stage set for personal and family growth. There is also a standard dose of road events, notably the camper breaking down soon after the voyage begins and a playfully 'western' element suggested by the destination. The camper itself is representative of a particularly Belgian sensibility characterised by dark humour. It features a living area, as a version of 'home', a crucial element to this film, a dashboard-mounted snow globe with a yellow-clad biker who resembles Eddie Merckx and a malfunctioning cassette player/radio that often plays Dutch language lessons and seems to have a mind of its own. Early frontal travelling shots frame the travellers along with the unavoidable map and the snow globe within this moving home that takes them to new places whilst symbolising the world they left behind, both in the form of domestic space and the contested 'family' relations within the language communities of Belgium. The initial border crossing from Belgium to France is marked by a subtle evocation of national borders in the form of an encounter with a French mechanic in which he discusses Belgian stereotypes after Michel reveals his origins by using Belgian numbers ('nononte-et-un').

As he travels, Michel's self-image improves and once outside their entrenched positions of everyday life, the artificial family starts to resemble a real one. These transformations are framed and reflected by a shifting landscape. The film is about constructing, reconstructing and inventing family, and much of this takes place against the backdrop of landscape. The protagonists are regularly framed using extreme long shots and travelling montages that highlight their shifting positions within a space. Unlike Sweden, the Balkans and Spain in other films discussed in this chapter, the terrain that leads to Brest holds little signification in itself. It is markedly different from the space left behind in Belgium and also represents a European 'Wild West' of sorts, and as such primarily serves as a blank canvas against which the heroes' transformation into a family unit is displayed. As Michel, Kevin and Christine all grow closer together, the scenery shifts from the slightly dilapidated housing complex where Michel and Kevin reside to the nondescript suburbs where Christine lives, junkyards and drab industrial areas – all of which seem nearing devoid of human presence – and finally to verdant countryside and, as the final destination approaches, beautiful seascapes. Before the road trip begins in earnest, Michel gets himself lost looking for his sister's suburban home. A montage of Michel retracing his steps and backtracking provides comedic expression for his alienation from family as well as metaphor for his current unclear place in the world.

The accidental kidnap victim 'Pascal Dumont' espouses a conservative vision of identity and cultural roots and serves as a reminder of the norms left behind. When he proclaims that the ragtag bunch will never win the contest because they do not have the appearance of a believable and 'true' family, Michel announces that have two days to resemble his image of a believable and 'true' family. He purchases a phony wedding ring for Christine and they trade old clothes for new, attempt to rename young Kevin 'Michel' – like his faux father and grandfather – and give him a new life story as they rest at various stops along the road. These efforts aptly represent examples of the attraction of the road for those who seek to forge new identities and escape entrenched or imposed conceptions of self. To discern if his efforts have been successful, Michel changes course from the Brest-bound route to test out his new family on his old family, namely his uncle and aunt. They reside near Michel's now crumbling boyhood home, which they also visit in order to initiate Kevin into the family history. In a nod to Belgium's cultural diversity and tradition of immigration, the family is from Naples, which as it turns out is also Christine's heritage. After Aunt Rosa learns that Michel's pretend wife speaks Italian, all is rosy and she pronounces that they make *una spendida familia*. Certain cracks in the foundation re-emerge, such as the uncle's resentment of Michel's choice to leave the family apple orchard to pursue a career as a singer. A life trajectory that runs from solid, organic and literally rooted to diffuse sharply contrast with the discourses of family expounded by Sofa Life's campaign, and it is telling that Michel opts to forge this alternative family not at home but on the road in a 'mobile home'. Michel, it would seem, is allergic to the very idea of fixity, an outlook perhaps representative of a reaction to his immigrant family's contradictory obsession with staying put. As for the orchard itself, Michel is shocked to learn that the once bucolic parcel is now the site of a massive construction project that renders it, much like the decrepit childhood home, fundamentally different. The trope of fundamentally altered and virtually unrecognisable home sites is prevalent in the 'return' road films discussed in Chapter 4, while the itinerary into childhood when combined with a protagonist who lives and makes a living with his mobile home recalls *Kings of the Road*.

The use of wide-open landscape on a continental scale in *Torpedo* also positions it firmly in Wender's lineage. As discussed in Chapter 1, *Kings of the Road* demonstrates a 'sense of movement only possible in a country with huge, empty open spaces of a kind we don't really have in Europe' (Roddick 2008). *Torpedo* manages to find some spaces that are wide open, although bounded by the sea (Figure 2.2), which is unusual in the typical American representation of open road movie space. The landscape in *Torpedo* that is most crucial to character development is not that which already signifies something (notably the past), the city and industrial spaces that are closed and fixed spaces, or as

Figure 2.2   The mobile home merges with the landscape in *Torpedo* (Matthieu Donck, 2012).

Deleuze and Guattari put it, 'striated' (1987) by the state, work, the economy and so on, but the neutral space that each traveller can freely 'conquer'. In her reading of French road movies, Laura Rascaroli has suggested that 'smooth' space – the opposite of 'striated' space in Deleuze and Guattari's formulation – 'suggests the possibility of renegotiating identities, travelling, communicating and starting anew' (Rascaroli 2013: 29). In *Torpedo* these spaces offer the chance to (re)define one's identity, and the travelling montages that trace the approach to a final destination involve a projection of space on self and self on space. In the open space, Michel and Christine grow closer and teach Kevin to ride a bike, something his real parents have never done, a scene that forms a mini-travelling montage in itself. Michel also lets Kevin take the wheel of the camper momentarily, to the consternation of all. Such moments underscore the ability of the road to put people in touch with something new and perhaps usually forbidden.

Laderman equates freedom in (American) road movies with 'movement across open space' (2002: 14–15). Here, however, the crucial factors in *Torpedo* are not the speedy traversal of space, but both the interactions within the vehicle in contrast with Michel's lacking home life and between the passengers and the spaces they travel through. While earlier scenes focus on character interaction within the mobile home, later travelling montages use techniques that turn the focus towards the landscape and the vehicle's place in it. The more rapid cuts and disjointed space of the initial urban road montage make way for longer takes of the vehicle plodding through the landscape of Brittany, often framed as tableaus in extreme long aerial shots. The significance of the spaces in the later portion of the film are derived from the blank slate they offer. Brittany as 'Wild West' here furnishes a new setting within which the characters can tell a new story while erasing past frustrations.

The film indeed ends with the trio finally forming a 'true family', albeit an unconventional and perhaps ephemeral one. Michel, Kevin and Christine embrace outside Sofa Life in Brest, with countless guns and cameras pointed on them by the police and the media. This bittersweet ending is characteristic of a particular darkly comedic sensibility prevalent in Belgian cinema (see Chapter 3). If this is the end of the road for Michel and his improvised family, they all seem happy and young Kevin – whose foster parents have reported him missing – refuses to leave Michel's side as the police ask. Meanwhile in the background a snow machine used for promotional purposes starts to rain white particles on everyone, notably the statue of Eddie Merckx that fronts the store. The diorama represents a large-scale version of the dashboard snow globe in particular and the spirit of quest in general that drove the voyage forward towards this destination. It is notable that Michel learned of his father's death by phone after they visit the orchard. Ostensibly this would have rendered the remaining portion of the voyage futile, since the initial goal was to please his father by bringing a sports hero home. In this way *Torpedo* follows a common road movie trajectory that involves a modified sense of purpose and often, although not always, a change of destination.

Saint-Jacques . . . la Mecque (Colline Serreau, 2005, France)

Lacking a vehicle and windows or windscreen to buffer the individual from – and frame – the world outside, walking road movies place travellers in the most direct contact with the spaces around them. While less common, and less commonly associated with the road category by critics and spectators, walking road films distil the essence of the road movie, paring it down but not deviating significantly from it, as the following discussion demonstrates. Walking road movies are more prevalent in European cinema and notable examples from French-language industries include *Le Far West* (Jacques Brel, 1973, France/Belgium), *Western* (Manuel Poirier, 1997, France), *Drôle de Félix/The Adventures of Félix* (Olivier Ducastel and Jacques Martineau, 2000, France), *Donne-moi la main* (Pascal-Alex Vincent, 2008, France/Germany), *Le grand'tour* (Jérôme Le Maire, 2011, Belgium) and *La marche* (Nabil Ben Yadir, 2013, France/Belgium). Some of these involve the common combination of walking and hitchhiking, but Serreau's film narrates a trek that takes place exclusively by foot. *Saint-Jacques . . . la Mecque*[7] exemplifies Laderman's observation that European road movies stage voyages as a way of 'tracing the meaning of citizenship as a journey' (2002: 15). It is also about coming together, but in a wider sense, for *Saint-Jacques* traces a voyage into a space where a left-leaning version of French republican ideas triumphs. Serreau has opined that the road is the 'last collective space' in society (Vavasseur 2014), and the communal spirit is on full display on foot given that walking is 'the most "egalitarian" of mobility systems' (Urry 2007: 88). Such an egalitarian approach is arguably most feasible in a walking film, in which a party too large to fit into a vehicle is compelled to interact over the course of many weeks as a group (particularly during stopovers) and as various micro-units while in movement (due to the narrowness of the path). These units represent a wide slice of French life and follow a progression that by now should seem familiar, from isolation towards solidarity or at least mutual understanding. Rosello's reading of *Le grand voyage* as a film that recounts two disparate voyages would initially apply here as well, only on a larger scale.

Saint-Jacques follows eight latter-day pilgrims and their guide on a voyage of three months from a starting point in France to the famous Catholic pilgrimage site, Santiago de Compostela. More than a century ago walking holidays became a popular undertaking intended to strengthen 'body and soul' (Urry 2007: 81). The general edifying motive and purported religious basis for the slog also recalls *Le grand voyage*. This quest is, however, a 'false' pilgrimage, at least in the traditional religious sense, and compared to *Le grand voyage* this trek is more evidently linked to tourism and a distinctly secular brand of self-improvement. None of the travellers appears to have been inspired to undertake the voyage out of purely religious motivations. A trio of troubled and long-feuding siblings are required to make the trek together in order to inherit their mother's fortune, a middle-aged woman tries to beat cancer and escape a loveless marriage and two teenage girls do it for some summer adventure. Lastly Ramzi (Aymen Saïdi) and Saïd (Nicholas Cazalé, who also starred in *Le grand voyage*), two young men of Muslim heritage, are along in one case to follow one of the girls and in the other because his friend told him that Mecca was the destination and, oddly, because the former convinced the latter's mother to bankroll this voyage that she was told would help her son learn to read. The road and the encounters it engenders prove to be antidotes to the sundry problems facing the travellers. Their various voyages – towards literacy, towards a flexible state of what for lack of a better term might be called 'integration', towards family reconciliation, love, self-understanding and self-improvement, and community in a French republican sense – are all set against and facilitated by a picturesque natural and historical backdrop. In other words, the process that Cristina Johnston suggests is taking place in what she calls French 'minority cinema', a 'negotiatory discourse emerging from within republicanism' (2010: 177), is facilitated both by getting away from habitual spaces and promoted by interaction with the particular natural and cultural landscapes traversed. As Chapter 4, on 'return' films, will consider in more depth, the preponderant form of French republicanism privileges an interpretation of the French constitutional principal of 'equality before the law' that leaves no room in public space for cultural difference and offers an inadequate response to the discrimination faces by minorities.

With this voyage taking place by foot, interactions with the landscape and cultures traversed are not mediated by windows or prescribed by stationary tracks and departure schedules as will be the case in *La vraie vie est ailleurs*, the final film under consideration in this chapter. While as viewers we are treated from the start to a feast of beautiful and changing landscapes captured by the camera of veteran cinematographer Jean-François Robin, several exchanges make clear that the characters do not initially appreciate the beauty that surrounds them. The guide laments that people complain about their problems and neglect to notice the world passing by. This changes as the characters are themselves transformed and open up to others and to the world around them. Walking, as one guidebook to the *Camino* puts it, provides 'different perspectives' and allows travellers to 'more fully appreciate the architecture and landscape, while coming into contact with different people, cultures and languages' (Ramis 2012: 5). The voyage ends at another 'far west', what the guide incorrectly calls the 'western-most point in Europe', the ultimate end of the road, where the camera captures the group standing together on a coastal bluff, visibly moved by the scenery. This example demonstrates that similar forms of transformation are at work in walking films as in driving road trips. The initial insularity of the voyagers invites certain comparisons to the process of 'inhabiting' the automobile rather than the road. Walking does, however, promote a more profound engagement with the surroundings once the connection is made.

Like the bicycle episode in *Le grand voyage*, many sequences in *Saint-Jacques* represent examples of non-motorised travelling shots and montages. As would be expected in a walking film, on-foot versions of travelling montages focus on space and character interaction rather than speedy movement through it, featuring slow pan montages over landscape. As they walk, the travellers virtually merge with their setting as they are surrounded by sheep and swallowed up by natural palettes of green or yellow in numerous tableau-like extreme long shots that capture the group as they traverse the countryside and pass numerous picturesque scenes. These shots are regularly combined to briefly encapsulate a day's worth of trekking. The way in which landscape is framed during pauses as a setting for character development is also particularly notable. By walking, and therefore avoiding the road, the voyagers also avoid the lorries, petrol stations and iconography of 'transfer points' so prevalent in most road films. In *Saint-Jacques*, stopovers allow for exercises in the type of communal solidarity that seemed to be sorely lacking at the onset, such as group cooking efforts, and for the pairing up that is often imposed in auto travel but not in this type of voyage, in which small groups form and break up as the day and the miles

Figure 2.3   Weary pilgrims pause in a setting evocative of the cinematic West in *Saint-Jacques . . . la Mecque* (Colline Serreau, 2005).

go by. This coupling allows for activities as diverse as romance and reading lessons. Ramzi, whose mother sent him on the trip in order to learn to read, has gradually done so thanks to lessons from a teacher in the group named Clara (Muriel Robin). In one scene she instructs Ramzi in the foreground, set against a natural backdrop that dominates the frame, a very different setting from the striated social space at home where Ramzi is seen as an educational failure. Once again, getting outside the habitual spaces and social interactions proves profitable for the travelling subject and allows for a new space to tell one's story. Much like *Le grand voyage* ventures beyond the representational clichés and entrenched binaries of the home front, Serreau's film suggests that if the principals of republicanism have fallen short within the typical spaces that minorities such as Ramzi find themselves both in life and in cinema, the road provides an antidote.

In this transnational voyage national borders are less important than the variety of natural lines of demarcation, such as between desert and forest. The crucial turning point for the group as a whole takes place in the Navarre portion of the trek, amidst the landscape of the Spanish desert (Figure 2.3). The region is well-known for its resemblance to the American West and brings to mind the filming locations of Italian 'spaghetti westerns', which were often shot in Spain, as well as the settings of many famous American road movies and westerns.[8] Once again the desert is drawn upon to wink at the American road – a bar that they enter features distinctly Western décor – and to geographically symbolise new beginnings. Road movie scholars have observed that vast territories and boundless horizons make the desert an ideal locale for the road film, a genre in which traditionally 'freedom becomes rediscovered as movement across open space' (Laderman 2002: 14–15).

The space traversed in *Saint-Jacques* is not only significant for its climate, physical landscape and cinematic intertextuality. The traditional pilgrimage route, a long-time transnational space of encounter, and the history of Spain also inform the voyage. As in the prior examples, 'escape' in this film is again not about getting outside society but is concerned with new ways of relating to others within it. Over time, popular walking paths become 'iteratively impressed into the ground' (Urry 2007: 63) and indeed in this case the route travelled hardly lends itself to complete flight from society given that pilgrims have been following it for over one thousand years. The continued importance of the route for tourism and religious treks alike was more recently acknowledged when it was named the first 'Council of Europe Cultural Route' (Council of Europe 2014). In both cases the cultural significance transcends the nation. National differences and imbalances are acknowledged and the significance of Spain as a destination resonates in a variety of ways. Like in *Torpedo*, where we encounter on the road the invisible ethnic diversity in Michel and Christine's respective family heritages, a wealthy young pilgrim thinks back to her childhood maid, who was Spanish, and professes that the woman 'practically raised her'. This passing reference provides a reminder of Spain's role in the twentieth century as a major source of immigration into France (Hargreaves 2007: 144). Spain's perceived difference from France is brought to the fore when a priest along the route is forced to confront the religious and cultural diversity inherent in postcolonial Europe through the lens of what is portrayed as a progressive French outlook. When the priest tries to bar the dark-skinned pilgrims in the group from staying in his convent, their fellow travellers demonstrate solidarity by announcing that they too will not stay under his roof and reproach him for what one derides rather superciliously as Franco-era thinking. This exchange, while perhaps all too conveniently allowing the French travellers to display their perceived cultural openness in relation to Spain while overlooking France's own issues, does again demonstrate an exchange of ideas made possible on the road. It seems clear that no such display of *fraternité* would have been offered at home, or even on the road at the onset of the voyage. Here the setting is also telling given Spain's position as a crucial space in Fortress Europe and new site of immigration (Amago 2007: 12). Lastly, the film's French title, which refers to a confusion between Muslim and Christian pilgrimage sites is also suggestive of Spain's historical experience as Muslim–Christian borderland. Though unlike in films such as Gatlif's *Exils* the travellers do not venture through Andalusia, formerly occupied by the Moors, Spain was and is now again point of contact between Europe and the Muslim world thanks to its proximity to North Africa.

In the way it repurposes striated space, *Saint-Jacques* furnishes a good example of the ways by which many European road films espouse a hybrid version of the perceived American and European approaches. Space and culture are reformulated here, but the space traversed is far from the 'smooth' and ostensibly uncharted desert, being marked both by centuries of travel promoted by the Catholic church and by more recent efforts of the Council of Europe to use the route to promote closer ties between Europeans of different nationalities. *Saint-Jacques* subverts this design – and the religious purpose of the route – by mapping a distinctly secular and republican voyage onto a route designed to promote religious piety and shared myth-building. The cultural subversion and mixing suggested by the French title is acted out as the voyage comes to an end: as the group arrives in Santiago, Ramzi climbs to the top of a monument built to mark the visit of the pope and yells 'Allah Wakbar'. As in *Le grand voyage*, a communal trip is capped with an individual expression of religion connected to the very different goals held by individual travellers. This public display of religious belief would seem to flout the otherwise secular and republican quality of the collective voyage, and by doing so recall very current French debates about the place of religion, particularly Islam, in public space. In the end, however, the travellers have come together in both cases but are willing to accept difference. This is perhaps another example of common ground that can be forged on the road and away from the usual parameters of debate. This distinctly republican tale, the director suggests, can only take place in the course of a voyage.

If the travellers are able to refashion the cultural-religious spaces striated by man, the natural landscape of their route still imposes itself on them. The physically trying voyage ends at the aforementioned 'western-most point in Europe', where the protagonists' gazes over dramatic scenery suggest that they will return home transformed.

The film does not end here, instead opting to return to France in order to follow the 'life voyages' of the protagonists and render visible the transformations yielded through the voyage. Transformation is of course a staple road movie element but one that generally is only intimated by an ending that places the voyagers back on the road. This return to France confirms an alignment of *Saint-Jacques* with the oft-cited notion that road movies are primarily concerned with home. Following their return, the once-squabbling siblings are reunited at their childhood home, Ramzi can read and is adopted by the family of his teacher Clara, the alcoholic Claude has shaped up and Saïd and his love interest Clara are finally together. The final image is a freeze-frame of this couple forged on the road, underscoring the film's message of *mixité sociale*.

LA VRAIE VIE EST AILLEURS: FROM NON-PLACE TO LANDSCAPE

Swiss director Frédéric Choffat's 2006 film *La vraie vie est ailleurs*, a debut feature that garnered a good deal of attention in his native Switzerland for the young director, is an exemplary European road film. Several national frontiers are crossed – of cultural and linguistic significance rather than actual border lines, which are not represented – putting into relief linguistic differences and border-crossings of various sorts both literal and figurative. It offers the opportunity to consider the train as a mode of road movie transport and to introduce the small but clearly discernible trend of an opening up towards Europe in the French-language Swiss film industry (which we will return to in Chapter 4). The protagonists travel by train, a format that while less common in what we would typically consider a road movie, is prevalent enough in European cinema to merit inclusion here. While train travel is quite common in European cinema, a relatively small number of European travel films are built around this mode of conveyance. Notable examples of those that are include *Les rendez-vous d'Anna* (Chantal Akerman), *Ceux qui m'aiment prendront le train/Those Who Love Me Will Take the Train* (Patrice Chéreau, 1998, France), *A l'est de moi* (Bojena Horackova, 2008, France) and the experimental film *Sibérie* (Joana Preiss, 2011, France). Akerman's film focuses on the spaces of train stations, often the platforms and underbellies, rather than any picturesque scenery.

The connection between the cinematic experience and watching the passing world through an automobile windscreen has been widely discussed in the context of the road movie, but as Ian Christie points out, there are a number of links between viewing from train windows and the cinema screen, as if 'sixty years of railways had prepared people to be film spectators' (1994: 17; see also Orgeron 2007: 14). However, since they involve neither the participative element of driving nor the effort of walking, rail films would seem to offer up the most passive form of road movie travel and therefore provide the best opportunity to test the notion that modern transportation results in a travelling experience defined by 'passivity and indifference' (Eleftheriotis 2010: 101). The railway revolutionised travel in the nineteenth century and provided new ways of 'moving, socializing and seeing the swiftly passing landscape' (Urry 2007: 37). For a variety of reasons travel by rail is not particularly well-suited for road cinema and this is reflected in the small number of films constructed around train voyages. First and foremost, the linearity and inelastic nature of rail travel itself is not immediately conducive to either the escape or the variation that is often at the heart of road cinema. Put differently, once aboard a train the travelling subject has precious little agency in terms of forging his or her route, nor are they particularly likely to be subject to the vagaries of the road event. European road films have juxtaposed the perceived freedom of travellers in cars with passing trains, which connote 'controlled, regulated, destination-oriented travel' (Laderman 2002: 262). In his discussion of *Kings of the Road*, Laderman contrasts the driving undertaken by Robert and Bruno with the prospect of travel on a passing train, the 'train Robert *should* be on' (2002: 262; original emphasis). A similar idea is suggested in the scene from Laurent Cantet's *L'emploi du temps*, in which the protagonist who is driving to avoid work and domestic life 'races' a train (O'Shaughnessy 2013: 158). In other words, if automobiles represent at least the illusion of escape and liberation, rail travel seems overly regimented and constricting. Train travel is associated with 'clock-time', a development that Urry contends 'initiates the dream of speed both in travel and in a much more general way throughout society' (2007: 99). This emphasis on speed, combined with the constraints of travelling on rails, means that the train journey as a process is viewed as 'dead time', meaning that 'no consideration is paid to the pleasures and uses of "travel time"' (2007: 99). Travel time is, of course, generally at the heart of road movie narratives.

Railways also led a transformation from 'dwelling' in the natural environment to seeing it as a separate entity to be viewed through the window of a moving vehicle, and travel 'through' the landscape at a high rate of speed 'generated many new views, a panorama of new, fast moving landscapes' (Urry 2007: 102). As Eleftheriotis demonstrates, such 'mobile vision' is commonly associated with a process of 'knowledge acquisition' (2010: 78) and the 'dizzying experiences of mobile vision challenge established and traditional certainties as they push travellers out of the stability of home and into unknown and uncertain territories' (2010: 77). As a brief scene of high-speed rail travel in *Aaltra* (Chapter 3) demonstrates, however, contemporary European rail travel does not necessarily furnish an ideal opportunity to consider the landscape. While this impulse to see the world differently is a fundamental one in road cinema, train travel also does not engender encounters with the people and cultures inhabiting the traversed spaces. Neither does it tend to promote plentiful and meaningful encounters between fellow travellers. If the first concept is self-evident, this last idea seems counterintuitive, because train travel did create new spaces and contexts of interaction: rail travel was seen as placing together strangers within 'novel, enclosed spaces' (Urry 2007: 104), thus generating 'new sociabilities' (2007: 105). Train riders, however, 'found new ways of keeping social distance' (2007: 106). Often this involved simply looking away or reading, but the possibilities for self-enclosed travel have grown immensely with technologies such as headphones, portable computers and mobile phones (2007: 106). Michel de Certeau encapsulated both the imposed and hierarchic nature of train travel and the impossibility of personal connections when he theorised train travel as an extension of the non-place, a 'module of imprisonment that makes possible the production of an order, a closed and autonomous insularity'(1984: 2).

All of this has rendered the train a generally inauspicious setting for road movies. In *Vraie vie* the norms of rail travel are transgressed in order to forge three seemingly typical road narratives within uncommon settings. The meaningful encounters that influence the three disparate narratives' trajectories take place in one case in a station, the result of a missed connection, and in the others the product of exceptional circumstance in which people come together on the train to breach the rules in a way that is entirely outside the norm.[9] Choffat's film initially suggests a rather bleak outlook on travel and presents us with an uninspiring and drab slice of European non-spaces of the station and within the train. Much like in Akerman's *Les rendez-vous d'Anna*, any 'landscape' is limited to train stations and their environs, hotel rooms, glimpses of darkness caught from train windows. We see none of the famous sights of Geneva or, due to the darkness outside, even passing images of the landscapes traversed. The film opens in the underground passageways of the main railway station in Geneva. There the highly mobile camera sets the tone for the film, following three characters as they make their way to different platforms, saying goodbyes or buying flowers. These travellers exemplify some of the primary reasons that Europeans are in motion within the Schengen Zone. One is headed to Berlin, where his partner has just given birth, another to Naples, where her parents are from, in order to remake her life there, and a third is travelling to a scientific conference in Marseille, where she hopes to secure continued funding for her research. Each, as we shall learn as the narrative unfolds, can said to be 'lost' in a metaphysical sense. This is entirely conventional in road movies, although the mode of travel employed here means that this will not translate into literal terms. Instead it finds a visual manifestation or leads to being stranded or waylaid in a known location rather than literally lost. Their doubts about the direction of their lives will be resolved to some extent en route, thanks to a series of fortuitous encounters.

The narrative cuts amongst these geographically disparate threads. In atypical fashion, we initially do not know where the travellers are headed or why. Like the characters we also start out lost; each early glimpse in the station offers only minimal insight into the reasons for their voyage, but the stories will be revealed as they recount them to others they meet. The sharing of stories is part of a symbolic movement that accompanies the physical progress of the train, a progression from isolation towards human contacts, or at least a new orientation in life and vis-à-vis others. Klaus Eder has theorised such storytelling as a crucial part of the construction of 'soft borders', narrative boundaries between Europeans and non-European or divisions within Europe such as Northern and Southern (2006: 258, 266). In line with the process of coming together that I pointed out is central to European road cinema in general and to the films featured in the present chapter in particular, each voyager moves from isolation to social contact. These contacts were not meant to be – they are both out of the ordinary and against the normal order – and therefore undermined the production of the 'order' and autonomy that de Certeau argues is characteristic of rail travel. In this sense each point of contact falls within the logic of the 'road event', encounters or incidents that imposed unexpected directions on the traveller (and the narrative).

Such encounters, represented as chance events in the narrative, in fact reveal a number of interwoven points of contact rendered possible by contemporary European policies and by recent European histories of migration. In one episode, the Berlin-bound man misses the last connection, forcing him to spend the night in the station, where he finds himself alone with a Czech woman who lived in Paris and is now headed for Romania. This connection is made possible by an irregularity: typically in the railroad system regulated by 'clock-time' the first train would have delivered him to his subsequent train and no personal connections would have been made. In another storyline the scientist crosses paths with a man on the train who claims to have been robbed and left without means to pay or to identify himself. When the conductor, the personification of the panoptic order of the train, informs him that this issue will be taken to the police upon arrival, the scientist intervenes and pays for his fare. She will later offer him hospitality in the form of a hotel room couch. The final voyager is a young woman of Italian origins who was born in Switzerland and is now relocating to Naples. She strikes up an unlikely and initially undesired friendship with the Italian train conductor who, in another anomalous gesture, imposes himself into her compartment, insisting that he has a policy against allowing women to travel alone on the *Trenitalia*. Perhaps ironically in contrast to the latter case, it is an individual brand of surveillance that renders this connection possible. Once he is settled in the compartment, her separation from the outside world continues through a series of mobile phone conversations. Only later does she put the device aside and engage with her unwanted cabin mate, sharing a conversation about her Italian origins and sense of not belonging in Switzerland.

The individual transformations correspond with movement from the non-space of the train station to the distinctive spaces of personal contact: Marseille and Naples in two cases and an encounter amidst the non-place of a train station zone in the third instance. In each narrative strand, travellers step outside the habitual uses of space in rail travel to forge meaningful connections with people and spaces. If the characters never entirely 'inhabit' the spaces around them, those spaces do have a significant role in their metaphorical voyages. Landscape is filmed in a highly subjective manner; when characters are full of doubt and their figurative paths are unclear and we see only darkness in subjective point-of-view shots looking out the train window. To hone in on one example, visible landscape emerges after characters in the third story

Figure 2.4   Train travellers merge with landscape in *La Vraie vie est ailleurs* (Frédéric Choffat, 2006).

line have lived a transformative experience in their voyage, as when the two Naples-bound voyagers wake up to a splendid vista of morning light reflecting on the Gulf of Naples. The reverse shot that follows (Figure 2.4) utilises reflections to project the landscape onto the characters, who are standing side by side, seemingly jointly experiencing the view as a revelation despite that fact that both have seen it before. We might think of it as 'striated' space on a personal level; the *cuccetista* is familiar with it from his passages on board the train and the woman knows it from annual family holidays that were presumably quite regimented and imposed by family history. But more than a voyage into family past, this 'return' is her own gesture, a leap into the void to begin a new life. As in *Saint-Jacques*, *Le grand voyage* and *Torpedo*, landscape becomes a background onto which new ways of seeing self and the world can be projected. The experience of travel has rendered striated space smooth. The notion of starting anew and breaking from the past is reinforced by the woman's parting gesture to the *cuccettista*: she gives him the fondue set that her Swiss friends had bestowed upon her as a parting gift in the opening scene. Emblazoned with a Swiss cross, it represents her connections to that nation. The film closes with final glimpses of each character. The Italian–Swiss woman buzzes alone through the streets on a Vespa (a Neapolitan cliché brought up earlier by the *cuccettista*), the Marseille-bound woman smiles as she looks out over the Mediterranean from her hotel balcony and the German-bound man writes about his son's birth in a journal that recalls Robert's notebook in *Kings of the Road*.

Scholars have observed the 'contradictory' (Urry 2007: 100) spatial process that is fundamental to rail travel. Railways 'seem to shrink space through bringing some places closer together and to eliminate many places in between' while simultaneously expanding 'space by connecting places that otherwise never would have been connected' (Urry 2007: 100). *Vraie vie* harnesses both of these processes, taking advantage of the latter to emphasise connections between Switzerland and other places in Europe and manipulating the former to forge meaningful links along the way. This gesture would seem to align Choffat with his countryman Lionel Baier's attempt to open Switzerland up to Europe via cinema (a film by Baier will be considered in Chapter 4; see Van Heuckelom 2014: 38, 50). Indeed the film's narrative leitmotif of opening one's space to others is an apt metaphor for the same process on a national and cinematic level. What Europe looks like at the conclusion of the voyage/process is very different from the image presented at the onset: a space connected by a series of networks and interpersonal links. Stylistically, this film demonstrates how certain components of the road movie model are adopted and adapted by European directors to address particularly European contexts and issues.

Conclusion

Using mobility studies as a framework, this chapter has considered a variety of modes of transit employed in European road films. The films were selected to represent diverse forms of mobility, but also to provide an overview of the primary motivations for being on the (cinematic) road in France, Belgium, Switzerland and beyond. We have examined a Belgian film set in primarily in France, which is separated by a subtle yet distinguishable line of demarcation, a Swiss film that explores a variety of places beyond that nation's national borders, French films in which the most crucial scenes take place in Spain and Sweden and another multinational French co-production that spends very little time France. Together these films provide considerable insight into what Europe looks like from the vantage point of road cinema. A notion of what French-language European road cinema looks like is also formed in this chapter. The hallmarks of contemporary European road cinema include voyages towards togetherness, understanding and solidarity; a narrative circularity that often places travellers back on the road at the end of the film; varied forms of mobility; and regular references to the tropes and iconography of American road cinema. The 'Far West' of American cinema legend is often channelled to symbolise a process of mapping new spaces and telling one's own stories outside the constraints imposed by society. If this chapter focused on connections between societies, nations and geographic spaces, the following two chapters will hone in more on the specific contexts of Belgium and France respectively and consider the effect of national particularities on road cinema production.

NOTES

1. Other examples of this include films *Robert Mitchum est mort/Robert Mitchum is Dead* (Olivier Babinet and Fred Kihn, 2010 France/Norway/Poland/Belgium) as well as *Aaltra* (Chapter 3) and *L'iceberg* (Chapter 3).
2. As Higbee argues, the choice between religion and education is significant in the French republican context because school is seen as one of the pillars of republican values (2013: 166).
3. A number of articles and books have considered what James Austin (2009) calls the 'immobility' of cinematic representations of the *banlieue*. In addition to Austin, see Higbee 2007, 2011 and 2013; Gott 2013a and Tarr 2005.
4. Despite subsequent quarrels, the first sign of rapprochement occurs in Bulgaria, where waylaid for the night in a snowstorm Réda finally asks the question that he initially only dared pose to his mother: why did the older man not opt for a faster plane voyage?
5. 'I really like the image he represents, that of the old Belgium. He might even be the last Belgian. No one knows if he is Flemish or a Walloon, he's simply Belgian!' (my translation). See: <http://www.cinergie.be/webzine/torpedo_de_matthieu_donck_avec_francois_damiens_2011_05_12>
6. Road films that reimagine the parameters of the traditional family unit and of sexual citizenship include *Western* (Manuel Poirier, France, 1997), *Plein sud/Going South* (Sébastien Lifshitz, France, 2009), *Origine contrôlée/Made in France* (Ahmed Bouchaala and Zakia Tahri, France/Luxembourg, 2001), and *Comme des voleurs (à l'est)/Stealth* (Lionel Baier, Switzerland, 2006; Chapter 4).
7. The English translation of the title, *Keep Walking*, fails to express the mix-up between the Catholic pilgrimage site Santiago de Compostela and Mecca referred to in the original French.
8. See Gott and Schilt (2015) for a discussion of the Navarre desert setting in the French road film *Plein sud*.
9. Notable predecessors of this type of narrative include Krzysztof Kieślowski's *Przypadek/Blind Chance* (1987, Poland), which involves three possibilities that stem from different encounters on a train or in the station and *Tickets* (2005, Italy/UK), which also combines three intersecting stories directed respectively by Abbas Kiarostami, Ken Loach and Ermanno Olmi.

3. COWBOYS, ICEBERGS, ANARCHISTS AND TOREADORS: THE PARADOXES AND POSSIBILITIES OF THE FRANCOPHONE BELGIAN ROAD CINEMA

Films covered: *Quand la mer monte* (Yolande Moreau and Gilles Porte, 2004), *L'iceberg* (Dominique Abel, Fiona Gordon and Bruno Romy, 2005), *Eldorado* (Bouli Lanners, 2008), *Les folles aventures de Simon Konianski/ Simon Konianski* (Micha Wald, 2008) and *Aaltra* (Gustave de Kervern and Benoît Delépine, 2004, France/Belgium)

'Where are we?' Thus is the question posed by one of a motley pair of travellers in Bouli Lanner's acclaimed 2008 *Eldorado* (Belgium/France) after both passenger and driver drift into sleep on the road, causing their car to careen into seemingly uncharted wilderness. As we have seen in the previous chapter, the road movie has increasingly become a privileged mode of expression for contemporary European directors attempting to answer this very question. Filmmakers have hit the road in order to come to terms with a protean European landscape marked by shifting conceptions of identity and citizenship in the wake of events such as the collapse of communism, EU expansion, the Schengen Agreements and various 'new migrations' (Mazierska and Rascaroli 2006: 139–41) that have ensued. In short, road movies have experienced what Wendy Everett terms a 'boom' in Europe precisely because they are uniquely suited to represent 'postmodern identity as essentially fluid and migratory (2009: 165–6). This chapter will consider this broadly European issue from the vantage point of the Belgian cinema industry, in the process bringing to the fore questions of how national specificity asserts itself within what is in many ways a fundamentally transnational cinematic category and to what extent this specificity is representative of 'Belgian-ness'. This chapter takes a cue from the travellers in *Eldorado* and attempts to answer the questions: 'what, and where, is Belgian road cinema?' Doing so involves considering the European-ness of Belgian film as well as its national specificity and connection to wider French-language cultural categories and industries.

So far we have used Jason Wood's attempt to delineate road cinema as a starting point for a basic categorical definition for this protean and malleable category of filmmaking: 'in archetypal terms, road movies commonly entail the undertaking of a journey by one or more protagonists as they seek out adventures, redemption or escape from the constricting norms of society and its laws' (2007: xv). In order to delineate geographically based distinctions within the genre, we have also turned to David Laderman's argument that while the classic American strain of the road movie espouses rebellion against cultural norms, the European variety tends to be concerned with travelling 'into the national culture, tracing the meaning of citizenship as a journey' (2002: 248). The Belgian films under consideration here represent a hybrid of these two conceptions. As a group, Belgian road films follow the European model as defined by Laderman by staging travel 'into culture' while simultaneously questioning social norms. This transgression against norms often takes a form that parodies the outlaw associations of the American road movie strain. Revolt in Belgian road movies should not be seen as an attempt to travel outside culture per se, but as symptomatic of a desire to evade certain dominant conceptions of national or communitarian culture and identity. Although these voyages generally engage with national culture – or cultures, in the case of Belgium – it should be emphasised that the limits of the nation-state no longer adequately contain the cultures and spaces explored in Belgian road cinema. Citizenship in contemporary Belgium is reframed as inherently linked to mobility, a stance that rejects fixed, monolithic identity formulations and the closed spaces associated with national identities and conceptions of Fortress Europe. Building on Everett's observation, identity in the Belgian road movie is presented as always fluid, often migratory and above all cyclical. As the films under discussion demonstrate, where the American template favours linear progression and movement away from society, travel in Belgian films is more commonly circular.

Any attempt to classify French-language Belgian cinema requires some delicate balance. On the one hand, then, Belgian road cinema is in many ways representative of the wider French-language European trends sketched out in the previous chapter. On the other hand, however, it also retains a certain dose of national specificity and a particular, unique Belgian quality that will become apparent in the following case studies. As discussed in the introduction, cinema from the nation that the French refer to as 'le plat pays' (the flat country), after an eponymous song by singer and road movie director Jacques

Brel, often contains certain distinguishable traits. More than one Belgian road film has been qualified in publicity material or press reviews as a 'very belge trip' ('very Belgian trip'). In this chapter I will focus on Belgian productions and co-productions in order to determine to what extent national boundaries affect and motivate the voyage and the fashion in which it is filmed. What European road movies often do involves transcending national boundaries and calling into question ingrained and monolithic conceptions of identity, the 'constricting norms' as Wood puts it (and soft borders in Eder's nomenclature) that delineate lines of difference between home and abroad and national and stranger. On the surface it would appear somewhat problematic to approach the object of our study through a specific and limited national framework. Belgian cinema, however, remains particular enough to merit a dedicated chapter but at the same time is inextricably linked to wider (and especially French) production and reception contexts. While Belgian films are considered elsewhere in the book in relation to the thematic approaches of each respective chapter, in this chapter Belgium is the primary theme.

Before continuing it is worth pausing to consider from a film production standpoint the parameters of 'Belgian' cinema. The ten-year period between 2002 and 2011 saw the release of 211 French-language Belgian productions and co-productions. The vast majority of these are co-productions, mostly in cooperation with France. Of the top twenty-five of these films in terms of tickets sold in Belgium, all were co-productions. Furthermore only four films in the top 100 were exclusively Belgian productions (Anonymous 2012: 24–5).[1] This interconnectedness with the much larger French market, and by extension the global market for French-language cinema, forms an important subtext in several of the films explored in detail in this chapter. Although Francophone Belgian films distributed abroad surely benefit to some extent from the larger market for French-language films, there is also a 'competition' problem (Anonymous 2012: 22) at home that tends to lead to Belgian films getting lost amidst the sea of French productions. This state of affairs also has a significant effect on the talent pool of French-speaking Belgian actors. Whereas Flanders has a thriving domestic television industry that grooms actors for big screen productions, Francophone Belgian actors must generally forge their reputation in French films. This often means making a name in Paris before they get significant work in Belgian films. Prominent examples of this artistic trajectory include Cécile de France, Benoît Poelvoorde and Jéremie Renier (Anonymous 2012: 22).

THE CINEMA AND POLITICS OF THE BELGIAN 'MELTING POT'

Even beyond the complex (co)production relationships to France, on the surface Belgian road movies are as a group marked by a number of significant paradoxes. Most notably, while vast spaces and boundless horizons made the American West the archetypal locale for the road film, a genre in which 'freedom becomes rediscovered as movement across open space' (Laderman 2002: 14–15), at some 30,000 square kilometres Belgium shares the measurements of the small state of Maryland. Despite its limited size, no single place provides a more fitting context for identity-mapping projects than Belgium, a nation whose inherent linguistic and cultural complexity has long presented challenges to the creation of a unified national identity. The Belgian, as Piet Van de Craen contends, was a 'European citizen who had European ideas *avant la lettre*' (2002: 24–33). Belgium is a small country with three national borders in close proximity, and as a federated state with three official languages it comprises a variety of internal frontiers, both administrative and cultural-linguistic. This complex make-up appears to provide an ideal laboratory for cinematic identity quests.

Not a major site of immigration before World War II, Belgium has nonetheless experienced a certain structurally assured ambivalence about identity since the nation's founding in 1830. In his recent work published to promote the 'post-Dardenne' generation of filmmakers, journalist Boyd Van Hoeij contends that what separates Belgian cinema from its French neighbours is its multiplicity of voices, a side effect of the nation's makeup and history. Belgium has been a 'melting pot' of various cultural and linguistic influences (2010: 164). Lieve Spaas argues that factors such as the recognition of French, Dutch and German as official languages; the creation of a federal state in 1993; the presence of large numbers of European civil servants; and postcolonial, Jewish diaspora and other post-war migrations have resulted in 'a mosaic of different groups of people' (Spaas 2000: 8). In short, perhaps no place in Europe better exemplifies Everett's observation that it is impossible 'to drive far in Europe without crossing borders: political, linguistic, cultural, social . . .' (Everett 2009: 168). Spaas also points out that the Belgian cinema industry has been characterised by both internal and external diversity. Well-known filmmakers Charles Dekeukeleire and Henri Stork made both Francophone and Flemish films, while others such as Boris Lehman (Switzerland), Marion Hänsel (France) and Michel Khleifi (Lebanon) have diverse origins (Spaas 2000: 9). Sam Garbarski was born in Germany and claims Polish-Jewish origins, while Nabil Ben Yidar was born in Brussels to Moroccan immigrant parents.

Belgian filmmakers are fond of citing this diversity as a creative influence. Ben Yidar, director of *Les Barons*, a successful 2009 film about minorities living in the working-class Molenbeek community of Brussels and the road film *La Marche* (2013), a France–Belgium co-production about the 'Marche pour l'égalité et contre le racisme' that took place in France in 1983, contends that Belgium's complexity is reflected in its cinema (Van Hoeij 2010: 142). Lanners, the most prolific Belgian director of road films, points to an instinctively diverse Belgian 'cultural subconscious' behind his work:

> I was born in the German-speaking region, near the German and Dutch borders, a situation that causes people to speak several languages with ease. We mix, we move from one language to another, from one culture to another. In the region there is an enormous spirit of openness towards difference, which makes me refuse to accept what is happening in Belgium right now. (Van Hoeij 2010: 88; my translation)

It is not surprising that such 'movement' amongst cultures and languages has been translated into literal cinematic motion. However, while Belgian cinema has embraced diversity, the nation itself is sometimes considered to be amongst the most xenophobic in Europe today. The above quote from Lanners refers to communitarian disputes as well as the fact that the country has active right-wing parties. Many Belgians seem to be resistant to immigration and multiculturalism. In recent polling, Belgians were second most likely amongst Europeans to agree with the statement 'immigrants are a threat to your way of life' (Mulcahy 2011: 104–6, 159). Debates over immigration and integration have been brought to the fore by social disturbances and clashes between residents and the police in Molenbeek in 2009 and 2010 and by a polemic over an article in which Luckas Vander Taelen, Green Party parliamentarian and self-described proponent of multiculturalism, labelled his Brussels neighbourhood an immigrant 'ghetto' (Vander Taelen 2009). Such discussions of xenophobia should be nuanced, however. Brussels in particular is extremely diverse ethnically. Some 46 per cent of the capital's residents have roots outside Belgium, with the largest minority populations being Moroccan and Turkish at 13 per cent and 4 per cent, respectively (Vandezande 2011). A certain level of acceptance of this diversity can be noted. Socialist Prime Minister Elio Di Rupo is the son of working-class Italian immigrants, while foreign nationals who have resided in Belgium for at least five years were accorded the right to vote in local elections in 2004. Similar proposals have faced vociferous opposition across the border in France.

This brings us to another fascinating paradox of the Belgian case. While xenophobia is often articulated in terms of a fixed, 'imagined' notion of identity under the menace of outside forces, Belgium's inherent multiplicity has made it difficult to formulate a firm and static conception of precisely what Belgiumness is. Spaas points out that for many in its polyglot population, 'Belgium is a place rather than a nation' (Spaas 2000: 8). Thus Francophone road movie directors in Belgium face a very different paradigm from their French counterparts, for whom the road format offers the possibility of elaborating a flexible, transnational and multicultural alternative to a vision of France as a closed and monolithic space (Gott and Schilt 2013: 3). In the Belgian context, the very concept of a fixed identity has proven to be elusive. Indeed, some have seen this perceived lack of fixity as a positive. Proponents of *belgitude*, a cultural movement that arose in Wallonia in the 1970s and 1980s, celebrated hybridity and considered Belgium to epitomise anti-nationalism (Deprez and Vos 1998: 16). More recently the Belgian paradox has led to seemingly contradictory impulses. As ratification of the Maastricht Treaty opened the door for increased supranational integration, linguistic and communal squabbles risked pushing Belgium towards national disintegration (Craeybeckx et al. 2000: 271). With such incongruities in mind, Klaus Eder's distinction between hard and soft borders offers a conceptual starting point for a discussion of Belgian cinematic voyages in post-Berlin-Wall Europe. While hard borders are inscribed in law, the 'soft borders of Europe are encoded in other types of texts indicating a pre-institutional social reality, the reality of images of what Europe is and who are Europeans and who are not' (Eder 2006: 256). As hard borders lose some of their consequence for European citizens, Belgian road movies participate in the task of formulating 'soft borders', exploring the significance of national boundaries and cultural porosity in a unified Europe and postcolonial world.[2]

The Parameters of Francophone Belgian Road Cinema

The road movie format has been popular with Francophone Belgian directors attempting to grapple with the geographic and political paradoxes outlined above. This chapter will analyse five films: *Quand la mer monte* (Yolande Moreau and Gilles Porte, 2004), *L'iceberg* (Dominique Abel, Fiona Gordon and Bruno Romy, 2005), *Eldorado* (Bouli Lanners, 2008), *Les folles aventures de Simon Konianski/Simon Konianski* (Micha Wald, 2008) and *Aaltra* (Gustave de Kervern and Benoît Delépine, 2004, France/Belgium). The latter is a majority French production but qualifies as an 'honorary' Belgian film via its itinerary and casting. Before turning to these case studies, I will outline some general tendencies in the Francophone Belgian road movie of the past decade. I have identified a corpus that includes more than twenty films. This output is significant, particularly considering that on average only eleven Francophone films are (co)produced each year as majority Belgian productions. The road movie's recent currency in Belgium demonstrates that the appeal of approaching identity questions through the optic of mobility is strong even in – and perhaps, especially in – small nations. This is not to say, however, that road movies are an entirely new development in Belgium. In a review of *Eldorado* for the French culture magazine *Les Inrockuptibles*, Jean-Baptiste Morain (2008) points out that the Belgian affinity with road movies goes back to *Far West* (1973), Jacque Brel's second and final directorial effort. That quixotic film sets the tone for a particularly Belgian sensibility that can be readily identified in many of the films covered here. Morain makes the intriguing suggestion that despite – or perhaps because of – the limited geographic scope of the nation, Belgian road films as a group have traditionally been more concerned with the vastness of space, something he describes as a particularly 'European dream' of boundlessness. This he contrasts with a number of French films, including *Le corniaud* (Chapter 1), in which even when vast distances are traversed the terrain encompasses a horizon that lies within the vision of the human eye (Morain 2008). The case studies contained in this chapter will bear out this observation while simultaneously drawing attention to the paradoxes/contradiction inherent in this vision of space.

Recent Francophone Belgian road movies include *Hop* (Dominique Standaert, 2002), *25 degrees en hiver/25 degrees in Winter* (Stéphane Vuillet, 2004, Belgium/France/Russia/Spain), *La visite* (Nicholas Guicheteau, 2004), *Congorama* (a Canadian/Belgian/French co-production by Québecois director Philippe Falardeau that starts and finishes in Belgium, 2006), *Dikkenek* (Olivier van Hoofstadt, 2006), *Au cul du loup* (Pierre Duculot, 2011, Belgium/France), *Le grand'tour* (Jérôme Le Maire, 2011), *Où va la nuit/The Long Falling* (Martin Provost, 2011, France/Belgium), *Mobile Home* (François Pirot, 2012), *La tête la première/Headfirst* (Amélie van Elmbt, 2012, Belgium/France), *Torpedo* (Matthieu Donck, 2012, Belgium/France [covered in Chapter 2]), *La marche* (Nabil Ben Yadir, 2013, France/Belgium), *La tendresse/Tenderness* (Marion Hänsel, 2013, Belgium/France/Germany) and *Yamdam* (Vivian Goffette, 2013). Bouli Lanners stands out as Belgium's most avid road filmmaker. In addition to *Eldorado* his features *Ultranova* (2005, Belgium) and *Les géants* (2011, Belgium/France/Luxembourg) are firmly in the road category, as is *Les premiers, les derniers*, which began filming in early 2015. His films have also been the topic of Benoît Mariage's documentary film *On the road again, le cinema de Bouli Lanners* (2011, Belgium).[3]

Two additional films by the Abel, Gordon and Romy team, *Rumba* (2008) and *La fée* (*The Fairy*, 2011), are less obvious examples in which the road plays a significant if not pre-eminent role. It should be noted that the films on this list, with the notable exception of *Hop*, tend to trace voyages by Belgians of European origin who are privileged with passports and money. Others do not fit within the most typical conceptions of the road category but address similar concerns from outsider perspectives. *Illégal/Illegal* (Olivier Masset-Depasse, 2010, Belgium/Luxembourg/France), considered in-depth in Chapter 5, which tells the story of a Russian immigrant's battle against deportation, might be considered a variation on what Laura Rascaroli has termed a 'pre-departure' road film (Rascaroli 2013: 22). *L'envahisseur/The Invader* (Nicolas Provost, 2011, Belgium) joins a migrant from Africa at the end of his voyage to Belgium. Due, however, to his economic and social marginality, the protagonist remains in constant motion after his arrival, restlessly moving through Brussels in search of work and from one temporary abode to another. In a similar vein, Laderman has argued that much of the output by the Dardenne brothers could be read as iterations of the urban road movie subcategory. Both noun and verb forms of 'traffic' have been featured as prominent motifs in their oeuvre since *La Promesse* (1996), particularly in *Rosetta* (1999), *L'enfant/The Child* (2005), *Le silence de Lorna/Lorna's Silence* (2008; considered further in Chapter 5), *Le gamin au vélo/The Kid with a Bike* (2011, Belgium/France/ Italy) and *Deux jours, une nuit* (2014), in which the protagonist spends most of the narrative in constant motion in an attempt to save her job. Whether mobility is realised or frustrated, the flow of humans and goods within a global economy and in particular within a post-Berlin-Wall Europe is a central concern in these films (Laderman 2013: 173–86, esp. 173–4). Moreover, while only *Le silence de Lorna* features a road trip as such, each of the films above closes with the protagonist (back) on the move, demonstrating the characters' inability to gain solid footing in the world.

MAPPING BELGIUM WITHIN EUROPE AND THE WORLD

The five films examined in more depth here explore the significance of national boundaries and 'soft borders' in a unified Europe and postcolonial world. Each example 'maps' the place of Belgium in the wider world differently. *Quand la mer monte* (henceforth *QLMM*) looks across the border with France to examine Belgium's place in French-language cultural spheres. It also addresses the internal national divide in an alternative context by framing an encounter between a Walloon and a Fleming in France. In terms of its relationship to the road genre, *QLMM* is an ideal starting point. Discussions of mapping, the role of the random 'road event', and the film's parodic outlaw angle will provide an introduction to how these key tropes are employed in a particularly Belgian context in subsequent examples. Next on the list is *L'iceberg*, which stages an atypical voyage towards the north, in the process underscoring the possibilities and perils of open borders. The traveller in this film has a brief but remarkable encounter with clandestine migrants, the less-privileged mobile counterpoints to most Belgians' travels. Both *L'iceberg* and *QLMM* are noteworthy as rare examples of female road movies, suggesting a re-evaluation of conceptions of gender and family roles.

While venturing beyond the borders of Belgium is the norm in the works discussed here, *Eldorado* remains within the national boundaries but in the process keeps them firmly in focus. The border becomes both a spatial limitation and a metaphor for national identity. In this sense *Eldorado* – like the other four films – aims to answer both the question posed by its travellers, 'where are we?', as well as the auxiliary question with particular resonance in Belgium: 'who are we?' *Les folles aventures de Simon Konianski* (henceforth *Simon Konianski*) embraces a multiculturalist vision of citizenship and high-lights contemporary Belgian diversity. The return voyage to family origins it stages ultimately leads to a reconciliation between the titular protagonist's conceptions of cultural openness and the pull of cultural roots. Finally, *Aaltra* frames road travel within a different set of contextual references points, staging a voyage across Europe in which economic imperative for mobility takes precedence over personal and cultural quests. [4]

QUAND LA MER MONTE: A FEMALE 'OUTLAW' ON THE ROAD IN THE FRANCO-BELGIAN BORDERLANDS

An offbeat blend of escapist voyage and comedy, *QLMM* is based on the experiences of Belgian actor and co-director Yolande Moreau while touring for her one-woman comedy show, 'A Dirty Business of Sex and of Crime'. The opening sequence shows Irène (Moreau) removing her wedding ring before applying makeup, marking the show and its associated travel as an idealised, escapist alternative to the constraints of her home life. As such, the film offers a novel female twist on the road movie trope of escapist male fantasy. As has been discussed in prior chapters (see Chapter 1 in particular), women are commonly objectified in road movies, with the goal of the trip frequently being to encounter and seduce females and otherwise seek relief from the perceived limitations of domestic life (Mazierska and Rascaroli 2006: 166; Hayward 2005: 313). Here the tables are essentially turned, demonstrating again how European films adopt and adapt road cinema models. Irène's domestic life is illuminated by fragmentary phone conversations with her husband on banal domestic topics such as colour choices for new tiles being installed in the house. Things get interesting for Irène when her new car inexplicably breaks down in France, where she is on a tour of towns close to the Belgian border. A drifter named Dries, played by Flemish actor Wim Willaert, comes to her rescue and an unexpected connection is sparked. The 'road event', propelling the protagonist in unintended directions, is once again presented as an unforeseen obstacle within the context of the narrative. However, as an almost ubiquitous plot element in the road movie, such events can hardly be seen as a surprise by the viewer. It is worth recalling here Timothy Corrigan's observation that 'in the road movie events act upon the characters' (1991: 145). With this trope in mind, the Belgian road movies discussed here should be considered to encompass a combination of action and reaction to the shifting parameters of identity, economy and mobility in contemporary Europe. Unexpected encounters and events will play a role in each protagonist's experience with mobility, suggesting that mobility and travel are experiences that, much like the road event, are to varying degrees beyond the power of individual subjects to control.

Dries is an economic outsider, working odd jobs and living in a garage used to store the parade giants typical in the *Nord* and surrounding regions on both sides of the Franco-Belgian border. His heavily accented French clearly marks him as a foreigner. It is noteworthy that Irène, a Francophone Belgian, and Dries, of Flemish extraction, meet not in Belgium but in northern France. In this way, the contentious issue of Belgian politics and culture is broached in an indirect but unmistakable fashion, with the linguistic question avoided due to the fact that the protagonists meet in a place where it would seem logical to speak French. Indeed it is significant that the entire narrative of this Belgian–French co-production takes place over the border in France. Belgium was a major source of immigration to France from the mid-nineteenth through early twentieth centuries. Franco-Belgian connections go further back. Part of historical Flanders was annexed by France in 1668 and vestiges of that culture remain in Lille and throughout French Flanders. The fact that Flemish communities on the French side of the border are Francophone or Picard-speaking serves to underline the traditional importance of the political or hard border. This history notwithstanding, the formation of the Lille-Kortrijk-Tournai Eurometropolis, touted as a 'polycentric, bi-national, and tri-cultural metropolis', demonstrates that EU policies are rendering these hard borders crossed by Irène increasingly inconsequential.[5] The porosity of soft or cultural borders forms an important subtext to the film. The fact that Irène (just like Moreau) earns a portion of her living performing in France underscores the fact that Francophone Belgian films and actors tend to be similarly mobile. By far the largest market for these films is found across the border in France, where ticket sales accounted for over 90 per cent of box-office receipts for *QLMM* and 75 per cent for *Eldorado*.[6]

Dries represents the attraction of life on the road and on the margins of society. When he becomes a fixture in the audience-participation portion of Irène's show, it is clear that the boundaries of art and life are beginning to blur for the heroine. As their affair picks up speed, the film takes on a whimsical outlaw angle with a night-time excursion through off-limits industrial space surrounding an oil refinery. Such parodic reconfiguration of the tenets of the American road genre is common in European films, which as Everett puts it tend to 'use and abuse' the classic road movie template (2009: 165). It is here that the most overtly fantastic and surrealist – a hallmark of Belgian culture evident in many of the Belgian films considered in this book – moment occurs when Dries lowers a drawbridge on command whilst Irène visualises him as a knight on horseback. The act of trespass results in an encounter with the police, whose interest is piqued by the large stash of twenty-euro notes and faux-blood-stained garments that serve as props in Irène's act. The unlikely pair of quasi-outlaws is set free after Irène produces contracts demonstrating that she is on tour for her 'Sex and Crime' show, whose title the officer (played by Dardenne brothers' stalwart Olivier Gourmet) reads with scepticism. The misunderstanding having been cleared up, Irène finally realises that her road trip has transformed from temporary escapism into a potentially dangerous reaction to everyday life. She proceeds to break off relations with Dries and returns home.

Visually, *QLMM* draws on the standard road movie arsenal of travelling shots, which alternate with scenes from the encounters between Irène and Dries, her phone calls home and segments of her show. On the road we see perspectives outside and inside the car in addition to driver point-of-view shots of highway and countryside. The landscape captured by travelling shots ranges from vineyards to power lines and is altogether rather nondescript. Visually stunning exceptions come from luminescent night-time shots of refinery lights that create an almost magical, surrealist world and a two-shot, frontal windscreen frame composition in which reflections of passing plane trees merge with the image of the characters seen from outside. Such frame compositions of the windscreen (or mirrors) are often employed reflexively, to 'foreground the crucial act of looking or seeing while driving', as Laderman (2002: 16) describes the technique. Often, characters appear as reflections in the glass, which 'helps visualize aesthetically the theme of self-exploration as a projection of self through space' (2002: 16). Here the visual melding of people and landscape is suggestive of transformation, although the opacity caused by the reflection points to a darkening of the mood. Indeed at this juncture the road is nearing an end for Irène and Dries. The fact that this shot is the only occasion in which we see Dries driving is also noteworthy given the film's rare status as a female-led road film. Ultimately Irène maintains her place behind the wheel and remains in control of the narrative. While the hard border between nations is insignificant for Irène, who earns a living performing in French on both sides of the divide, the symbolic value of border crossing is crucial to the film's exploration of identity questions. Being in motion and outside her habitual place affords her the opportunity and the context to re-evaluate her personal life and by extension question the role of women in traditional family and social structures. The relationship between Wallonia and Flanders is also explored under a different light. By framing this encounter outside the borders of Belgium, the film might encourage viewers to consider the relationship between the communities in European terms rather than strictly national ones.

One salient and unique – at least when compared to North America – feature of the European landscape that merits mention here is the roundabout, which makes brief but symbolically significant appearances in *QLMM* as well as in *Simon Konianski* and *Aaltra*. Irène must circle around a smaller version of the Eiffel Tower on each of her two trips to Dries' temporary home. He signals the route as they drive past by saying 'Paris', followed by a whistle and a circular hand gesture. The diminished size of the famous Parisian landmark suggests that they are 'lost in the provinces', while the directional element of the gesture (repeated on the next trip by Irène) builds on the recurring motif of quite literally 'being lost'. The reference to Paris is not incidental. Belgium has traditionally been culturally marginalised in French culture. As journalist Henri Vivier puts it, Belgians are commonly regarded as no more than 'provincial cousins' by the French (2007: 248). Within the cinematic context, the reference to Paris carries a self-reflexive element, for Moreau launched her acting career in French productions, specifically a short by Agnès Varda followed by a small role in another notable female road film by that director, *Sans toit ni loi/Vagabond* (1985, France). She would eventually make her name in the French sketch comedy television series *Les Deschiens*. Returning to the film, Dries' attempt at drawing a map that will allow Irène to navigate a warren of one-way streets fails, forcing her to spend a chaste night at his makeshift apartment. Her navigational difficulties recall the initial travelling sequence in the film, which is interrupted when Irène must stop for directions in the midst of a sprawling suburban development. Her query is met with a jumble of incomprehensible and confused instructions. Both in improvised hand signal form and in more traditional written form, the map in *QLMM* underscores the theme of self-discovery and the need to find one's way in a new and perplexing landscape. To once again cite Conley's argument, maps in cinema serve an ontological function, encouraging us to consider 'where we come from and where we may be going' (2007: 3). Maps are staple elements in road cinema and will be significant for their presence or absence (suggested by getting lost) in each of the following works. As for the roundabout, which I will return to in the context of *Simon Konianski*, circular motion is symbolic of the cyclical nature of travel in each of the films addressed here except perhaps in *Aaltra*. Like the heroes of most the other films, Irène returns home at the end of her quest, suggesting that Belgians can be connected to a particular place while remaining flexible, open and unmoored in terms of outlooks on citizenship and identity.

L'iceberg: Open Roads (and Seas) and Closed Borders

Another female road narrative, *L'iceberg*, by Brussels-based directing and acting team Dominique Abel and Fiona Gordon along with co-director Bruno Romy, is certainly the quirkiest addition to the list of films discussed in this chapter. The Belgian Abel met the Canadian Gordon in the 1980s while both were studying at the Jacques Lecoq theatre school in Paris. *L'iceberg* is the first of four comedies sharing their unmistakable style that has drawn comparisons to Tati, Kaurismäki, and Laurel and Hardy. The films of Abel, Gordon and Romy are characterised by a strong dose of absurdist, physical comedy and by sparse dialogue. While *Rumba* and *Le fée* also contain road movie elements, the quest narrative in *L'iceberg* makes it the most obvious choice for discussion here. This film is perhaps best described as an accidental road movie, with the primary 'road event' that changes the course of the protagonists' lives serving as the impetus for the voyage rather than changing its course. As the narrative opens, Fiona (Gordon) and Julien (Abel) are, at times quite literally, sleepwalking through an extraordinarily banal existence in a staid suburban development. One night when closing down the fast-food restaurant she manages, Fiona inadvertently shuts herself in the walk-in freezer while stowing a massive sack of *frites* and is forced to spend a frigid night locked in with this frozen foodstuff. Fiona's absence initially goes un-noted by her husband and two children, under the morning spell of the workaday routine and beholden only to their clock. Rescued by a flock of scurrying employees in the morning, Fiona seems to have emerged well-chilled but otherwise unscathed and unchanged. Thawed out by a warm drink she returns to full robotic managerial mode; her first utterance is not 'thank you' but 'get to work'.

It is only after Fiona returns to her routine that the experience is revealed to be transformative; she has acquired an obsession with the frozen world. Her newfound affinity for ice leads to the second transformative experience, in the form of an unintended voyage inside a freezer truck. Unlike the protagonists of *QLMM* and *Eldorado*, Fiona is travelling without a car and is therefore more subject to the vicissitudes of chance and the will of others. The initial segment of her voyage is cut short after we learn, along with the police, that Fiona is not alone in her frosty hiding place. Following an ellipsis we find her alongside a group of African *clandestins* being scrutinised by two assiduously dour officers. The *mise en scène* of her encounter is symbolically charged. In the darkness of the truck numerous pairs of eyes become visible to the viewer and then to Fiona, a reminder that migrants crossing Europe from the south and the east often do so, whether literally or figuratively, in the dark (see Chapter 5).[7] As the discussion of landscape in Chapter 2 made clear, the pleasure of viewing scenic and novel territories is part of the experience of road cinema both for protagonists and for viewers. In this scene *L'iceberg* nods towards a fundamental difference in how mobility in Europe is experienced according to one's citizenship status. Many films that trace migrant voyages, from *Reise der Hoffnung/Journey of Hope* (1990, Xavier Koller, Switzerland/Turkey/France/UK) to *Nulle part terre promise*, demonstrate the restricted visual possibilities of clandestine voyages by depriving the spectator of the 'scopophilic "touristic" pleasure' (Loshitzky 2010: 27; Gott 2013c).

The only overtly political moment in the film is powerfully rendered without a single word being uttered. Sketched on the pavement are two boxes, delineated with chalk and marked respectively as 'Yes' and 'No' in English, the lingua franca of many migrants traversing Europe and therefore also the unofficial language of those who police its borders. As a large group huddles within the confines of the space labelled 'No', Fiona hides two young migrants behind her frame within her own comparatively spacious 'Yes' box, rotating in comical step with the officer scrutinising her in order to shield the children.

The physical comedy signals a refusal of realism that inscribes Fiona's silent gesture of resistance with a stubborn and whimsical optimism prevalent in other deliberately anti-realist films such as Aki Kaurismäki's 2011 *Le Havre*.[8] The choice by Belgians to resist the policies of their government to detain and deport undocumented migrants has become relatively common in recent films from that nation such as *Illégal*, discussed in Chapter 5, and *25 degrés en hiver* (2004). Meanwhile the choice of English to label the containment squares suggests a pithy critique of immigration policies that are not only Belgian but linked to a monolithic Fortress Europe. The episode invites a connection between travel and rebellion, or at least newfound awareness. When at home Fiona is a veritable automaton and unquestioning participant in society, but on the road she becomes enlivened with purpose. As such the film adheres to the road movie convention, identified as crucial by Laderman, of embracing the journey as a form of cultural critique (2002: 1). The road allows Fiona, quite literally in this case, to see the world through the eyes of the migrants. In this sense, the 'positive' and 'negative' road movie strains merge briefly in *L'iceberg*. Such categories provide a starting point for a fundamental division of contemporary European road movies. While positive films are more closely 'associated with open roads and by extension mobility, those on the negative side are primarily concerned with the implications of closed borders' (Gott and Schilt 2013: 3). These divergent categories are not contradictory, indeed the:

> European propensity to control borders and police immigration is responsible for the constant reproduction of internal barriers, whether social, cultural, psychological, or legal. These are the same static and inflexible parameters that positive road movies react against through recourse to movement as a liberatory trope. (Gott and Schilt 2013: 4)

Fiona's brief encounter with clandestine migrants invites us to see her fugue within the context of other, less fortunate travellers, and to consider how the various trajectories crisscrossing Europe fit (and do not fit) into contemporary identity structures. At the same time, her travels are motivated by a desire to escape the restrictive structures of her life.

Fiona's voyage continues via bus, onto which she is comically pulled along against her volition but seemingly without her active resistance in a stampede of elderly travellers at a roadside plaza. Again, the 'road event' proves fortuitous, as the bus takes her over the French border to the sleepy Norman coastal town of Barfleur. As in *QLMM*, this border crossing is culturally and linguistically insignificant for the protagonist. Seeking to venture further afield in her quest for ice, a ready supply of boats and an encounter with a post-traumatically mute sailor named René provide the impetus for Fiona to create her own 'map', a drawing of an iceberg at sea with a childish, arrow-marked route plotted for a sailboat. Her next voyage will be by boat, after Fiona uses the map to convince René to ferry her to an iceberg. After a variety of misadventures, the sailboat (ominously or fortuitously named '*Le titanique*') smashes directly into the object of her quest. Fiona, René and husband Julien, who has awakened from his torpor and somehow joined them at sea in an attempt to woo his wife back, are rescued by an Inuit fisherwoman named Nattikuttuk who first appeared in an opening monologue explaining that she will be recounting the story.

Though it takes a decidedly different approach from *QLMM*, *L'iceberg* also ventures beyond national borders in an attempt to answer existential questions through voyage. In two telephone exchanges in which we are privy to the words uttered only by one speaker – Julien in one case and Fiona in the next – the characters frame the geographic location of their partner as a fundamental existential question. The inquiring refrain 'but where are you?' is repeated with comedic obstinacy by Julien, who by this time has noted his wife's absence. Meanwhile, after he leaves home to find her, Fiona is compelled to repeatedly ask her children the same question by telephone about him. This identity quest leads to a positive denouement, with Fiona and Julien having reconciled and the solitary René simultaneously finding his words and a partner in the fisherwoman.

L'iceberg adopts rather conventional road movie tropes, including the quest for self-understanding and the desire to see exciting locales, which frequently merge as they do here, into a unique format. In this film, as in the other fruits of the Abel, Gordon and Romy collaboration, the idea of travel is more important than the physical trip itself, or at least the cinematic depiction of the road travelled. As Hayward suggests, road movie iconography is typically marked 'through such things as a car, the tracking shot, wide and wild open spaces' (2005: 313). All of these staple elements are to be found in *Eldorado*, which I will address next. The car – and the choice and control, or at least the illusion thereof, it affords the driver – is notably absent in *L'iceberg*, as is the conventional travelling shot. In its place, the directors opt for a clearly artificial rear-projection technique to express motion through space on the bus and on the boat. The latter form of transit is, of course, rare in road movies, which tend to ply dry land. From a spatial perspective, the film initially crosses from Wallonia into northern France, perhaps one of the simplest and unremarkable among European borders, linguistically and culturally speaking. Only later does *L'iceberg* conform to the 'wide and wild open spaces' template by heading off into uncharted territory at sea.

While the exact locale of the iceberg is not revealed – and it is telling that the object of Fiona's quest is itself mobile – the fact that the fisherwoman identifies herself in an opening monologue as a speaker of Inuktitut, an Inuit language spoken in Canada (including Quebec, among other places) suggests that the intrepid voyagers have indeed ventured rather far afield. While travel is foregrounded differently from the other films under consideration here, voyage is again depicted as a transformative experience that offers the temporary possibility of escape for the protagonists, who return home seemingly changed by their experience. Again, this voyage is cyclical, leading the protagonist back to her initial starting point. We might also read into the two encounters with 'others', one on Belgian soil and the second well beyond, a message relating to cultural debates on identity, borders and hospitality. Fiona attempts to aid the clandestine migrants she encounters in Belgium and her gesture is later reciprocated when she finds herself in a foreign land, or in foreign waters.

Eldorado: The Wide Open Belgian West

As the title suggests, *Eldorado* conforms to several key visual and iconographic conventions of the classic American road movie while also evoking *Candide*, a famous French contribution to travel literature.[9] While the previous films brought couples together in order to stage the voyage as a potentially romantic escapist fantasy, *Eldorado* revisits the male 'buddy' format popularised by *Il Sorpasso* and subsequently *Easy Rider* (Laderman 2002: 67). Lanner's odd couple also recalls the protagonists in *Western* (1997), another notable French-language road film that mobilises and then distorts American generic traditions. In that acclaimed film by Manuel Poirier, Paco, a travelling shoe salesman, is hoodwinked into giving a Russian drifter named Nino a lift only to have his passenger reciprocate by stealing his car. They meet again in the nearest town and after Paco puts Nino in the hospital in retaliation they strike up an improbable friendship that leads them to hit the road together. *Eldorado* opens with a similar premise. Yvan (Lanners), an auto trader who regularly travels to the United States to buy vintage cars, is driving in his newest acquisition to the sound of rock 'n' roll that recalls the 'vigorous music soundtrack' common in American road films (Laderman 2002: 16). He arrives home to find that his house has been burgled and the perpetrator is still on the premises. Armed with a muffler, a choice that symbolises his line of work and the mobile route the narrative will soon take, Yvan goes upstairs to find the frail and fretful culprit hiding under his bed. He immediately pegs Elie, as the thief identifies himself, as a drug addict in search of cash for a fix. For unexplained reasons Yvan is loath to involve the police and a long standoff ensues. Yvan injures Elie with the muffler as the latter attempts to flee but the two come to a truce. The car dealer drops his would-be robber off at a remote corner, from where Elie plans to hitch a ride to his parents' house located 'close to the French border'. When Yvan returns to the crossroads later in the day, the pitiful Elie announces that nobody passes by that forlorn spot and convinces the former to drive him to his destination (Figure 3.1).

Figure 3.1   Yvan sizes up Elie as they make their way towards the border in *Eldorado* (Bouli Lanners, 2008).

The remote locale that serves as the starting point for this road trip is more evocative of North America than Belgium. A reviewer in *Le Monde* compares the landscape to Canada, while Morain suggests that Lanners 'transforms the flat countryside into the Far West' (2008). The interplay of theme and topography provides another link to *Western* as well as to Brel's *Far West*. Much like *Eldorado*, the title of those films evokes the 'Wild West' and the cinematic western, an antecedent to the road movie that is referenced in *Saint-Jacques . . . la Meque* and *Torpedo* (see Chapter 2) and many other European films (Hayward 2005: 313; Laderman 2002: 9). Despite their joint projection of the American West onto smaller European landscapes shot in Cinemascope, *Western* and *Eldorado* have very different approaches to space. Poirier distils the vast spaces conjured by his title into a very small swathe of France's own 'west', limiting the film's narrative space to some twenty square kilometres. Meanwhile Lanners and cinematographer Jean-Paul de Zaeytijd (who also shot *Simon Konianski*) expand Belgium to its limits and, in an almost surrealist sense, beyond. Lanners has expressed the belief that the 'lateral tracking shot is the most beautiful invention the world has seen' (Regnier 2008). Travelling shots and montages in *Eldorado* take a variety of perspectives on Yvan's 1979 Chevy as it courses through seemingly outsized wilderness and desolate, expansive fields. The travellers stop to bathe in a vast, untamed river that would not seem out of place somewhere on the map of America symbolically adorning the protagonist's bedroom wall where the earlier standoff took place.

Eldorado's relationship to time is equally noteworthy. It is unlikely that such a river stopover would be needed given the small dimensions of the

Belgian space being traversed. Considering that Yvan's home in the eastern portion of the country is separated from the western border region where Elie's parents live by less than 150 kilometres, it is hard to imagine the trip taking a good portion of two days, even with Yvan's stated preference for side roads over motorways. Yet the voyage somehow seems interminable; the duo drive a while, pauses to fix a minor radiator problem and have a few too many drinks with a creepy fellow car aficionado, then drive some more. The latter sequence uses jump cuts to demonstrate progression from dusk to darkness. Such montage techniques are commonly employed to compress voyages into neatly encapsulated sequences. As Laderman notes, the 'montage approach sublimates car travel to an idea or sensibility, in contrast with the linear, destination-oriented concept of travel' (2002: 18). Such meandering trajectories are often fitting given the road genre's penchant for voyages with no particular destination in mind. However, in *Eldorado* the protagonists do indeed have a precise geographic goal and this montage sequence brings them not to their destination, but to a forlorn campground in a forest. It is at this point where Elie and Yvan drift into sleep and let the car veer off the road, forcing them to spend the night in an abandoned camper. More than a case of the 'road event' imposing itself, this accident is the direct result of Elie's failed scheme. In order to help Yvan stay awake, his travelling companion suggests taping his head to the roof of the car. When the driver drifts off, in theory, he will be awakened by the tape tugging at his sagging scalp.

Beyond humour, such an event – just one example of what a *Variety* review qualified as 'ridiculous mishaps', something that European audiences might simply read as typical of Belgian cinema – also serves a parodic function. Lanners plays with the conventions and expectations of the road form to instil it with a unique authorial, and perhaps Belgian, touch. A series of oddball characters, starting with the Dutch-speaking Messiah figure, and absurdist 'abuses' of the American road genre all contribute to this Belgian flavour. On the road the duo meet a collector of cars that have struck pedestrians who claims to see the future, followed by a nudist who introduces himself as Alain Delon, a name shared with the French acting icon with whom Lanners played in the big budget European co-production *Astérix aux jeux olympiques* (Frédéric Forestier and Thomas Langmann, 2008), which was released the same year. As with the mini Eiffel tower in *QLMM*, this reference to the dominance of France – in this case French cinema – serves as a reminder of Lanner's role in that industry. Elie and Yvan also briefly become small-time 'outlaws'. After waiting for a seemingly indifferent petrol station clerk (who remains off-camera) to ring up their purchases, the pair makes off with beer, candy and windscreen washer fluid in an absurdist wink at roadside robbery scenes in films such as *Thelma and Louise*.

Much like his tape scheme, Elie's plan to go home to his parents also reveals itself to be ill-conceived. He has clearly not made his presence known for quite some time and rather than reconciling with them, he quarrels off-screen with his father while his mother questions Yvan. Elie has also hatched the plot to have Yvan pretend to be a good friend in order to make his own life seem more stable. When Elie meekly acquiesces to Yvan's suggestion that they help out by doing some chores in the garden, the explanation for the unlikely buddy movie pairing is revealed. While Yvan was in the States acquiring cars his brother died from an overdose and Yvan reproaches himself for not having been there for him. Helping Elie fix his life therefore represents the opportunity for some degree of redemption. Indeed progress appears to have been made until, on the way home, Elie convinces his new friend to stop in town to obtain heroin for a DIY euthanisation of a dog they rescue after it was tossed off a railroad bridge and left for dead. Elie absconds with the money allotted for the animal's dose, leaving Yvan to return to the road to bury the now deceased canine and head back home. Thus while the film has some uplifting moments, often driven by the upbeat if contemplative rock soundtrack, it ends on a dark note and seemingly denies its characters the transformative experience one expects in a road movie. There is little obvious personal growth; having spent endless time driving, seemingly exhausting the possibilities that Wallonia has to offer, apparently nothing has changed for Elie and little for Yvan. One might, however, read into Yvan's voyage a certain degree of personal growth in the attempt to dispel his demons by helping Elie.

Despite Lanner's taste for the iconography and road movie conventions of America, *Eldorado* is the sole film discussed here not to narratively venture outside Belgium. It also engages more explicitly than the others with Belgium's internal cultural and political divide. The unexplained opening sequence features a monologue in Dutch by an older bearded man claiming to be Jesus. Thus while ongoing disputes between Flanders and Wallonia are never specifically mentioned, their spectre lurks below the surface. At his parents' home it is revealed that Elie is in fact named Didier, marking him with a dual identity suggestive of a bumbling Belgian version of Kieślowski's double-lived Veronika/Véronique. The association of Didier/Elie with the Belgian nation is reinforced by his penchant for singing the national anthem, to the great surprise of Yvan, who declares that nobody knows the words anymore. Given the film's dark undertones, it is tempting to read both the hapless Elie and the protagonists' orientation issues as rather bleak symbols of the state of Belgium. Despite this pessimistic tone, the fact that Lanners turned to the road movie to explore the parameters and possibilities of Belgian identity suggests that mobility must play a crucial role in mapping the new parameters of the nation. Fittingly, the only map present in the film does not correspond to the roads travelled by the protagonists, but instead to America as a symbol of escapism that Yvan ultimately rejects by apparently returning home rather than by setting off into the sunset in – classic or clichéd – American road movie fashion. This cyclical gesture invites us to draw another connection to *Candide* by suggesting that, having travelled across Belgium, Yvan will perhaps now be able to focus on tending his own garden.

SIMON KONIANSKI: COWBOY HATS AND YARMULKES

An unusual blend of road conventions, humour and Holocaust memory work, *Simon Konianski* has drawn comparisons to the offbeat films of Wes Anderson and the Coen brothers but stages a 'return' narrative with a uniquely Belgian spin (Chapter 4 will consider 'return' films from France and Switzerland). The film opens with a montage of tracking shots of the titular protagonist driving through a neighbourhood of post-war high-rise apartments in Brussels. As his short voyage nears an end, the camera hones in on a high-angle shot of the car manoeuvring through a roundabout, a symbol of Simon's initial stasis – he is travelling in circles – and the cyclical nature of European routes and roots. He is unemployed and lacking both orientation and inspiration and as a result is in the process of moving back into his elderly father's apartment. Unrealised mobility will eventually give way to open roads in this whimsical, comedic take on what can be termed a 'return (to origins) road movie' (Gott and Schilt 2013: 5). The features of this category will be discussed in more depth in Chapter 4, but I opted to place *Simon Konianski* within the discussion of other Belgian films because it seems so representative of that nation's filmmaking and identity debates. Both 'return' and 'origins' must be applied to Simon with care, for he was born and raised in Belgium and demonstrates no interest in his Jewish heritage. Whereas the previous films involve personal identity quests and allude to Belgium's inherent internal complexities, the voyage in *Simon Konianski* is linked to family history and highlights the post-war diversity of that nation. Simon's parents immigrated to Belgium from what is now Ukraine, a trajectory from the East followed by some thirty-five thousand survivors of the Holocaust (Mosley 2002: 166). Simon is compelled to retrace this route in reverse, accompanied by his son and elderly aunt and uncle, when his father Ernest's last testament stipulates that he be buried in his native village, a place called Ostrov. In the process Simon reconnects with his family history and comes to the realisation that attachment to his Jewish heritage and self-identification as a citizen of contemporary Belgium and Europe, are not mutually exclusive principles.

Since 1989 the return road movie has gained currency as a significant subcategory of the French-language road movie. As we will consider further in Chapter 4, the popularity of 'return' voyages is reflective of a desire to remap national identities within the parameters of an enlarged EU, within which hard borders have lost some degree of their significance. These films consider ways by which it is more conceivable to hold more ambivalent positions on national identity and be Belgian (or French or Swiss) and retain, or rediscover, a connection to another identity (Wagstaff 2007: 162).

Simon Konianski crosses borders, literal and figurative, from the Cuban music accompanying the opening scene by Beny Moré to the drive across Europe. This choice of music would seem to represent an odd contrast to the geographic setting of the film and the route of family discovery undertaken in the subsequent voyage. However, Cuban mambo music traces its roots to slaves that were brought to the island from central Africa, including lands in the Congo that would later come under Belgian colonial rule. This marks the musical score as another subtle nod to Belgium's past and to the circularity of identities embraced in Belgian road cinema.[10] The film's transnational stance – and Belgium's 'melting pot' status – is underscored by dialogue in French, German, Yiddish, Spanish, English and Ukrainian, four of which are spoken by Simon with widely varying levels of skill. As in the other works under consideration here, mobility becomes the catalyst for the formulation of new outlooks on citizenship and identity. While Ernest lives in the past and remains firmly attached to the tenets of Jewish religion and culture, Simon is entirely indifferent to tradition. Though Belgian or European identity per se is never explicitly evoked, Simon clearly positions himself as a citizen of a secular and diverse nation. The film is peopled with characters with origins in diverse locales such as Spain and Brazil, although not the Maghreb, Asia or (directly, at least) Africa. Despite his family's attempts to find him a Jewish wife, Simon remains infatuated with his Spanish ex-partner Corazon, with whom he shares custody of their son Hadrien. Such a framing of divergent generational outlooks is common in the French-language return movie. Quite often, as in *Simon Konianski*, the road trip allows younger protagonists to reach an accommodation between their own more assimilated outlook and family tradition.

The fashion in which the road movie form is mobilised to depict such processes of accommodation is exemplified by a sequence occurring in Ukraine as the travellers are nearing their destination. Unbeknownst to Corazon, Simon has taken his son with him on this trek into family origins. The boy starts out wearing a cowboy hat, one of several winks in the film at the western origins of the road movie template and another nod to the outlaw trope that commonly appears in European road movies. The latter angle is reinforced by the pistol inexplicably brought along by Uncle Maurice. A 'road event' will once again intercede, leaving the car out of commission in a Ukrainian field. Father, son and coffin then hitch a ride in the limousine of travelling singers belonging to the Hassidic Loubavitch movement. En route, they are regaled with traditional music while one of the performers convinces Hadrien to trade his cowboy hat for a yarmulke. The fact that the spot where they are dropped off is not their intended destination reminds us of the sometimes tenuous links that connect memory, culture and place. The family home was once in Poland but shifting borders have left it in the Ukraine. Likewise the fact that Ostrov, which signifies 'river island' in numerous Slavic languages, refers to dozens of villages in the region makes it a difficult locale to zero in on, much like Fiona's mobile destination in *L'iceberg* and the abandoned village in *Ten'ja* (Chapter 4). In a comedic touch that serves to parody the road movie's typical preoccupation with speed, the final segment of the trip takes place on a horse-drawn cart driven by a helpful peasant. At the cemetery in Ostrov, Simon reconciles with an apparition of his father that began to appear to him in the course of the voyage, as well as with relatives with whom he had clashed and left along a Polish roadside. Road cinema offers fertile ground for reconciliation in no small part because it tends to confine travellers within a small space inside a vehicle (Laderman 2002: 13). In *Simon Konianski* one of the antagonists is deceased, thus shifting the importance from character interaction taking place within the car to the interaction between Simon and the cultures and spaces encountered outside it. Simon and Hadrien, initially accompanied by elderly relatives who finish the voyage separately after numerous squabbles, stop at gatherings where extended family and old family friends reminisce, at the border post separating Ostrov from Poland and at the Majdanek concentration camp where Ernest was imprisoned. The Majdanek stopover and earlier news reports of the Israel–Palestine conflict that often form the backdrop to family disputes give the film an overtly political angle briefly present in *L'iceberg* but absent in the other primary films considered in this chapter. The death camp, along with references to occupied and enclosed territories, provides a cogent reminder that camps and policed borders remain an unavoidable element of the European landscape for certain voyagers (Loshitzky 2010: 119).[11]

In the fashion of most of the other films addressed in this book thus far, *Simon Konianski* cinematographer Jean-Paul de Zaeytijd employs a variety of tracking and framing shots common in road movies to chart the protagonists' movement across space. *Simon Konianski* also ends with the heroes still in motion, as in the prior examples. Before boarding a return flight from Lviv alongside his family, Simon phones Corazon to make plans to travel to the beach, suggesting that his newfound outlook complements rather than replaces his former stance. It is clear from his unflagging interest in his Spanish ex-girlfriend that even after his rediscovery of family heritage Simon still eschews his family's communitarian reflexes. In a fashion similar to the 'return' road films addressed in the following chapter, *Simon Konianski* paints a picture of identity that may contain multiple allegiances, whether to different physical places or to different cultural and religious outlooks. Transformed by the road, the 'new Simon' is simultaneously in touch with his roots and at ease in a diverse Belgium that, as the presence of Corazon suggests, is a microcosm of Europe.

AALTRA: IMPORTING TRACTORS AND EXPORTING THE BELGIAN APPROACH TO CINEMA

The Belgian-ness of the four films analysed so far has become an exportable commodity in Europe. Lanner's French friends Gustave de Kervern and Benoît Delépine have cast him in no fewer than five of the six offbeat road movies they have directed. While the films are French productions, Lanners has commented that the directors expressed the desire to work with what he terms a more laid-back, 'Belgian' approach (Van Hoeij 2010: 89). The final film under consideration in this chapter is a Belgian–French co-production that exemplifies this approach. The director–actor duo Gustave de Kervern and Benoît Delépine have collaborated on six feature films and whether the narratives lead through Belgium en route to Finland as in *Aaltra*, to Guernsey in search of fiscal exiles as in *Louise-Michel* (2008, France) or crisscross France (*Mammuth*, 2010, France), their collaborations have a distinctive feel that connects them to many of the Belgian films addressed above.

Whereas the voyages in the first four films in this chapter were primarily motivated by very personal quests or cultural discovery, *Aaltra* situates its travelling protagonists within a world defined primarily by economic and political imperatives.[12] In a fashion similar to *Louise-Michel* and *Mammuth*, earlier efforts by the same directors, *Aaltra* frames a voyage within the context of globalisation, Europeanisation and the free movement of citizens and goods across European borders, two of the 'four freedoms' central to the European project since the Treaty of Rome (Verstraete 2010: 4) This is demonstrated by the variety of languages spoken in the film, including French, Dutch, English, German and Finnish. *Aaltra*, shot in black-and-white cinemascope, is a darkly comedic film that engendered comparisons to the directing style of Kaurismäki and the acting talents of Laurel and Hardy and earned the label of the funniest film in recent years by one French critic (Ostria 2007). Delépine and Kervern consciously stake out a place in Kaurismäki's road movie lineage, something made clear by the fact that the 3,000 kilometre route undertaken by *Aaltra*'s voyagers leads to Finland, culminating with a cameo by the Finnish director whose name is synonymous with quirky and dark European road cinema.

Aaltra reformulates common road movie conventions and, to an even greater extent than the other films discussed here, contorts and abuses the tropes, themes, techniques and expectations of travel cinema. It then proceeds to reassemble the pieces in order to refashion road movie mobility, with an utterly eccentric twist, and to bring the travellers to some version of their destination and an ultimately somewhat typical – albeit characteristically quirky – personal transformation. If it ultimately celebrates the possibilities and joys of the open roads and reaffirms the role of travel in the creation of identities and the possibility inherent in escape from the habitual spaces of existence,

Aaltra first thrusts to the forefront the perils of mobility and the danger of dissipation and unrootedness inherent in globalisation. It does so by initially staging a descent from socially perceived physical and economic mobility towards socially perceived immobility (Urry 2007: 8) by the two protagonists who will ultimately come together to form a highly unlikely travelling duo. Delépine's 'employee', designated in the credits only by his professional function in society, loses his car, wife, cell phone and job which he worked as a telecommuter, and ultimately finds himself in a wheelchair after an accident. Similarly Kervern's 'agricultural worker' – a label that implies more instability than the French terms that would be translated into English as 'farmer' and imply a closer, rooted, link to the earth – suffers an injury that confines him to a wheelchair following an incident with the employee and loses his already precarious livelihood when his equipment is repossessed by the bank. In the process of their voyage the film will foreground issues of differential mobilities and highlight a question not commonly posed amidst what Everett has called the European road movie 'boom' (2009): the difficulty of travel by wheelchair (Figure 3.2). At another level, the film also uses wheelchairs as a symbol of the challenges of navigating an ostensibly borderless Europe that has become, economically and socially, literally and figuratively, what sociologist Viard terms a 'society of mobility' (2011: 18). In this context, economic and social immobility is, as it also is quite literally in at least one instance in the film, a threat to personal well-being. To be immobile is to be relegated to a solitary existence on the fringes of society and outside the social fabric (Viard 2011: 106), and it is above all to escape their social isolation that the protagonists hit the road.

Figure 3.2   The motley protagonists await a ride in Gustave de Kervern and Benoît Delépine's 2004 film *Aaltra*.

Aaltra is above all remarkable as a 'wheelchair road movie' ('un road-movie en fauteuil roulant') as Samuel Douhaire in *Libération* calls it.[13] However, the directors also provide their heroes with a comically staggering array of mobility options. Virtually every imaginable form of land transportation is employed in this film: train, car, motocross bike, tractor, ambulance, gurney, ferry, wheelchairs, an electric mobility cart, and the latter two on or in a variety of vehicles, from car to mobile home. Despite the sheer range of modes of transit that the travellers must call on – exemplifying an often surrealist version of Rabelaisian excess on display throughout the directors' oeuvre – and the narrative's context of globalised trade that provides the impetus for the voyage, mobility in the film is represented as above all difficult. The characters are regularly marooned by the side of the road and generally move slowly and painfully as when they undertake a bumpy and loud crossing in an old town full of cobblestones. In one case they spend many nervous hours stuck in their chairs at the beach as the high tide rises perilously close to their necklines before they finally find a swimmer who fishes them out and pushes their chairs back onto solid land.

The variety of forms of travel is rendered necessary by two important 'road events'. First, the accident that disables the protagonists is the result of a road-side confrontation between Delépine's 'employee' and Kervern's 'agricultural worker'. The employee, incensed that the worker's puttering tractor and noisy motorbike interrupted a business videoconference and blocked his drive to the office – both of which lead to the ultimate loss of his job – drives out to the field where the latter is working and attacks him on his tractor. A mishap ensues and both are stricken by what appear to be identical injuries. From this point on they are unwitting yet inseparable companions: sharing a diagnosis, hospital room, ambulance ride home and ultimately a trek to seek compensation after the agricultural worker discovers that their injuries were the result of shoddily constructed farm equipment. The second event occurs after the pair has travelled side by side – if not together, for each would prefer to be on his own but they are constantly lumped together on account of their wheelchairs – by train on the first leg of their journey and spend the night waiting for a connection. After buying tickets for their respective onward voyages (one to Finland, the other to a motocross race in Namur, Belgium) they visit a bar together and are robbed and left penniless in the street. Without ID cards and money they are unable to pick up their reserved tickets and must improvise a path that ultimately leads to Finland. In order to reach their destination they rely on their wheelchairs, mendicancy that crosses the line into petty theft and the kindness and solidarity of strangers who offer rides, pushes, nourishment and hospitality. The motley pair also resort to their own particular brand of gleaning that is decidedly more crude than, if not entirely incomparable to, that on display in Agnès Varda's road documentary *Les glaneurs et la glaneuse/The Gleaners and I* (2000, France): helping themselves to partially consumed food and drink in a biker bar and snatching a snack from a young boy's hands.

These comically ornery, greedy and altogether inconsiderate travellers regularly outstay their welcome. Indeed a good deal of the film's comedic power is generated by the gap between the innate sympathy that characters and, presumably, the audience are predisposed to have for the wheelchair-bound protagonists and the craven nature of these voyagers. The two wheel-chair-bound protagonists benefit, and take advantage of, a latent sympathy that more readily mobile travellers or passers-by feel for the disabled. They occupy and charge a fare to park in a handicapped spot, accost a man on the street who refused to give them money, and far outstay their welcome at the home of a German family. The latter's offer of a plug with which to charge the mobility cart (stolen earlier by the 'employee' from an elderly couple) turns into several meals and an overnight stay, all marked by overzealous use of the cart's horn by the 'employee', who beeps incessantly to demand delivery of food and beer. Finally fed up, the exasperated host drops the two off unceremoniously by the side of the road next to a graffiti-covered panel that perhaps appropriately reads 'Highway to Hell' in English. Numerous other episodes mine this theme of 'disabled' individuals that are entirely unworthy of the sympathy and magnanimity that they are generally treated with. In one instance, when they stop at a motocross event in Belgium, the 'employee' cons a driver into letting him take a spin on a vintage prized racing bike that is exceptional in that it is automatic and does not require the use of legs, which he promptly absconds with and crashes in a distant field. Until they reach the end point of their voyage, the travellers seem to forge no true connections with any of the numerous people they encounter, suggesting that while their rout is officially devoid of hard border crossings (indeed they travel without ID cards of any sort), soft borders between individuals and groups abound in Europe, something underscored by the lack of subtitles provided to translate the Dutch, German and Finnish that the protagonists encounter.

The event in Namur also furnishes an overt Belgian touch and dose of offbeat humour when Belgian actor–director Benoît Poelvoorde makes a cameo. He gets into an argument with the protagonists, demonstrating that often the 'hosts' found along the road are just as unpleasant as these 'guests', and offering him the opportunity to cite some numbers that are said differently north of the border. Such references to Europe's soft, or cultural borders, in this case the version of French spoken in Belgium, are a staple in Belgian productions involving encounters with French speakers from France. Another Belgian cameo coincides with an example of how the film injects the traditional road movie wayside points and iconography with a particularly European and quirky flare that is characteristic of Delépine and Kervern's work and of Belgian cinema in general. After the travellers arrive in Finland they stop in a biker bar where Bouli Lanners croons a vaguely Finnish and utterly absurdist karaoke version of Bobby Hebb's 'Sunny' to a roomful of disinterested bikers. In yet another wink to Belgium, in the backdrop during his performance are wall advertisements for Flemish beers.

Such stopovers also represent novel twists on generic road movie standards. In place of petrol stations and other typical roadside waypoints, the wheelchair-bound voyagers are prone to stop in places that bring into relief their atypical form of conveyance and relative lack of mobility. At the Namur rally they observe motocross drivers zip through terrain that would be utterly impassable in their wheelchairs. At a punk show in a bar they sit motionless amidst a riot of dancers moving in furious concert with the ear-splitting music. In the aforementioned biker bar, a close-up of the highly stylised, painted mural displays a virile biker with an alluring woman, reminding us of the dissimilarity of the heroes to preponderant images of hyper-masculine (cinematic) mobility. Yet despite the biker reference, the most rebellious figure on display in *Aaltra* is not a bank robber or motorcycle gang member but a character in a decidedly more European lineage. A leftist the protagonists meet at one stop attempts to inspire them by quoting with aplomb French anarchists such as Albert Libertad (1875–1908), who lost the use of his legs in childhood and was known for fighting the police with his crutches. Libertad is also a particularly suitable borderless road movie hero due to his stance against identity cards. Delépine and Kervern also channel 19th century anarchist circles with the title *Louise-Michel*, which references teacher, organiser and *communarde* Louise Michel (1830–1905). Both examples demonstrate that European road cinema does not lack for its own rebellious figures to draw upon. Later, after the motocross event – at which their relative lack of mobility is once again thrust into sharp contrast with the motorised spectacle (they are asked not to stand in front of the stage for the trophy presentation) – the 'agricultural worker' is inspired to proclaim his desire for revolt, to 'smash up everything' ('de tout péter'), perhaps channelling either Albert Libertad or the punk dancers encountered early in the voyage.

The wheelchair-bound duo's reliance on the kindness of others to give them a push or to be willing to pick them up by the side of the road and stow their chairs, places them in sharp contrast with images of effortless and rebellious mobility evoked by the leather-clad bikers. However, once they adjust to their new form of mobility, the road opens up and travel becomes an at least occasionally enjoyable experience. In one scene they celebrate in rather ironic fashion with a victory cheer after they successfully roll along a flat stretch of roadway past the national border between the Netherlands and Germany. This is followed by a memorable downhill segment of road demonstrating that the exhilarating brand of travelling shot need not necessarily be the exclusive purview of travellers blessed with automobility. The camera tracks the wheelchair and cart from behind before cutting to a shot of the runaway wheelchair almost being lost from sight around a curve in the road from the perspective of the 'employee', whose motorised cart – generally a more advantageous form of locomotion, as on the uphill stretch that preceded the border-crossing – is unable to keep up with gravity. The joy of speed is short-lived, however, for thirty-four seconds after the start of the downhill montage the 'agricultural worker' careens into a roadside barrier at the bottom of the hill and topples over. Another juxtaposition of mobility and stalled movement occurs in a scene in which they wait for an extended period of time at the side of the road. A long two-shot from across the road frames their stasis against an occasional vehicle that zips by, almost visually imperceptible. Several shots taken from an almost extreme-long distance from the other side of the road frame the waiting protagonists at an angle that emphasises the emptiness of the road and highlights their isolation amidst a vast landscape. The editing suggests that they have spent a long time in this spot, cutting from one shot of them gazing off down the road to another, identically framed, in which they doze. This is immediately followed by the most readily mobile segment of their voyage, at the end of which the duo finally experience the joy of speed that had generally eluded them and, ultimately, the satisfaction of having found their destination.

Once they are finally picked up from their roadside exile – to their bewilderment by a van transporting four sleeping nudists – the travellers are delivered directly to the ferry pier. The sudden upturn in their mobility continues on the other side of the Baltic, where several Finns kindly push the wheelchair while prattling on in the local tongue until an abrupt cut shows the duo at the peak of their mobility. A medium two-shot frames them above the waist, excluding from vision their injured legs, from a slightly low angle that frames the duo against the open skies and seemingly endless forest. They are attached to a trailer pulled by a car and the speed of the vehicle pushes the wind through their hair, eliciting the 'employee' to shed the neck brace that he had worn since leaving the hospital and emit a celebratory cry. The shot demonstrates the progression that has taken place during the voyage: a movement towards physical healing, a coming together of the protagonists, who are framed side by side and on entirely equal terms and equal levels of mobility for the first time, as well as the end of their voyage. The arrival at their final destination is staged with a twist. As in *L'iceberg* and *Simon Konianski*, the two other films discussed in this chapter narrating A to B voyages, the final destination in *Aaltra* is not exactly where or what the voyagers intended when they set off. Their first attempt to file for compensation for their injuries brings them not to 'Aaltra', the manufacturer of the faulty farm equipment, but to 'Valtra', where they are told that the other company makes imitations of their products. 'Aaltra' is a visibly smaller and lower-budget enterprise and in place of the six million euros they sought the travellers instead accept an offer of employment and a drink from the owner, played by Kaurismäki. Like all of the other workers, the latter is in a wheelchair, seemingly suggesting that the duo have finally found a place that corresponds to the wheelchair symbol that adorned the employee's cart, which served to advertise his 'identity', or at least as a projection of how both travellers were seen by others. That symbolic identity replaces the familiar stickers seen in this and other films – and indeed omnipresent on European roads – adorning the back of automobiles that announce national identity. This unexpected ending situates the voyage in relationship to the personal development and identity quest elements, but also more starkly within the context of economic factors, including boundary-free trade and professional mobility within the EU. The notion that finding a solid landing spot necessitates travel would seem paradoxical. In this sense, however, we can read the pair's physical injuries as symbols for the effects of globalisation on previously rooted people for whom mobility is imposed as their jobs and ways of life are uprooted through the process of *délocalisation*. Thus in this film, as in much of their work, Delépine and Kervern are attuned to the notion that the most prominent expression of globalisation has been 'in the transformation of localities' (Morley 2000: 14). A similar fate awaits the protagonist in *Louise-Michel*, whose factory is packed up and moved under cover of night, or even the entirely less sympathetic Roger in the Dardenne brothers' *La Promesse*, who becomes implicated in human trafficking in order to obtain a solid footing in the decaying industrial town of Seraing in the form of a building he is saving to purchase.[14] Like the characters in those films, the employee and the agricultural worker also partake in mobility that is part of the process that necessitated their displacement. Unlike the aforementioned films, however, *Aaltra* engages with this circular mobility in an ultimately 'positive' road movie format that allows the protagonists the opportunity to use the newfound flexibility to their benefit by moving until they find a place where they feel that they fit in. As their final approach atop the trailer shows, they have gained back a good deal of their lost mobility in the process, although their means of movement will forever be different.

Conclusion: Belgian Road Cinema's Openness and Blind Spots

As this chapter has aimed to demonstrate, Belgian road movies undertake metaphysical explorations of the links between identity, geography and mobility. The generally cyclical voyages in these films suggest that a project of mapping identity must take into account the circular routes and multiple connections that are intrinsic to contemporary Belgian and European identities. By venturing onto the road and subsequently returning home (or in one case finding a new home), each of these films frames identity as open and posits that Europe's soft borders are flexible. While grounded – to avoid the term rooted – in a particularly Belgian context, these films present parameters of identity that are sufficiently open as to encompass a cultural vision with space for cowboys, yarmulkes, icebergs, faux outlaws and apparently real anarchists – and to follow the Spanish thread from Corazon in *Simon Konianski* to another Belgian road film, *25 degrees en hiver* – roadside toreadors and, to some extent, undocumented migrants from beyond Europe or the EU. It could be argued that this is done in a uniquely Belgian fashion, characterised by strong doses of surrealism and humour and following in the lineage of the hybridity proponents in the *belgitude* movement. Whether or not these gestures should be labelled as particularly Belgian, it is clear that mobility in each of these films is harnessed in the service of a particular form of resistance to traditional, enclosed conceptions of citizenship and belonging. In this way they conform to the road movie model of rebellion against constricting norms. These films push the limits of identity by crossing hard borders, and do so at a time in which European preoccupations with border security have tended to encourage 'monolithic interpretations' (Thomas 2012b: 18) of European identity. Indeed 'others' – whether of the internal Belgian variety, European or African – are a constant presence in the films addressed here. These others are at times marginal, like Dries in *QLMM* and the clandestine migrants in *L'iceberg*, and at other times well integrated into Belgian life, as is the case of Corazon in *Simon Konianski*. In most cases encounters with alterity are facilitated by voyage, while in *Simon Konianski* travel opens the possibility of the protagonist coming to terms with his own distinctive heritage within an always already diverse Belgium. *Aaltra* only mentions ethnic others in passing, but in doing so and in framing that discussion as a case of amnesia on the part of the man who broaches the topic and of general indifference of his interlocutors, the film does subtly but successfully bring the issue to our attention. In this episode, the duo get a ride from an elderly man (Robert Dehoux) they encounter in a parking lot, who in a meandering monologue inside a car recounts being greeted in a village in colonial Congo as if he and other Europeans has arrived 'from Heaven'. His recollections of being greeted with chants of 'Bwana' is a clear reference to King Baudouin's voyage to the Belgian colony in 1955, documented in the film *Bwana Kitoko*[15] by André Cauvin, who was enlisted by the Belgian government to document the king's trip. The role is credited as *l'amnésiaque*, clearly highlighting a tendency to overlook unpleasant aspects of history, a habit shared by Belgium and Europe in general. In the course of three minutes, the man tells this story twice, in slightly varying forms, and the camera pans slowly between close-ups of the man's testimony and the two disinterested hitchhikers in the back seat. The close-ups on the gentleman have a documentary quality, and the cut *in media res* from the parking lot to the memories being shared inside a car without any context as to how the conversation started almost induces us to imagine the presence of a documentarian who has asked the man to share his memories. After some talk about deceased aunts, the man admits that 'Now all that I remember is what happened in the Congo.' It is a phrase that might elicit thoughts of numerous well-documented atrocities, but in the narrative the story falls on indifferent ears. Preoccupied with reaching their destination – the rally in Namur – the pair demonstrates no interest in stories from Belgium's colonial past. This three-minute driving sequence, in which the camera remains focused on the inside of the car with the exception of a quick cut to a direction panel indicating that Namur is approaching, demonstrates the power and possibility of road cinema and the encounters it can engender. It also points out the short-comings of destination-oriented travel that leads voyagers to privilege arrival over the experience and encounters that the road has in store. The episode, completely extraneous to the voyage narrative, is nonetheless an important example of how road films can facilitate travel into culture and history.

With non-European subjects appearing only in *L'iceberg* and *Simon Konianski*, we might have expected to see even more of Belgium's cultural diversity on display in these films. Yet I would argue that they still embrace diversity and openness by inviting us to think of 'who are we?' and 'where are we?' as questions that, while inextricably linked, are not always directly cor-relative. In the process they demonstrate the increasing difficulty of answering such questions within strictly national parameters. The popularity of the road format amongst Francophone Belgian directors clearly indicates that mobility is seen as a privileged way to address these issues. By crossing borders in a variety of ways, Belgian road cinema marks itself as eminently European, unmistakably transnational and restlessly mobile. The following chapter will consider films that, much like *Simon Konianski*, chart protagonists on 'return' voyages. The case studies from France and Switzerland share a similarly mobile and flexible outlook on identity with the Belgian films addressed here while also represent-ing an even more culturally diverse slice of new European identities.

NOTES

1. A good number of films that are officially considered minority Belgian co-pro-ductions are not popularly associated with Belgium or Belgian cinema. Examples of this include *Potiche* and *Indigènes*. Co-productions are much less common in Dutch-language Belgian cinema. Of the top ten Flemish releases between 2005 and 2010 in terms of domestic ticket sales, only one was a co-production (*Ben X*, co-produced by the Netherlands).
2. Laura Rascaroli (2013) applies Eder's theories to her analysis of 'pre-border cross-ing' films, in which mobility is ultimately frustrated or unrealised.
3. While the Flemish cinema industry has shown less affinity for the road movies format, some notable examples can be cited, including Geoffrey Enthoven's multi-lingual *Hasta la Vista/Come as You Are* (2011), with dialogue in Dutch, Flemish, French, English and Spanish and *Paradise Trips* (Raf Reyntjens, 2015, Belgium/ Croatia).
4. Though this angle will not be highlighted in my analysis, it is worth noting that

comedy, ranging from offbeat and slightly dark in *Eldorado, Simon Konianski* and *QLMM*, to slapstick in *L'iceberg* and surreal and absurdist in varying doses in all of the above, reveals itself to be a common thread in these examples as well as a dominant tendency in Belgian road movies in general.

5. See http://www.eurometropolis.eu/

6. *QLMM* had 28,984 box-office entries in Belgium compared to 372,708 in France. For *Eldorado* the figures are 46,562 in Belgium and 141,154 in France (AMSFWB nd).

7. Clandestine migrants being smuggled across Europe in the back of trucks are a common sight in films such as *Nulle part terre promise/Nowhere Promised Land* (Emmanuel Finkiel, 2008, France) and *Morgen* (Marian Crişan, 2010, Romania/France/Hungary).

8. Kaurismäki's film also features a European citizen who attempts to shelter a young African migrant from the authorities.

9. *El Dorado* is a 1966 western by Howard Hawks starring John Wayne and Robert Michum and the mythical lost city of gold famously visited in an early forerunner of the travel film, Voltaire's *Candide*. 'Eldorado' was a car model produced from 1953 to 2002 by Cadillac.

10. The Cuban music also may point to another circular movement of sorts in the Spanish-speaking world, represented in the film by Simon's ex, Corazon.

11. An episode in Emmanuel Finkiel's 1999 film *Voyages* (Poland/France/Belgium) recounts the return of Holocaust survivors to Auschwitz. Films such as *Last Resort* (Pawel Pawlikowski, UK, 2000) and *The World is Big and Salvation Lurks Around the Corner* (Stephen Komandarev, Bulgaria/Germany/Slovenia/Hungary, 2008) provide a reminder that internment camps remain present in Europe. *Hope* and *Illégal*, both analysed in Chapter 5, film unofficial camps used by migrants on the way to Europe and an official police detention centre for migrants.

12. Both protagonists lose their jobs, placing the film within a broader tendency to explore and critique the world of work that Martin O'Shaughnessy (2007) traces back to the 1990s. Starting in that decade a proliferation of French productions and co-productions concerned with job loss and its aftereffects can be identified. The diverse range of films that examine responses to the loss of individual and sometimes collective livelihood include *Western* (Manuel Poirier, 1997), Robert Guédiguian's *La ville est tranquille* (2000), Laurent Cantent's *L'emploi du temps* (2001), *La question humaine* (Nicolas Klotz, 2007), Kervern and Delépine's *Louise-Michel* (2008), *Erreur de la banque en votre faveur* (Gérard Bitton and Michel Munz, 2009), *De bon matin* (2011) by Jean-Marc Moutout, *Ma part du gâteau* (2011) by Cédric Klapisch and Jean-Pierre and Luc Dardenne's *Deux jours, une nuit* (2014). Like *Aaltra* and *Louise-Michel*, *Western* and *L'Emploi du temps* explore these issues using the road movie template.

13. *Aaltra* is perhaps the only French-language 'wheelchair road movie'. Jean-Pierre Sinapi's 2000 film *Nationale 7* is a less evident example of a road film. It is narratively anchored in one place, although the protagonists undertake a number of short voyages and the roadside setting means that there are a number of iconographic resemblances. Geoffrey Enthoven's multilingual *Hasta la Vista/Come as You Are* (2011, Belgium), with dialogue in Dutch, Flemish, French, English and Spanish, follows a journey to Spain by three young men in wheelchairs or mobility scooters.

14. See Laderman 2013.

15. *Bwana* note: refers to the name bestowed upon the king by some who greeted him, translated as 'handsome man' in Swahili.

4. TRAVELLING BEYOND THE NATIONAL: MOBILE CITIZENSHIP AND FLEXIBLE IDENTITIES IN FRENCH-LANGUAGE RETURN ROAD MOVIES

Films covered: *Voyage en Arménie/Armenia* (Robert Guédiguian, 2006, France), *Ten'ja/Testament* (Hassan Legzouli, 2004, France/Morocco), *Comme des voleurs (à l'est)/Stealth* (Lionel Baier, 2006, Switzerland)

In 2011 *Cahiers du Cinéma* devoted an entire issue to the recent tendency in French cinema to view France itself as an object of interest. From regionalism to immigration, from the colonial heritage to contemporary citizenship, Stéphane Delorme identifies the rise in the past ten years of a veritable obsession with France and its inhabitants, in and beyond cinema (2011). Over the same period, and looking back a bit further to the mid-1990s, the road movies that this book is concerned with have been plying similar terrain. As I have argued in previous chapters road cinema has become an increasingly popular vehicle for filmmakers attempting to come to terms with the complexities of contemporary identity within France and Belgium – both particularly rich case studies – but also within 'New Europe' and a postcolonial world. A close look at the corpus of French-language road cinema of the past twenty years reveals a genre that actively reformulates the limits of national and European identity by (often literally) redrawing the map. As is common in road cinema, this concern for home – whether it be France, Belgium or Switzerland – is translated into voyages beyond the boundaries of protagonists' home nations. Hitting the road has allowed directors of diverse origins and backgrounds to re-imagine boundaries and transcend the typical spatial signifiers that dominate political, cultural and media debates. Within the context of 'return' films in in particular, what is called into questions are binary distinctions between local and global, home and away, and cultural identities linked to 'home' and 'host'.

If *Cahiers de Cinéma* opted for a white silhouette of France on a black background for the cover of its issue, I will argue here that the return road movie opens the door to a reading of contemporary national identity as a flexible concept not strictly delimited by the geographic boundaries of the nation-state. At the same time, nor are identities aligned with the ethnic or cultural origins of the protagonists. Put differently, 'return' films complicate simplistic notions of home that would align that concept uniquely with origins or be defined by assimilation. Although these films narrate voyages to far-flung locales, they are fundamentally about the places that the protagonists call home more than the destinations. Indeed numerous scholars have pointed out the essential function of home or the concept of home in road movies, where it serves as a basic point of comparison that travels and experiences are measured against. As Pamela Robertson argues in reference to road movies in general, 'the trip away from home serves to both increase appreciation of home and to reformulate family bonds' (1997: 271, 283). The combination of these factors makes 'return' road movies particularly important contributions to our understanding of citizenship in contemporary Europe. 'Return' films formulate alternatives to the often divisive 'production of locality' found in diasporic cinema, which frame more traditional parents and more Western offspring grappling over identity within the space of the home, which is often represented as in conflict with the society outside (Berghahn 2013: 13). As in films like *Le grand voyage* and *Torpedo*, the potentially more harmonious outlooks on intergenerational relations are rendered possible by the voyages outside the habitual spaces of conflict.

This chapter will consider the how these films intervene in and intersect with French debates over republican identity constructions before branching out to compare and contrast a Swiss contribution to this cinematic category. Return films have been particularly prevalent in France, most obviously because of that nation's long tradition of immigration; they have also recently emerged as a significant subcategory of European road cinema.[1] My consideration of a corpus that includes films from France and Switzerland aims to hone in on the specificity of the return movie within French identity debates while also extending the analysis to other nations within the scope of this book. In the course of my analysis I will also selectively refer back to *Simon Konianski*, which, although a clear representative of the 'return' category, seemed to fit better within a discussion of Belgian cinema. Belgium's more recent history of immigration has also made it increasingly fertile ground for such cinematic return narratives whereas Swiss cinema, if more of an outlier, is arguably being pushed towards a greater opening to (internal) otherness by a small but notable group of directors, in particular Frédéric Choffat (discussed in Chapter

2), Greg Zglinski, Fernand Melgar, Andrea Staka and Lionel Baier, whose film *Comme des voleurs (à l'est)/Stealth* (2006) will be discussed in detail. When combined, cinematic 'returns' from the three nations encompass immigration and diversity related to postcolonial and inter-European factors.

The two dozen films making up the wider corpus this chapter was drawn from demonstrate the flexibility of individual allegiances and identifications within these shifting spatial parameters. The popularity of 'return' voyages is reflective of a desire to remap French and other national identities within the parameters of an enlarged EU, within which physical and administrative frontiers have fallen. It is now conceivable to be French, Belgian or Swiss and retain, or rediscover, a connection to another identity, whether Polish, Czech, Armenian, Spanish, Italian or Maghrebi (Gott and Schilt 2013: 5). Following a discussion of the political and social factors at play, this chapter will take two approaches to the films in this cinematic category. The variety of perspectives and destinations they espouse will first be discussed in general terms in order to highlight and classify the different motivations and causes behind these cinematic voyages. I will then turn to a more detailed analysis of two particular films that exemplify flexible, layered outlooks on French republican citizenship, *Voyage en Arménie/Armenia* (Robert Guédiguian, 2006) and *Ten'ja/Testament* (Hassan Legzouli, 2004). *Comme des voleurs (à l'est)*, a film made beyond the borders of the Hexagon, will then be considered in comparison to the French films. The latter portion of the chapter aims to assess how shifting borders and allegiances are navigated in the return film, with particular attention to the contentious issue of 'second (and third) generation' subjectivities.

'NEW' EUROPE, NEW IDENTITIES: SITUATING (CINEMATIC) CITIZENSHIP IN THE REPUBLIC AND BEYOND

The recent popularity of the return subcategory corresponds to attempts by scholars and institutions alike to re-evaluate how identity and citizenship are perceived, constructed and policed. Contemporary citizenship is increasingly characterised by what Nira Yuval-Davis has termed 'multi-layered citizenship' (1999), in which identity has become unmoored from its unwavering, 'imagined' attachment to the nation. Within France and Europe it is now possible to follow Doreen Massey's suggestion that 'instead . . . of thinking of places as areas with boundaries around [them], they can be imagined as articulated moments in networks of social relations and understandings . . .' (1994: 153). Patrick Weil has applied a similar perspective to the French debate on immigration policy, arguing that institutions have not yet taken into account new parameters of population movements and of flexible identities. The state, he contends, must reimagine how it approaches immigration, which is no longer primarily a voyage with the permanent goal of sedentary settlement, but an ongoing process of 'migration in movement' (2005: 46). Weil's observations refer to retired immigrant workers who wish to travel back and forth between their native land and France. He also extends the question to address the shifting allegiances of younger generations, who are the most common travellers in 'return' films. Weil cites a case study on the relationship of Maghrebi-French youth towards citizenship as illustrative of the variety and flexibility of vantage points on citizenship held by young people:

> In the course of their life, these young people will perhaps circulate from one approach to self-identification to another. They may also wish to identify with a religion or with a career, a gender, or a political or union affiliation. (2005: 106)

In short, individual agency plays an increasingly important role in identity construction. While the above observations by Weil refer specifically to the French context, they, like those from Massey and Yuval-Davis, will be germane to return films from Belgium and Switzerland.

Within a particularly French context, public debates over evolving conceptions of citizenship have played out in cinema and subsequently replayed in academic approaches to French cinema and French studies in general. In *Minority French Cinema*, which focuses on *banlieue* and gay cinemas, Cristina Johnston contends that certain films undertake the 'construction and reconstruction' of social links, a process involving dialogue between mainstream and 'minor' communities (2010: 12, 38). While cinema can bring to the fore the 'fragmented subjectivities which can be seen to emerge' in members of minority groups as they attempt to reconcile difference with republicanism, Johnston insists that what emerges from her analysis is not a communitarian model but a 'negotiatory discourse' that attempts to reclaim republicanism (2010: 177). Johnston's assessment builds on recent interventions in the debate by Jack Dahomay, who envisages a renewal of republicanism from within that does not exclude cultural difference. Dahomay is situated alongside Michel Wieviorka and others within a current of French thought that seeks to update republicanism in order to keep it relevant to contemporary society (Johnston 2010: 15).

The other popular, and arguably dominant, interpretation of republicanism draws on a more traditional reading of the French constitutional principal of 'equality before the law'. Régis Debray, a leading proponent of this traditional republicanism, has warned that the 'dictatorship of particularities' represents a menace to the Republic (Johnston 2010: 14). This articulation of French citizenship is viewed as outmoded by Johnston and is flatly rejected by Carrie Tarr, who in her own study of *Beur* and *banlieue* cinema opines that the 'multicultural nature of contemporary postcolonial France-and the inequalities in the way its diverse cultures are valued-would appear to be self-evident' (2005: 1).

While the French return road movies under consideration here are fundamentally concerned with rendering difference and diversity visible, I would position them between the 'traditional' and 'negotiatory' outlooks on republican citizenship. On one hand, they elaborate difference as a question of individual subjectivity that is unrelated to the spirit of 'communitarianism' so commonly seen by traditionalists as a risk to social coherence. In this individualist sense, return road movies are consistent with an orthodox republican vision of a community comprised of 'public similars' as much as of 'private others' (Laborde 2001). Furthermore their outlook is not entirely incompatible with Debray's traditionalist assertion that the French Republic 'is composed of citizens, not communities' (1998: 7). On the other hand, however, the protagonists of these films do not see themselves as minorities, choosing to avoid or reject communitarianism and to identify – at least initially – entirely with mainstream society at a national or regional level. Their connections to and contacts with points of 'origin' are transmitted not by ethnic or cultural communities, but by personal factors. Thus these narratives portray subjects who do not call into question the public–private separation at the heart of the traditional republican stance.

While these contemporary, flexible parameters of identity referenced by Wieviorka, Johnston, Dahomay and Weil are in part explained by France's history as a colonial power and postcolonial site of immigration, the role of European unification and the ongoing process of constructing a unified European identity should not be overlooked. As Peter Wagstaff puts it,

> the crossing of borders is a defining characteristic of what it means to be European . . . Migration therefore brings to the definition of nationalism and national allegiance the possibility of ambivalence: multiple allegiances may co-exist, emphasizing the porosity of borders and the permeability of cultures. (2007: 164)

Gary Marks and William Wallace have suggested that although attempts to forge 'Unity in Diversity', as the EU slogan puts it, have not resulted in the transfer of identification from the nation to Europe, there has been a 'shift towards multiple loyalties with the single focus of the nation supplemented by European and regional affiliations above and below' (quoted in Wagstaff 2007: 162). In other words, the notion that everyone in France must be or become French has come under pressure not only from immigrants, but from regional and transnational factors linked to the EU. The elimination of obstacles to movement within the EU has led to population shifts, most notably from East to West. The focus of the present chapter, however, will be on how new parameters of identity have affected the offspring of previous waves of immigration who hold allegiances that are not only layered, but also frequently latent, particularly in the case of invisible minorities with European points of origin. Contemporary France faces both postcolonial and post-Wall paradigms, in which mobility is the order of the day, as Eva Mazierska and Laura Rascaroli put it in the first study of the European road movie genre (2006). In short, subjectivity in road return films tends to be malleable and mobile and is not aligned with a multiculturalist vision or agenda.

The return phenomenon is not limited to France. The Swiss, and as we saw in Chapter 3, Belgian identity debates share some important similarities with the French situation. Before expounding briefly on points of comparison and contrast, it is worth noting that the Belgian production *Simon Konianski* and the Swiss film *Comme des voleurs (à l'est)*, while pointing to some national specificity, take generally universalist stances on the issue of second generation (and beyond) subjectivities. Many of the issues outlined above within a specifically French republican context also apply to the non-French protagonists in these films. Belgium's structurally assured internal diversity, the presence of large numbers of European civil servants, and significant post-World War II influx of immigration have resulted in a situation that is similar to that of France in terms of desire to tell so-called 'second generation' stories as a way to come to terms with ambivalent subjectivities. As *Simon Konianski* demonstrates, however, the parameters of what it means to be Belgian differ. The European term 'mosaic' is apt in Belgium because less pressure is exerted to conform to a monolithic conception of national identity. As for Switzerland, while it is not a member of the EU, the nation has been a fully participating part of the Schengen Zone since 2009 (having voted to join it in a 2005 referendum), and has experienced, to a very different degree, the immigrant flows that have marked post-War and post-Wall Europe. Like Belgium, Switzerland also contains significant internal linguistic and cultural diversity.

PARAMETERS AND APPROACHES:
MAPPING THE RETURN ROAD MOVIE CATEGORY

Return road movies involve travel away from the Hexagon, Belgium and Switzerland, often by young people of diverse backgrounds who were born – or at least established early on – in those countries. The parameters of the 'return' road movie require some clarification. Because of the nature of 'return' voyages and the long distances often involved, I have employed the road movie label in a slightly broader sense in this chapter, applying it both to films that narrate travel in traditional road movie fashion and the smaller amount of those that elide to some extent the act of long-distance travel but depict the ensuing displacement. In both cases, the (re)discovery of ancestral or family home is generally displayed via travelling shots and montages. Perhaps to an even greater extent than the films addressed in prior chapters, 'return' road films incorporate elements of both American and European traditions. Most return quests are marked less by rebellion than by a desire – generally perceived as European – to trace 'the meaning of citizenship' (Laderman 2002: 248). Yet the examples addressed here are driving films in what is considered the classic American vein.[2] Stylistically, this means that they tend to make liberal use of the car-centred road format, which offers travellers the freedom to map their own route and furnishes a fitting template for the exploration of self-evaluation and the projection of self through space. The use of windows and mirrors as framing devices allows protagonists on identity quests to look forwards and backwards simultaneously, providing a level of self-reflection that becomes an 'effective metaphor for someone riding on the edge of self-identity' (Everett 2009: 172). The rapid passage of car and riders through the landscape is portrayed in montages of travelling shots. Let us recall that such shots, as Laderman puts it, are intended to convey 'a visceral sense of traveling at a hyper-human, modernized speed'. This is in contrast to the conventional tracking shot, which tends to be related to walking or running (2002: 15). The juxtaposition of shots from different perspectives, angles and distances, both on characters and the space surrounding them, permits films to map character development and transformation as it occurs. In other words, travelling montages foreground negotiation amongst characters and between people and the terrains they are traversing. A final crucial ingredient of the road cinema that often plays a particularly central and weighty role in 'return' films is the 'road event', the detours, diversions and roadblocks that impose an illusion of randomness and often divert or stall the quest for narrative purposes. In 'return' films, the generic logic of the road event pushes the characters towards closer proximity with local culture and people in the place of their family origins.

As for the idea of 'return', Alec Hargreaves points out that the applicability of the term, strictly speaking, ends with the first generation immigrant: 'For young people born and brought up in France, resettlement in the "home country" would not in fact be a "return" at all, but an act of emigration tearing them away from their deepest roots ...' (2007: 122). However, most return road movies do not involve resettlement. Rather, 'return' here refers broadly to a multiplicity of trajectories towards a site of, or associated with, the protagonist's origins. A direct genealogical link to a particular place is often involved, although I have included in my list films that stage less literal quest into the family or personal history, typically cultural or religious in nature, of the protagonists and/or the director. Three sometimes overlapping categories might be outlined: the first generation return, frequently staged late in life or posthumously for burial; the second or third generation return, the most common narrative; and the symbolic return, carried out to a place of some signification to family history (Gott and Schilt 2013: 5–8).

French 'return' road movies have forged routes to Central and Eastern Europe, North Africa, the Caribbean, Eurasia, Asia and the Middle East. While the majority of these films stage journeys to the former French colonies, the multiplicity of trajectories they represent underscore the fact that French identity is always already more complex and transnational than prevailing discourses of 'imagined' identity might admit (Gott and Schilt 2013: 5). As Mireille Rosello has pointed out, scratching the surface of Frenchness often reveals that the 'White' component of the highly symbolic *Black, Blanc, Beur* multicultural trio that gained currency in the 1990s is not necessarily Franco-French but might represent a variety of less visible alternative subjectivities and outsider perspectives (1998: 8).[3] The other possibilities are nearly endless, given the fact that in 1991 one in four people residing in France were themselves immigrants or had immigrant parents or grandparents (Hargreaves 2007: 6). Despite France's long tradition of immigration, as Gérard Noiriel has argued, French national identity was already moulded before large waves of immigration started, leaving the immigrants to navigate Frenchness as a vertical hierarchy of assimilation. Yet contrary to prevalent narratives, previous identities are not always left behind at the French border, or even at the door of the republican school, long considered the great equaliser (Noiriel 1996: 184–5; Grillo 2007). An examination of return films, with Weil's notion of flexible identities in mind, offers some insight into how outsider subjectivity, even when invisible, can awake from dormancy at key junctures in the protagonists' lives. This leads to some intriguing questions about contemporary identity in France and Europe. Notably, does a history of immigration combined with the reflex of facing '(at least) two ways at once', as Gilroy describes the diasporic stance (1993: 3), lead inevitably to a different and perhaps more sceptical approach to a monolithic conception of national identity?

With such a diversity of routes in mind, this chapter aims to build on recent scholarship on the 'return' category and the French road movie in general. A chapter by Will Higbee in *Screening Integration: Recasting Maghrebi Immigration in Contemporary France* (Durmelat and Swamy 2012) addresses three films narrating return voyages to the Maghreb (*Ten'ja*, *Exils* and *Bled Number One*, all released between 2004 and 2006) and theorises the increasingly prevalent return narrative within the context of Maghrebi-French identity debates and the 'myth of return' once embraced by some immigrants. Higbee convincingly suggests that the wave of popularity of such films could be linked to the fact that 'by the first decade of the twenty-first century, the French-born descendants of Maghrebi immigrants are, by and large, more integrated than in the 1980s and 1990s' and therefore more free to investigate connections with their North African heritage in lieu of working to establish their place within French society (2012: 72). I intend to expand the parameters of the debate. Moving beyond France to Maghreb voyages allows for a multifaceted assessment of the road movie's role as conduit for identity quests and, by extension, of the status of 'accented' identity (to adapt Hamid Naficy's well-known formulation) in contemporary France and Europe. In a nation of immigration, the newfound interest in ethnic and cultural heritage – though at times in conflict with traditional interpretations of the official tenets of French republicanism – is more than simply the domain of Maghrebi-French subjects, but a universal response to the contemporary landscape. Juxtaposing films that stage returns to North Africa with those that address wider geographic points of origin reminds us that, as Rosello argues, Maghrebi-French identity is never autonomous and 'always attached to other connotations, other communities, other problematics' (1996: 149–51).

POINTS OF DEPARTURE AND ORIGIN: 'RETURN' TRAJECTORIES

The films under consideration here will survey a range of points of origin, each adding a layer of complexity to contemporary French and European identities. The diverse starting points of these voyages are representative of the unique spatial remapping and identity reformulation at work in the return road movie. The first two films discussed in-depth are linked by their rather literal and multigenerational representation of the return narrative. In both – just as in *Simon Konianski* – a second-generation subject travels to their father's birthplace, whether following the elderly patriarch or escorting his remains. The French cases, *Ten'ja* and *Voyage*, which depict travel to Morocco and Armenia respectively, juxtapose regional identities with concepts of 'origins'. *Comme des voleurs* takes a different perspective by framing the quest by a Swiss man to learn about family roots that date back to pre-World War II Poland. Like *Voyage*, these two case studies narrate voyages that cross the pre-1989 East/West divide.

Parental quests represent the primary preoccupation of the return road subcategory. Some films offer less literal twists on this trope or alternative formulations of 'return'. *Le grand voyage* (Chapter 2) narrates a 'return' to the director's cultural and religious heritage, makes it clear that these films need not trace routes to literal points of origin in order to explore the implications that familial and cultural traditions hold for contemporary identity formulations. Similarly, in *Gadjo Dilo/The Crazy Stranger* (Tony Gatlif, 1995, Romania/France), Stéphane is a young French man who travels to Romania in search of a singer revered by his late father. While not a literal return for the protagonist, the film's exploration of Gypsy culture and music does represent a voyage into Tony Gatlif's family heritage. The director was born in Algiers to a Berber father and Roma mother. In his *Exils/Exiles* a couple of twentysomethings with origins in Algerian do 'return' there for the first time in an attempt to discover family history. Zano is the son of repatriated *pieds-noirs* and Naïma is a woman of Maghrebi origins. She initially exhibits no interest in this aspect of her identity, a stance that undergoes gradual transformation in the course of their trek. Mehdi Charef's film *La fille de Keltoum/Keltoum's Daughter* (2001, France/Belgium/Tunisia) also marks a return to Algeria, both narrative and personal. Charef was born in Algeria ten years before that nation's independence from France. His fictional returnee Rallia was raised in Switzerland by adoptive parents and is on the road in order to find her mother and perhaps exact revenge for her perceived abandonment. Benoît Jacquot's *L'intouchable/The Untouchable* (2006, France), is perhaps the most unique and geographically far-flung quest, spurred by the surprise revelation that the father of protagonist Jeanne was Indian.

Trois couleurs: Blanc/Three Colors: White (Krzysztof Kieślowski, 1994, France/Poland/Switzerland), *Voyages* (Emmanuel Finkiel, 1999, Poland/France/Belgium), *Monsieur Ibrahim et les fleurs du Coran/Monsieur Ibrahim* (François Dupeyron, 2003, France) and *A l'est de moi/East of Me* (Bojena Horackova, 2008, France) are notable as films to focus primarily on the first-generation return voyages of immigrants – the only 'returns' that can be literally read as such – each made possible by the fall of the Berlin Wall. *Blanc*, inspired by the French republican theme of equality, provides some insight into one 'white' community that is simultaneously positioned inside and outside. Polish immigrants and their descendants in France – the product of several waves of migration primarily dating back to the 1920s – represent complex layers of belonging and exclusion, as demonstrated by the 'Polish Plumber' so prevalent in the 2005 EU Constitution debate (Raissiguier 2010: 91). *A l'est de moi*, equal parts autofiction and documentary travelogue, is also notable because while it retraces the director's initial voyage to France in the 1970s, her return is staged to the titular points further east rather than to her native Czech Republic. In the process the film questions the very concept of return and points to shifts in the cultural, economic and physical borders of Europe. The director's voyage leads her to Ukraine and Russia because, she theorises, her country of origin is no longer part of the 'East'. In the episodic *Voyages* Holocaust survivors return to Poland on a guided tour.

Cheb (Rachid Bouchareb, 1991, Algeria/France), *Bled Number One* (Rabah Ameur-Zaïmeche, 2006, Algeria/France), *Française* (Souad el-Bouhati, 2008, France/Morocco) and *Paris à tout prix* (Reem Kherici, 2013, France) stand apart for their depiction of return as an involuntary process. In the first two the protagonists are victims of the '*double peine*', the practice of deporting those convicted of a crime who do not hold French citizenship after their sentence has been served. *Bled Number One* is a companion to Ameur-Zaïmeche's 2001 film *Wesh wesh, qu'est-ce qui se passe?* Both feature the director himself playing the protagonist Kamel, who in the earlier film must adjust to life in the *cité* after being released from prison. While *Bled Number One* opens in Algeria, Kemal's past is inescapable: he is referred to by Algerian relatives as '*le Français*'. Similar to *Ten'ja*, both *Cheb* (Roubaix) and *Française* (Amiens) open in northern France before shifting the narrative space to the Maghreb. In the case of the latter, the forced voyage is not imposed by the French state but by ten-year-old Sofia's parents, who pack up the family in search of what is seen by all aside from her as a better life in Morocco. Like Kamel, when 'over there' Sofia is marked as a perpetual outsider, aligned with French values and culture and therefore not quite Moroccan. Her childhood in an orderly housing project in Amiens is primarily seen through the lens of happy childhood memories; pleasant outings with family and a French best friend in the Pas-de-Calais countryside are highlighted while the family financial situation and father's work life are not contextualised. Thus the initial return by parents creates an ultimately unrealised desire for 'return' in the opposite direction to an idealised France. *Paris à tout prix* generates humour by staging the deportation of an upwardly mobile fashion designer to her native Morocco because she failed to update her residency permit.

Though there are several comedies on my list, *Il était une fois dans l'oued* (Djamel Bensalah, 2005, France) merits mention as a particularly unique contribution to the category. Bensalah's film stages three concomitant varieties of return: the annual summer trip to the '*bled*' by a first generation immigrant, the 'return' of his son for marriage to a young Franco-Algerian woman and the apparently imagined return of a young Frenchman who has created a seemingly fictional Algerian identity for himself . Much of the film's humour is generated by Johnny Leclerc's (alias Abdel Bachir) idealisation of his adopted/invented heritage, aptly symbolised by his obsessive quest for an 'authentic' *chorba* that seems to exist only in his mind's eye. Food, as we shall see in *Voyage en Arménie* and *Ten'ja*, tends to play a significant role in return narratives. Indeed culinary traditions are a prominent symbol of cultural allegiance in diasporic film (Berghahn 2013:13).[4]

VOYAGE EN ARMÉNIE: 'ARMENIANNESS' REDISCOVERED

At first glance, *Voyage en Arménie* (henceforth *Armenia*) represents a radical geographic departure from the spaces depicted in much of Robert Guédiguian's work. A self-described creator of 'district cinema', Guédiguian's first twelve films were set in Marseille, primarily in his native Estaque neighbourhood. *Armenia* is just his second film, following the 2005 *Le promeneur du champs-de-Mars/The Last Mitterand*, to be set primarily outside his native city. However, as Laura Rascaroli convincingly argues, his cinema 'accentuates the identification between local and transnational' by highlighting the global aspects of the Midi without the mediation of Paris and by ignoring references to the nation.[5] Moreover identity is not geographically fixed in Guédiguian's cinema. As Rascaroli points out, his films are fundamentally concerned with 'the disappearance of "place" as the locus of the development of feelings of belonging and identity' (2006).

Armenia narrates a return prompted by the wishes of a first generation father. However, unlike in *Simon Konianski* and *Ten'ja*, Barsam opts to return to the place of his birth before he dies. He prods his daughter to make the voyage by absconding unannounced. Anna, played by Arianne Ascaride, Guédiguian's wife and a fixture in his films, is a Marseille heart doctor who feels compelled to make the trip for professional as much as personal reasons. Although her diagnosis calls for an immediate operation, Barsam prefers to live out his remaining days in the tranquillity of his native village. Anna's search for her father is rendered difficult by her unfamiliarity with his Armenian past. With no more than an old photo to work with, she must enlist the help of Armenians, starting with Marseille expat businessman Sarkis Arabian. As will be the case in the other films discussed below, locals guide the 'returnee' in her quest: Manouk, an elderly unofficial taxi driver; Gayané, an employee at the French embassy; Schaké, a young woman who longs to emigrate and serves as Anna's interpreter and symbolic Armenia daughter; Yervanth (long-time Guédiguidan regular Gérard Meylan), an army hero and one-time Marseille resident; and Simon (played by Jalil Lespert, who I will discuss below), a French doctor of Armenian origin who is working at a free clinic run by Yervanth.

Anna travels to Armenia by air, a voyage rapidly represented by a cartoon image of a plane crossing a map of Europe in a fashion that highlights the very dramatic changes in the outlooks on and realities of travel since her father made the initial voyage in the opposite direction. The actual 'road' element of the film is comprised of a series of smaller voyages Anna undertakes once in Armenia in order to find her father. I suggested in the introduction that travelling shots are a key defining characteristic of road cinema, separating them from 'travel' cinema and what might be classified as films about 'leaving and arriving' (Mazierska and Rascarli 2006: 25). In *Voyage* automobile travelling montages punctuate Anna's stay in Armenia and help to narrate her discovery of that nation's culture and her family history. Travelling shots allow viewers to share Anna's initial impressions of the new side of post-Soviet Armenia (garish neon signs lining the road from the airport) and her first encounter with a more traditional slice of Yerevan. The latter involves a daytime voyage in Manouk's taxi, accompanied by non-diegetic traditional music and assembled via eyeline matches that show us the highlights of the capital city, condensed by a series of jump cuts from Anna's perspective. Later her flight to the countryside after she temporarily finds herself on the bad side of Sarkis and his organised crime associates also involves auto travel (with her driving for the first time). Other travelling montages that are key to Anna's discovery of Armenia involve a helicopter trip guided by Yervanth that offers dramatic aerial vistas of mountains and revered architectural sights and a drive with Yervanth and others to the country that features a travelling shot from what appears to be Anna's perspective on Mount Ararat.

Anna ultimately locates her father after a series of setbacks and at least one somewhat implausible plot twist. In the process, she is transformed from someone who claims to have no interest in – or sense of – identity to feel a visceral connection with the land and its people. Anna's identity is initially most strongly linked to her profession, a position underscored by her insistence on wearing uncomfortable professional attire while on the road. Her metamorphosis is sparked by the kindness and solidarity shown to her by Armenians, including assistance locating her father, guided tours to sacred Armenian sights and impromptu exaltations of Mount Ararat. The fact that this national symbol, featured on the official coat of arms of the Republic of Armenia, lies across the Turkish border demonstrates that thinking of identity outside the boundaries demarcated by the state is indeed nothing new.

France and Armenia have long shared strong ties, particularly since 1915, when the former accommodated some 500,000 refugees from the genocide perpetrated by Turkey. Yet as in Guédiguian's Marseille-centric 'district cinema', France is hardly mentioned in *Armenia*. Rather, the film focuses on Armenian ties to Marseille, the city that was the point of arrival for many of the 1915 migrants. Anna introduces herself as a 'doctor from Marseille' to Franco-Armenian doctor Simon. Later when clinic owner Yervanth helps Anna out of a jam, he claims to be 'doing it for Marseille'. As for the mobile clinic, although it is named 'Dispensaire France-Arménie', the letters are dwarfed by large murals adorning the trailer, one showing Mount Ararat (Figure 4.1), the other a panorama of Marseille's harbour. The city's image thus sits in as a metonymic representation of France. In this sense it is more than a site of Armenian diaspora, but a point of encounter for the multicultural Mediterranean region. As Joseph McGonagle observes, Marseille has traditionally been 'viewed as the epitome of ethnic diversity within France, and constructed as a uniquely hybrid and harmonious space' (2007a: 231). As the daughter of immigrants from Italy and Armenia, Anna exemplifies the port city's hybridity. Although denying any interest in identity, Anna does admit that her heritage has left a mark in the form of cooking; she is skilled at making pasta thanks to her Italian mother. As we will also see in *Ten'ja*, food is a prominent cultural signifier in *Voyage*. On her first day in Yerevan, her driver Manouk buys Anna an Armenian sandwich and instructs her on the correct pronunciation. It will be the first Armenian word she learns and the role of travel in her discovery of culture via food is underscored by the fact that she eats the sandwich sitting in the

Figure 4.1   The 'Dispensaire France-Arménie' in *Voyage en Arménie* (Guédiguian, 2006).

back seat, while Manouk eats his in a similar position in the front seat. It also seems significant that the second word she learns in this scene is the Armenian word for car. Returning to cuisine, Anna later dines with Armenians on three other occasions – situated between her various sorties by car in and beyond Yerevan – including a culminating feast at her father's new (old) home, with each mealtime conversation adding to her knowledge of the country. At one point, her guides use a traditional dinner in an apartment-turned-restaurant to explain both the indefatigable spirit of Armenians and the imperfect economic and political system they inherited from the Soviet Union.

While Anna's discovery of a nation struggling with the transition from communism to capitalism is charmingly rendered, *Armenia* is most remarkable for the way it frames generational conceptions of identity. The first image we see of Ararat is not from Armenia but inside an Armenian cultural centre in Marseille in the film's opening scene. In that space Barsam frequently socialises and plays cards while his granddaughter Jeannette (the director's daughter Madeleine Guédiguian) performs Armenian dance to the painted backdrop of the iconic mountain. When Anna visits the centre in search of information about Barsam's fugue, it becomes apparent that this is her first appearance there in a long while. This is rather typical, as ties between an immigrant and his home culture have traditionally been thought to end with the first generation. Yet the granddaughter's investment in a cultural heritage her mother has ignored provides a fresh twist.

The storyline is largely based on the director's personal experience and, like his protagonist, Guédiguian's father was Armenian. Also like Anna, Guédiguian never considered himself Armenian until he was invited to Yerevan for a retrospective of his films organised by the Armenian diaspora in France. He explains that his grandparents, who immigrated to France in the 1910s, never transmitted their culture to his father because they invested all of their energy into integration (Frois 2006). This is reflected in the film when Barsam tells Anna that he never taught her Armenian because he preferred that she focus on her more practical studies. Language has been demonstrated to be the crucial factor in successful integration in France and Barsam's stance is largely reflective of the norm for immigrant households (Tribalat 1995: 44–9). Yet in the course of the film it becomes apparent that he has long understated his ties to Armenia and in fact arrived in France much later than Anna believed. His own investment in 'Armenianness' appears to have redoubled after retirement and the death of his Italian wife. With a position in France economically and socially assured, Barsam was free to rediscover his roots, much like the retirees discussed by Weil. Similarly, facing no integration dilemma, his granddaughter Jeannette enjoyed the option of exploring the different facets of her family heritage.

Guédiguian's tradition of working with the same troupe of actors, notably Ascaride, Meylan and Jean-Pierre Darroussin (who plays Anna's husband), opens the possibility of a fascinating intertextual re-evaluation of his previous films. Thinking retrospectively of Meylan and Ascaride – who play Armenians in *Armenia* – as perhaps also being Armenian in their prior roles adds an additional transnational element to Guédiguian's depiction of Marseille. In *Armenia* Anna suggests that she starts feeling Armenian after noticing her resemblance to the people around her, a shift of perception symbolised by several shots of her gazing into a mirror. Although unlike in many films belonging to the road category, these frame compositions are not set inside a vehicle. Instead her frequent gazes into the hotel mirror complement her mobile visual explorations of the Armenia landscape, which include travelling shots of buildings, sites and the unavoidable Ararat as well as one frame composition from her vantage point that frames Manouk in his rear-view mirror.

While this process of seeing herself as Armenian because she 'looks' so could risk essentialising Anna's identity, I propose that an opposite process is at work. As an actress Ascaride can shift ethnicities, whether articulated or perceived, because as 'southern', as she is frequently described (Rascaroli 2006: 98) – or more specifically in the oeuvre of her husband as a Marseillaise – her identity is slippery. Though of Italian origin, Ascaride had already played an Armenian immigrant in *Brodeuses/A Common Thread* (Éléonore Faucher,

2004, France). Looking beyond Guédiguian's typical cadre of actors, casting Jalil Lespert as a Frenchman of Armenian roots is another interesting example of how roles are permeable for certain performers. The son of a *Pied-noir*, Lespert has played a diverse array of roles, from seemingly 'unaccented' French characters in *Ressources humaines* (Laurent Cantet, 2004, France/UK) and numerous other films to Sami Bouajila's *Beur* brother in *Vivre me tue* (Jean-Pierre Sinapi, 2002, France/Germany).

Both in his choice of actors who can shuttle between ethnic associations or be 'simply French' (or Marseillaise) and in his framing of food as a floating cultural signifier, Guédiguian highlights what Yuval-Davis terms 'multi-layered citizenship' (1999). Just as Ascaride can inhabit various ethnic associations (or be ethnically neutral) as an actress, Anna reveals that individual identity formulations can be positioned simultaneously on different levels between the extremes of traditional republicanism and communitarianism. In this sense her offhand comment that Italian culture – in the form of cuisine – was transmitted to her by her mother exemplifies how republican outlooks can be layered with often latent alterity. Anna's stated viewpoints on origins would seem to indicate that despite her culinary acumen, 'Italianness' held no attraction for her. Yet we might imagine that her position could be revisited after her voyage, or in the course of a similar trip to Italy had events led her there rather than to Armenia. The film ends in typical road movie fashion, with Anna on the move again, getting into a car that will take her to the airport and promising to 'return' again.

Ten'ja: Settled in the *Nord* and Unsettled in 'Return'

The voyage in *Ten'ja* begins with the death of the protagonist's father, who immigrated as a young man to the Nord-pas-de-Calais region to work as a miner. The father's final request was for his son to deliver his remains to his native Moroccan village of Aderj, returning by ferry, the same way he departed. The voyage is facilitated by two Moroccans who befriend Nordine (Roschdy Zem) and serve as his guides. Mimoun is a porter at the morgue, where Nordine makes his acquaintance while retrieving his father's remains following a customs inspection. Nora is a young woman Nordine picks up by the side of the highway – the first and most significant 'road event' – where she was left after an argument with her lover. Despite holding a university degree she is 'jobless with honors' as she puts it and though her parents believe she works as a civil servant, Nora supports herself as a wealthy man's mistress. Mimoun offers Nordine pointers on how to navigate Moroccan roads (and corruption) while Nora maps the route to Aderj and translates Berber lyrics on a cassette by one of the favourite musicians of Nordine's father.

Since the mid-1990s, a period that corresponds with a new turn towards politically concerned cinema in France, the north has been a popular setting for films addressing issues of marginality, disaffection and unemployment (Tarr 2005: 136). In *Ten'ja*, however, the place and status in France of self-employed taxi driver Nordine appears solid and unquestioned (Renault 2005; Higbee 2012: 61). Despite this fact, he has a rather nuanced sense of identity that is more than 'simply French'. The voyage to Morocco is Nordine's first because his father preferred to spend summer vacations in a camper at the beach rather than join the flow of Maghrebi workers making the annual pilgrimage. At the age of fourteen an attempted school trip was cut short by Moroccan immigration officials because he did not hold a Moroccan passport. Explaining his identity and citizenship is something that Nordine is compelled to do on several occasions. When he retrieves his father's body after customs inspection at the morgue an official asks him if he is Moroccan. The fact that his reply – 'you have my passport in front of you' – does not suffice is telling. Though Nordine eventually admits that he agrees with the official who considers him Moroccan, as his voyage continues the film makes it clear that nationality, represented by the passport, is inadequate as an articulation of his identity.

In the American road movie archetype, the identity of the protagonist is commonly fused with that of the vehicle (Corrigan 1991: 45). In *Ten'ja* the automobile plays a similarly symbolic role and Nordine's status in France is both highlighted and problematised by the lettering on his car. More than publicising his taxi business, the inscription 'Nord'in Auto' also serves as a moving advertisement for his multifaceted identity. Rather than feeling neither entirely French nor entirely Maghrebi, a well-documented position for '*Beurs*', the wordplay combining a French region with a transliteration of his name suggests that Nordine considers himself both French and of Maghrebi heritage, even if he initially displays limited overt interest in the particularities of the latter. This posture will evolve as the trek progresses and ultimately becomes a voyage of self-discovery. In the course of Nordine's travels the nuances of his French and Moroccan sides are divulged. As the name of his taxi service suggests, he identifies with Lille and the northern department where he was born and raised. This comes to the fore in discussions while driving with Nora and later with an émigré who returned after retiring from the mines and who approaches Nordine as a fellow 'northerner' (Figure 4.2). On the other hand, he is not simply Moroccan or 'Arab', as those of Maghrebi heritage are commonly called in France. His explanation of the family history reveals a rather complex interface of cultural origins and allegiances. When Nordine asks Nora to translate the lyrics of his father's preferred Berber musician from a cassette purchased at the souk, he explains that Berber was never used at home. The fact that his parents spoke Arabic while he responded in French demonstrates that his family history is one of constant negotiations between various elements of their identity.

The symbolism involved in the literal merging of driver and vehicle, made

Figure 4.2   Nordine's car bears his name in *Ten'ja* (Hassan Legzouli, 2004).

literal by the 'Nord'in' ensign, offers an update of the 'mythical fusion' of car and driver seen in so many post-war American road movies, which Laderman (2002: 11) traces back to Kerouac's *On The Road*. More than a signifier of Nordine's complex identity, the car plays a major role in the film as a technical prop that Legzouli employs to frame and visually narrate Nordine's transformation. Stylistically *Ten'ja* is aligned with the American influenced, auto-centric vein of the road genre. A variety of frame compositions of Nordine alone and later with passenger Nora, along with travelling montages from an array of distances and camera angles, chart the process of discovery of Morocco and rapprochement with his deceased father. Compositions framing windshields, windows and mirrors are often employed reflexively, to 'foreground the crucial act of looking or seeing while driving', as Laderman describes the technique (2002: 16). Inside the car, Nordine is framed in his rear-view mirror at key junctures, a shot that 'helps visualize aesthetically the theme of self-exploration as a projection of self through space' (Laderman 2002: 16). His first in-depth conversation with Nora is captured by a camera mounted on the centre of his SUV hood by a series of shots that cut from driver to passenger at an angle that divides the front seat in two, revealing only one character at a time.

The distance between them evoked by that sequence quickly makes way for budding romance and a reconciliation of Nordine with his Moroccan roots, which Nora comes to represent as his guide. This role is underscored in a frontal two-shot of him driving while she consults a Michelin map of Morocco, the red colour and visible title adorning its cover suggesting a symbolic visual link to Mimoun, Nordine's other guide, who dons a green and red Moroccan soccer warm-up suit. The map, coded here as symbolic of Morocco, as in many other road films, demonstrates Tom Conley's suggestion that maps in cinema encourage questions of 'where we come from and where we may be going' (2007: 3). Nordine's voyage is also mapped less literally by travelling montages that display his shifting relationship to the space he drives through. The film opens with a medium close-up of Nordine in his car, wearing a contented expression and seemingly enjoying the shelter it offers from the outside world that is rendered opaque by the brushes and foam of an automatic car wash. As the final destination nears, Nordine and his vehicle become integrated with the terrain. An assortment of shots frames the Moroccan countryside through windows and mirrors while the landscape becomes increasingly expansive in long and extreme long shots. His car, the interior of which dominates the visual field in the opening scene, grows smaller and nearly disappears into the landscape of certain shots. The 'Nord'in Auto' decals reappear frequently in these montages, suggesting a literal fusion of Nordine and the space around him as his voyage nears its destination.

Ten'ja also closes with Nordine on the move again, a gesture common in road movies. A culminating travelling shot often suggests a stance of constant movement, in this case leading back to France. The ending chosen by Legzouli suggests that Nordine's identity is flexible and might encourage us to revisit Higbee's assessment that the film 'attempts to reclaim the myth of return' (2012: 60). It is fitting that *Ten'ja* starts and ends with Nordine in his car. Like his profession, his identity is attached to the notion of mobility and is not inextricably linked to a set place. If he does return to, and ultimately forge a deeper connection with, the land of his family origins, it is a temporary voyage rather than a reverse migration. Thus I contend that the film problematises, and to some extent parodies, the return myth and the concept of origins in general. Nordine's rather static and folkloric image of Morocco is constantly – and sometimes humorously – refuted. When Nora takes him to a souk he expresses surprise at the sight of Western brand shoes and admitted he expected more (apparently 'traditional') pottery and rugs. Nordine also ignores Nora's warning about ordering a Moroccan dish, riposting that he is 'not going to eat fries in Morocco'. After the meal makes him ill, Nora sardonically chides him for thinking that 'eating cows' feet would make [him] Moroccan'. This is but one of three bouts of gastrointestinal illness Nordine faces on the trip; of the other two, one is chalked up to a 'poorly digested' soup and the other follows a ceremonial couscous dinner prepared for his father's wake by hospitable residents living near Aderj. While in *Armenia* food serves as a point of entry into Armenian culture for Anna, Nordine's unpleasant encounters with 'traditional' food – despite the hospitality it suggests – serves as a very practical reminder of his distance from Moroccan traditions and realities. As for his father's village, it is long abandoned, suggesting that everyone has left for greener pastures abroad or in Moroccan cities and that true return is in fact impossible. The final travelling montage that brings Nordine to Aderj abruptly ends with him driving in reverse after initially missing the almost imperceptible road that leads up to the disused settlement. The return myth is also called into question by the fact that, as pointed out by Higbee, Nordine's guides and new-found friends are marginal figures in Moroccan society (2012: 61). Mimoun dreams of emigrating while Nora struggles to find work. Nothing about their positions in society indicates that a permanent return to Morocco would be practical or desirable, even if Nordine wished to do so.

The closing sequence reprises an image seen numerous times in the film, starting with the opening shot: Nordine's face framed in the rear-view mirror. In this instance it merges with a happy Mimoun in the background, symbolising Nordine's new, hybrid self-image. However, I would not read, as Higbee does, the final image as representative of a harmonic blending of the French and Moroccan sides of Nordine's identity (2012: 64). Rather, Mimoun, who is dubbed Nordine's Moroccan 'brother' will soon become a deterritorialised signifier of an imperfect Morocco, having announced he hopes to rejoin his new friend in France as a first step towards his aspired destination of Australia. Thus the final shot arguably demonstrates that Nordine has come to terms with his Moroccan side, but he does not idealise that nation and indeed is content to see it in his rear-view mirror. The sequence opens with Nordine again showing his passport, this time to gain access to the secure international port area. Here the 'are you Moroccan?' query is reprised by the guard. Tellingly, Nordine does not understand the question and Mimoun must answer in the affirmative for his friend. Thus Legzouli passes on the opportunity to portray the voyage as having had a fundamentally transformative effect on Nordine's identity. In a similar vein, the director also resists the temptation to symbolically fuse Nordine with his Moroccan heritage via a permanent relationship with Nora. While there is a clear spark between the two, they part ways before Nordine makes the return drive, with Nora suggesting that he might consider returning to visit her. Even more important than the human connections he makes in Morocco is Nordine's imagined post-mortem reconciliation with his father. A series of conciliatory 'conversations' takes place, first with the vision of the father who appears while Nordine is suffering from the ill effects of his Moroccan meals and then between Nordine and his father's casket as it is lowered into the ground.

As in *Armenia*, the background of the actors furnishes an interesting subtext on the topic of layered and flexible identity. Nordine's identity negotiation resembles the personal experience of actor Roschdy Zem. Though of Moroccan origin, as a child Zem never partook in his family's summer return trips because his parents lacked the resources to bring each of their five children along (Lefort 1999). Similar to Ascaride and Lespert, Zem has been a diverse performer, taking on the role of Algerian characters in numerous films including *Vivre au paradis/Living in Paradise* (Bourlem Guerdjou, 1998, France/Algeria/Belgium) and *Indigènes/Days of Glory* (Racid Bouchareb, 2006, Algeria/France/Morocco/Belgium). He also joined the club of actors having played Armenians with the 2010 film *Tête de turc* (Pascal Elbé, France). This type of flexibility is aligned with the mobile stances on identity forwarded in numerous French 'return' films. While transnational hybridity is arguably a less prominent current in Swiss cinema, the films of Lionel Baier mark a notable exception to this rule. The subsequent analysis of the Swiss production *Stealth* will serve to demonstrate that 'return' films are not just the purview of nations that, like Belgium and France, are characterised both by postcolonial imprints and rich histories if immigration.

Stealth: Re-imagining Roots and Enumerating Identities

The final film under consideration is a Swiss production and the first in a planned tetralogy of road films narrating voyages in the four cardinal directions from the director's home base in Lausanne.[6] Lionel Baier's *Comme des voleurs (à l'Est)/Stealth* narrates the 'return' to Poland by a young, gay, French-speaking Swiss man of very distant – and at times seemingly entirely fictional – Polish heritage and his sister. If the other films discussed previously suggest that there is space within French and Belgian national identities for another layer of self-identification derived from family roots and transmitted by parents (and fathers in particular), the voyage in *Stealth* calls forth a more radical and playful reformulation of identity. In this 'joyful treasure hunt' (Hée 2007), Baier re-imagines the imagined parameters of Swiss identity that are traced back to the legend of Wilhelm Tell and the foundation of the Old Swiss Confederacy in the fourteenth century. The protagonist Lionel, played by Baier, is inspired to rethink what he learned in school about his Swiss, 'lake dwelling' ancestors by the Swiss pioneer John Sutter, the hero of Swiss-born Blaise Cendrar's fictionalised biography *L'Or* (translated as *Sutter's Gold*). As Kris Van Heuckelom convincingly argues, if

Tell has come to function as the cornerstone of Swiss mythology and embodies a collective selfhood which is defensive, protective and humanitarian, the nineteenth-century pioneer John Sutter – the founder of a

'New Helvetia' on American soil – may be seen as a transgressive figure who, unlike his legendary compatriot, defies boundaries and intrepidly charts new territory. (2014: 43)

The recurring image of Lionel reading Cendrar's book and the inclusion of several passages read in voice-over by the hero furnish a constant reminder of road cinema's roots in travel literature (see Laderman 2002: 6–13) and also highlight the fictionalised nature of identity construction in general: both the rather closed Swiss identity – often referred to as 'the special case of Switzerland' – at the heart of Europe and the perhaps genealogically accurate but entirely invented Polishness dreamed up by Lionel.

Lionel's sudden interest in the Polish facet of his family history is sparked by existential or metaphysical dilemmas (he is not content with his life and love, if not quite stuck in neutral as Simon Konianski is) and by an encounter with Ewa (Alicja Bachleda), a young, undocumented Polish woman working as an au pair in Switzerland. This lineage becomes an obsession leading to language lessons, incessant reading about Poland and of Polish authors, a new affinity for the Polish national football team (and seemingly for football in general), and compulsive and humorous discussions of what he obdurately perceives to be his Slavic physiognomy. The obsession ultimately leads to a spontaneous departure towards Warsaw by Lionel and his initially sceptical sister Lucie (Natacha Koutchoumov), who surprisingly is the one who initiates the voyage. In the process of digging up a past that their father would be content to leave hidden, Lionel and Lucie chart a course that thrusts them – and by extension Swiss cinema – into more direct contact with the realities of contemporary Europe. As Van Heuckelom argues, 'Baier's transnational cinematic endeavours may be seen as an attempt to align his native Switzerland more visibly and palpably with the geopolitical and sociocultural changes taking place in post-Wall Europe' (2014: 38).

Walter Salles once suggested that there are no Swiss road films because Swiss identity is – in contrast to his native Brazil – 'crystalized' (Berman and Pulcini 2006). With this comment in mind it is worth briefly considering some of the differences between Swiss outlooks on identity and the parameters that define the debates on belonging, citizenship and culture in France and Belgium. While French identity is to a significant degree linked to language and Belgium is marked by linguistically founded communitarian squabbles, belonging in and to the Swiss Confederation, which has four language communities, is not fundamentally linked to language. As Swiss sociologist Uli Windisch contends, despite rising frictions between French and German speakers (or more precisely speakers on the dialect Schwyzerdütsch), Swiss unity has traditionally been based on a shared 'political culture' rooted in direct democracy and federalism (2004:162–3). Switzerland has a large immigrant population, comprising 20 per cent of the current population. In order to assure that immigrants have 'integrated the political-cultural personality' that maintains Swiss unity, compared to France Swiss citizenship is more difficult to obtain and the process lasts longer. At the same time Swiss law also allows for dual citizenship for naturalised citizens, theoretically leaving space for another identity as long as one is judged to have properly adapted to Swiss political culture (Windisch 2004: 164). In the context of *Stealth*, therefore, it is notable that there is a different but comparable, particularly Swiss framework for the types of flexible identity stances commonly explored in return road films. This allowance for linguistic and cultural differences within a framework of solid political-cultural belonging allows us to read Baier's film (and his tetralogy) in a way that acknowledges both Salles' observation on the paucity of road films from countries with entrenched identities and Van Heuckelom's argument that the films represent an opening up.

By situating siblings Lionel and Lucie at the centre of the narrative, *Stealth* also connects family issues and national identities, using each as a conduit for a story about the other. As in the previous films under consideration in this chapter, the result is a perspective on identity and kinship that is mobile, layered and flexible. *Stealth*, however, brings another element into the identity equation through its treatment of Lionel's homosexuality in relation to his other identity frameworks (religious, familial and national). The road narrative is employed to frame interrogations of sexuality and the family unit while simultaneously taking a 'queer' approach to national and cultural identity.

Stealth puts family matters front and centre from the start. The narrative opens with Lionel picking up his partner Serge to go to church for Christmas Eve service, ministered by Lionel's father. The closed doors they find when they arrive at church for the service that has already begun clearly demarcate a space of restriction and rules that are connected to complicated family and domestic matters. Although Serge and Lionel's relationship has been (perhaps begrudgingly) accepted by his parents, within the space of the church Lionel is ambivalent about outward exhibits of his lifestyle, at one point rejecting Serge's attempt to hold his hand. The camera cuts from the service to a scene outside the family home later that night that will provide the inspiration for the voyage and the film's original title: Lionel and Lucie are outside setting up lights and ruminating on the less-than-cheerful memories of Christmases past. Lucie suggests, as they gaze inside at their parents and respective partners – neither of whom they appear to be currently in love with – that instead of entering they could instead flee 'like thieves in the night'.

Although Lionel and Lucie resist – temporarily – the impulse to flee their family, partners and lives, Lionel's obsession with Poland lead to in the short term to a departure from the normal patterns of his life. The first travelling montage of the film, serving as a preview of things to come, takes place not on the open road but in the urban setting of night-time Lausanne. In this sequence of just under a minute, close-ups of Lionel's face alternate with travelling shots from his perspective of night-time streetscapes. As he drives Lionel listens to a Polish lesson (the announcement of 'lesson one' underscores that this is a new interest), in which he learns how to introduce himself in the language of his recently discovered ancestors. Thus even before he actually hits the road to Poland, Lionel's Swiss identity has already started to metamorphose and blur with fantastic notions of Polishness. His discovery of Poland and its culture will be a voyage of both the literal and the symbolic varieties, as demonstrated by his greatly improved level of Polish that will be on display in Warsaw. The car montage immediately follows a cut from a sequence in which Lionel is daydreaming while reading Cendrars at an editorial meeting at 'Radio Suisse Romande'. That marker on the door of the premises also defines what until recently were the primary parameters for his identity – linguistic, cultural and professional – while a map of the world symbolically situated behind him suggests that he is not content with the limitations of being Suisse Romande or of working at the radio station. Lionel reads Cendrars in voice-over as a fade slowly merges the background of the office (and the map) with a golden-hued California landscape. Once the image of Lionel and his workplace have entirely disappeared, a Polish flag appears in the right foreground, waving in the wind against the imagined California backdrop. The next cut brings us to Lionel learning Polish in his car as the camera frames the Notre Dame de Lausanne cathedral in a travelling shot. The visual progression from the interior of the station to an imagined landscape and then to night-time Lausanne is accompanied by non-diegetic music that links the scene with another montage, in this case demonstrating Lionel's newfound Polish obsession. We see Lionel at the movies, reading Witold Gombrowicz in bed as Serge looks at a copy of the gay magazine *Têtu* – indicating both a 'switch' in terms of Lionel's self-perception and a link between reading and identity that is central to the storyline – watching the Polish football team and, finally, missing the cue for his radio cultural report segment because his nose is in another book about Poland. Simultaneously, the voice-over in which he reads about Sutter's dreams of the West ends shortly before another voice-over, in the form of a recorded Polish lesson, signals Lionel's newfound obsession with the East. The successive juxtapositions of map, imagined image, Polish flag and Swiss streetscape, all of which are blurred together visually and aurally, suggest a conception of physical place and national identity as flexible, and forward a profound connection between imaginary travel and actual motion.

Daydreams and night-time drives around Lausanne gradually make way for more dramatic and real changes in Lionel's life. If his sudden interest in his Polish roots was sparked by what the film frames as distinctively first-world existential dilemmas, Lionel's encounter with the undocumented Polish au pair

Ewa crystallises his desire to further immerse himself in Polish culture. When Ewa runs into trouble with her employers and ends up out on the street and at risk of deportation. Lionel takes her in and goes to Lucie, a social worker who assists undocumented migrants, for advice. Lucie's offhanded suggestion that a marriage of convenience could help Ewa stay in Switzerland leads Lionel to invite Ewa to live in the home he shares with Serge. Thus begins a gradual process of ostensible transformation in which Lionel changes his hair colour, redecorates his home, moves into Ewa's bed, dumps Serge and trades his French copy of *L'Or* for a Polish translation that she gives him. His voyage East begins some time later when at another family gathering Lionel announces that he and Ewa are to be married, provoking a quarrel with Lucie, who is sceptical of both his Polish obsession and ostensibly reframed sexuality. As she puts it, Lionel does not see a woman in Ewa, but an embodiment of Poland. Thus his attempt to un-queer himself and reassert a heterosexual identity leads him to walk an unconventional line. In the previous films the 'original' cultural identity is pushed upon protagonists by a father and therefore perpetuated by patriarchal family values. Meanwhile, as Daniela Berghahn has argued, 'queering the family' is a prevalent strategy for young diasporic or minority subjects, who share with older generations an outsider status vis-à-vis mainstream society that softens their intergenerational differences (2011: 130). In *Stealth*, however, the apparently 'insider' family risks being un-queered by Lionel in his attempt to reformulate what he sees as restrictive, transmitted conceptions of 'Swiss' identity. Paradoxically this un-queering of the family – who had accepted his relationship with Serge – is a simultaneously a subversion of the father's traditional notions of Swiss identity. Crucially, Lucie is also unhappy with her own relationship with live-in boyfriend Liberto (Spanish actor Bernabé Rico) and is feeling trapped within it by a pregnancy she has yet to reveal, and intervenes in order to provide a third option beyond what Lionel reads as a choice between drudging homosexual domesticity and Swiss-ness and what is surely destined to be unhappy heterosexual domesticity involving the Polish connection he longs for. In order to do so, Lucie 'kidnaps' Lionel, who is stewing in the car after the marriage announcement leads to an argument, putting into motion the road portion of the narrative. This sudden flight is an archetype of what of Walter Moser defines as the fundamental road movie impulse and calls the '*déprisé*' – which we might translate as rupture – from the sedentary forces (2008: 7). Moreover, as we have already seen in numerous cases, in road movies the car is often a space of reconciliation or of burgeoning friendship. In *Stealth*, the long-desired escape from the family unit creates an alternative domestic model on the road, a family defined by a combination of choice and of bloodlines (Gott and Schilt 2015).

The two primary travelling montages that show the siblings' route to Warsaw encapsulate virtually every typical component of road cinema, notably several key road events. The initial sequence brings them rapidly across several national borders in a fashion that recalls Philip Winter's quick, borderless hop from Germany to Portugal in *Lisbon Story* (Chapter 1). Although not a part of the EU, Switzerland is a member of the Schengen Zone and these Swiss travellers only answer a cursory question at the German border (in German) before being waved on and hitting the open road. Subsequent national frontiers are indicated by a series of road signs, a ready mobility in marked contrast with the situations of the migrants Lucie works with and those that the duo will encounter in Warsaw. In this insular and utilitarian four-minute road montage two-shots of the siblings in the car talking about their lives predominate. While the interactions within the car are significant, the space outside is not. The occasional cuts to point-of-view travelling shots of rather placeless slices of the European road only serve to mark rapid progress across the continent. The voyage to Poland is encapsulated into shots of power lines, lorries, motorway signage and roadside facilities such as service stations.

This portion of the trip closes with a significant road event. During a stopover to buy some clothing (they left hastily and without any baggage) in Slovakia, Lucie intervenes in a dispute between a Slovak skinhead and his girlfriend. Both the attacker and the victim turn on the siblings and the ensuing skirmish and car chase cause Lionel – and his Radio Suisse Romande car – to take a beating. Significantly the encounter also leads to Lionel meeting Stan, a young French-speaking Pole, while nursing his wounds in a supermarket washroom. The initial 'homecoming' for the siblings is quite out of line with Lionel's dreams of an, exotic, idyllic and cultured Poland. The pair wake up in a dingy parking lot outside a train station sign announcing Oświęcim, better-known by its German name Auschwitz, where the camera hones in on details that are drab and banal, but also grimly and highly symbolic (parked freight wagons, smoke emanating from a brush fire).[7] The demons of history make way for dreary conformity at their next stop, the aforementioned supermarket, which with its fluorescent lighting and shelves loaded with consumer goods epitomises the non-place and could have been found anywhere along the route of the initial travelling montage. Just as the demoralised – and bloodied, in Lionel's case – siblings resign to turn back, the encounter with Stan proves to be the 'gold' that Lionel dreamed of searching for. Thanks to Stan – who studied cinema in Paris – the voyage takes a Sutteresque 'Wild West' turn so common in European road films (see notably *Saint-Jacques* in Chapter 2), an example of how European directors apply American tropes and iconography to distinctively European contexts. Stan invites the siblings to recuperate from their saga at the family vacation home. Nestled in an isolated forest, the structure's strong resemblance to a North American log cabin is reinforced by appearance of a grandmother donning a cowboy hat. There Stan quotes John Ford's 1962 western *The Man Who Shot Liberty Valence* and the newly formed trio toast in Lionel's arcane literary Polish over shots of Żubrówka 'bison grass vodka' from a bottle bearing the image of that animal endemic to the Białowieża forest in the northeast of Poland but more commonly associated with the American West. The mapping of iconography popularly associated with the 'Wild West' onto an Eastern European setting inverts the earlier image of a Polish flag superimposed on a background of California landscape and playfully calls attention to the role that imagination (of Lionel Baier the filmmaker and Lionel the character) plays in this voyage. Once they are on the road again, a Swiss hitchhiker will bring up this West–East connection again when she remarks that Poland resembles the 'far West'.

That ultimate travelling montage incorporates virtually every ingredient typical of road cinema into the space of three minutes. This portion of the voyage begins with a classic crossroads: home to the left and to the right Warsaw, where Stan tells them they can find information on their ancestors. The duo are framed in a frontal two-shot through the windscreen as they debate their choice, the straight angle situating them side by side as equals, in agreement, while also suggesting the rapprochement that has occurred over the course of the voyage. In the road movie template the car is often a space of reconciliation and here the framing helps us interpret Lionel's question – 'where are we going?' – as both practical and metaphysical: they have made it this far, so what comes next? Unsurprisingly, they opt for the road towards Warsaw and the whimsical montage that follows demonstrates an elan that stands in sharp contrast to the fashion by which the route to Poland was filmed. Once in Poland and with their resolve to discover their origins restored, Lionel and Lucie are free to enjoy the experience of travel as Baier and cinematographer Séverine Barde (who also shot *La vraie vie est ailleurs*, discussed in Chapter 2) revel in the liberatory dimension of road cinema tropes.

Switching places is an important leitmotif in *Stealth* and the relationship of this montage to the first fits within this logic. Lucie was behind the wheel in the initial sequence and the first travelling shot was a low angle shot of power lines from Lionel's perspective. A similar shot opens the Warsaw-bound sequence, but this time from the vantage point of Lucie as passenger. The ensuing montage features a variety of travelling shots from within and outside the car. The roadside landscape of Poland is much more distinctive than the non-place aesthetic that predominated on the route from Switzerland. The siblings pass roadside stands and swerve past slow-moving Communist-era cars and families in horse-drawn carts with dogs chasing behind, once again recalling confrontations between cultures and different mobilities staged in films such as *Il Sorpasso*. Meanwhile the space inside of the car becomes a space of child-like play and the renegotiation of rules: Lucie faces backwards in her seat and playfully imitates her brother and splashes water in his face while he rumples her hair. Later she playfully sizes up passing trucks with her fingers, calling to mind a scene from Varda's *Les glaneurs et la glaneuse*. That film creatively explores the question of waste from the perspective of an immigrant and various people on the margins of society and by quoting it Baier both calls attention to his ludic approach and announces another dramatic turn that thrusts Lucie and Lionel into the world of Warsaw's marginal and undocumented migrants. The pair is put in that position by another fateful road event, in this case the improbable theft of their car – along with their passports and most of their money – by the Swiss hitchhiker, which, in keeping with the film's logic of switching, inverts the common Western cinematic representation (Kopp 2014) of Eastern Europeans as car thieves. After hitching the rest of the way to Warsaw they visit a market full of stalls manned by immigrants (primarily from the former USSR and Vietnam), trade their Western clothes for cheaper garb and use the difference to help buy false documents that they will use to access the records about their ancestors at the Polish national archives (Van Heuckelom 2014: 47). The most improbable twist of fate yet occurs at the archives, where Lionel and Lucie encounter a member of the Baier clan from Warsaw who is also doing research into the family tree. The Polish Baiers provide hospitality and Lucie ultimately decides to stay in Warsaw when Lionel returns to Switzerland by train, providing an unexpected twist to an otherwise typical road ending that places the protagonist back in motion and another example of changing. Lucie's apparent choice to raise her unborn child in Poland provides for a symbolic 'queering' of the family (Berghahn 2011), something that Lionel has already more literally achieved (Gott and Schilt 2015).

CONCLUSION

At least one critic has forwarded Russian nesting dolls as an apt image of identity as presented in *Stealth* (Hée 2007). Indeed Lionel's Polishness is hidden under the veneer and the socially produced notion of (Francophone) Swiss identity, but the notion of outer shells and inner cores seems inadequate and perhaps problematic and does not quite encapsulate the factors at work in a 'multi-layered' (Yuval-Davis 1999) conception of citizenship. Indeed this much is acknowledged in *Stealth* when Lucie opines that 'return to origins' is a fascist idea. Moreover, although Lionel symbolically sheds and sells his expensive Western clothes, he never discards his Swiss identity and returns home as the film ends. While all of the films covered in this chapter forward conceptions of identity that are flexible (Ong 1999) and multi-layered, the reflexive and auto-biographic element of *Stealth* aligns Baier's outlook on identity within what Denis Provencher has called 'performative "I" statements' in his research on sexual citizenship in self-identified queer Maghrebi-French individuals. Provencher suggests that these 'I' statements such as 'I am French,

Algerian, homosexual and muslim' opens the door to hybrid identity constructions within Western societies (Provencher 2013). At the moment he boards the train in Warsaw, Lionel would likely identify himself as simultaneously Swiss, gay and Polish, three elements that prior to his voyage did not seem to fit together in his imagination. Although there is certainly a reflexive and performative element to identity in return road films in general – and particularly in *Stealth* due to the fact that Baier plays a version of himself in the film – the 'and' element of that statement is also particularly important. This enumerative approach to describing one's own identity represents an alternative way of presenting complex and hybrid belonging, and is similar to, but more flexible than, hyphenated identity constructions (Swiss-Polish) or the Russian doll metaphor that involves a centre and various layers that are displayed to the exclusion of others.

Nowhere is the diversity of roots and routes constituent of contemporary French, Belgian and Swiss societies more evident than in return road films. In addition to Armenia, Morocco, Ukraine and Poland the films in this category (re)trace links to India, Germany, Romania, Israel, Spain, Quebec, the Congo, the Caribbean and the Czech Republic. As *Armenia* and *Ten'ja* demonstrated in the French context, a nationally based conception of citizenship can be supplemented and perhaps replaced by layered subjectivities that incorporate both transnational and regional elements.

The reframing of identity at work in these films is spurred by the very common experience of facing the death of a parent in three cases (again, looking back to the Belgian-directed *Simon Konianski*) and overall dissatisfaction with life in another, combined with the transformative power of travel. The result, for French, Belgian and Swiss citizens of Maghrebi or European ancestry, is the realisation that their identity need not be fixed, that one can be French, Belgian or Swiss and also other things. The return road movie represents a stance that appears to open the door, however slightly, to the acceptance of difference as the norm and of boundaries and borders as increasingly insignificant.

While generational distinctions have not disappeared, the increased mobility enjoyed by some in Europe over the past twenty years has allowed differences to be re-evaluated and reframed in more flexible terms. As signalled by the fact that each film ends with the protagonist back in motion, these terms are still not fixed. Just as I argued in the previous chapter that there is space in Belgian cinema for flexible identities, return road movies open the door to a reading of contemporary European identity as a flexible concept not strictly delimited by the geographic boundaries of the nation-state. Return protagonists hold complex attachments, always layered and frequently latent, to the cultures of their parents, grandparents or even more distant relatives. The return film is an ideal vehicle for the discovery, exploration and development of multifaceted identity stances such as those described as 'multi-layered' and 'flexible' citizenship.

Lionel and Lucie's gradual transformation into undocumented migrants – however ephemeral this status is for them since they simply would need to present themselves at the Swiss embassy to be rescued and reincorporated into the Swiss nation – draws our attention to a significant imbalance of European mobility. The presence of *sans-papiers* in Lausanne and Warsaw provide a link to the final chapter. *Stealth* clearly contextualises Lionel's wanderlust within a wider setting of less trivial voyages, simultaneously calling for more open conceptions of family, place and identity while also acknowledging the privilege that makes such obsessions possible. Chapter 5 will consider the case of voyages made in the opposite direction from 'return' films – from Africa to Europe or from east to west within Europe – and the continued unrootedness of the subjects who make this voyage. Whereas flexibility is a goal for the protagonists discussed in the present chapter, those who reach Europe in the films analysed in Chapter 5 yearn for the staid and moored domesticity that Lionel and Simon find unfulfilling.

NOTES

1. Examples of 'return' films from outside the French-language sphere of Europe include *Rabat, The World is Big and Salvation Lurks Around the Corner* and *Auf der anderen Seite/The Edge of Heaven* (Fatih Akin, 2007, Germany/Turkey/Italy), and *Prag/Prague* (Ole Christian Madsen, 2006, Denmark).
2. Where travel in American road films are generally staged by car or motorbike, voyagers in European cinema typically go by foot or rely on public transit (Laderman 2002: 248).
3. In the famous cases of Matthieu Kassovitz's film *La Haine/Hate* (1995) and the Goncourt-winning *La vie devant soi* by Émile Ajar, the white element of the trio is Jewish (Rosello 1998: 8).
4. Other notable films in the return category include *Souviens-toi de moi* (Zaïda Ghorab-Volta, 1996, France), *Congorama* (2006), *35 rhums/35 Shots of Rum* (Claire Denis, 2008), *Hello Goodbye* (Graham Guit, 2008, France/Israel/Italy), *Au cul du loup* (Pierre Duculot, 2011), *Le boneur d'Elza/Elza* (Mariette Monpierre, 2011, France), *30° couleur* (Lucien Jean-Baptiste, 2012, France) and *Tuk Tuk* (a television film by Kiyé Simon Luang, 2012, France).
5. This is also not his first eastward cinematic voyage: in *À la place du Coeur* (1998, France) Ascaride's character Marianne travels to Sarajevo. *La ville est tranquille* (2001) features a minor but symbolically important role for a family of Georgian immigrants.
6. The second in the tetralogy, *Longwave/Les grandes ondes (à l'ouest)*, was released in 2013. The third and fourth films are planned to be set in Italy and the UK, respectively, but Baier has interrupted the cycle with the 2015 release of *La vanité*.
7. This initially inglorious return staged by a recently self-identified Pole is not without meaning and situates the siblings' voyage within the Polish tradition of occupation and exile that has featured prominently in that nation's literature, which Lionel had been obsessively absorbing before the voyage (see Gott and Schilt 2015; Kalinowska 2002).

5. THE END OF THE ROAD? DARK ROUTES AND URBAN PASSAGEWAYS

Films covered: *Hope* (Boris Lojkine, 2014, France), *Illégal* (Olivier Masset-Depasse, 2010, Belgium/France/Luxembourg), *Marussia* (Eva Pervolovici, 2013, France/Russia)

This chapter changes direction in order to consider two related strands of cinema that are thematically and politically linked to road movies but are arguably less evidently classified as such. Previous chapters have considered road movies that engage primarily with open and soft iterations of borders. In those films, which I have labelled 'positive', it is only when European subjects venture beyond Schengen Europe that they face hard borders (explained most succinctly by Eder as police ordering travellers to stop), and in those cases the barriers generally prove to be only temporary. In this chapter I will consider two varieties of what I have more provisionally termed 'negative' films, in which subjects are confronted with hard borders, both on the way to and following their arrival in Europe. As Dominic Thomas contends, if 'migration has emerged as a key geometric coordinate of globalization today, then so too has the concern with *controlling* the planetary circulation of human beings (labour forces, asylum seekers, refuges), particularly when it comes to the African continent' (2012a: 157; original emphasis).

Hope (Boris Lojkine, 2014, France) narrates a voyage to Europe, through Algeria and Morocco, by two Africans, the eponymous female Nigerian protagonist and Léonard, a Cameroonian man she encounters en route. While unquestionably a journey narrative, the film's focus on obstacles and the protagonists' dramatic differences from typical road movie travellers result in a cinematic voyage that is unlike that of most road films. *Hope* reworks common road movie conventions that stage travel as a joyful platform for discovery and growth. *Illégal* (Olivier Masset-Depasse, 2010, Belgium/France/Luxembourg) and *Marussia* (Eva Pervolovici, 2013, France/Russia) both follow female (im) migrants from Russia as they attempt to secure footholds in Brussels and Paris, respectively. These two films would appear to be even more distant from the road movie template given the fact that the long voyages to Western Europe are already complete. The hero of *Marussia* is a relative newcomer to France whereas the narrative of *Illégal* picks up after the protagonist had already spent eight years in Belgium. Nevertheless the itineraries they undertake within the cities to which they migrated bear striking similarities to treks towards Europe. In this chapter I will compare and contrast these films, dealing with the increasingly prevalent and visible economic and political migrations to Europe with the European road movie template considered previously.[1] While I contend that these films are road movies, their framing of problematic mobility and problems of mobility suggests that they are pushing the limits of the road category.

Unlike most of the protagonists in the films covered in the preceding chapters, these travellers are not empowered with ready mobility bestowed by passports and bank accounts and are often on the road out of economic, social or political necessity. Their voyages involve South to North or East to West trajectories and they are frequently stuck in neutral and languish on slow, abortive treks encumbered by border patrols and cut short by unscrupulous smugglers. Even when migrants manage to arrive at their intended destination, as the protagonists in *Illégal* and *Marussia* have even before their narratives begin, they commonly remain in flux and transit. The filmmakers' focus on individual migrants furnish alternatives to the common representation of migrants in media and political discourse as 'numbers' rather than people. When migration is discussed, from within Europe and from beyond, terms of plenitude often predominate: migrants come in waves, influxes, streams (*flux* in French) or hoards (de Wenden 2011; Skrodzka-Bates 2014). These case studies are just two examples of the increasingly numerous films that take up the narrative thread where *Hope* and other similar productions end in order to explore the post-arrival realities of migrants who remain in constant motion in search of a job, shelter or food. While such post-arrival films are less readily identifiable as road movies, I argue that they are linked both narratively and, by their reliance on travelling shots, formally. They also share an indelible connection to the structure of road movies in general and that of migration road movies such as *Hope* in particular. As in prior chapters, the formal analysis here will focus on travelling shots and montages in both migrant and post-migration films and will focus on the similarities and differences in the look and sound of travel in 'negative' films as contrasted with 'positive' examples.

It is not by chance that each of the three films considered in-depth here focuses on female protagonists. Scholars of road cinema have noted a traditionally 'pejorative link between femininity and mobility' (Maziersk and Rascaroli 2006: 186) while recent waves of migration, particularly from Eastern to Western Europe, have been characterised as increasingly feminine in nature (Crisan 2012: 172). While films about clandestine voyages from the Maghreb and sub-Saharan Africa have generally focused more on male migrants, a significant number of directors have opted to make films about female migrants from Eastern Europe.[2] One of the impacts of the fall of communism in Eastern Europe was an increase of women who were trafficked across newly permeable frontiers. Recent popular cinema has offered up a primarily 'sensationalised and trivialised account of migrant sex work' (Skrodzka-Bates 2014: 119). Even less lurid representations of feminine migration in post-1989 Europe often tend to fall into a facile representational trap that invariably relegates Eastern European women to the status of exploited and helpless innocents who must be saved (generally by men) from fates such as deportation or worse. A common narrative trope involves women from Eastern Europe who are drawn to the West in hopes of reuniting with a male lover who has inevitably forgotten them or considered them to be no more than foreign conquest. This is the case in films such as Claire Denis's *J'ai pas sommeil/I Can't Sleep* (1994, France), *Vénus et Fleur* by Emmanuel Mouret (2004, France) and *Sauve-moi* by Christian Vincent (1998, France). Collectively these films point to a post-1989 cultural subtext in which women from the East are aligned with sex trafficking and sex tourism (Skrodzka-Bates 2014: 78). Numerous films frame women from Eastern Europe who are attracted to France, Belgium or Switzerland for different reasons yet who still face unique problems and issues related to their gender. One particular example that bears mention in a discussion of road cinema is *Le silence de Lorna/Lorna's Silence* (Luc and Jean-Pierre Dardenne, 2008, Belgium/France/Italy/Germany). That film follows the struggle of Lorna, an Albanian immigrant in Belgium, to buy a business with her Albanian boyfriend. However, when she believes she is pregnant she becomes a liability for the sordid transnational criminal enterprise she has relied on in order to reach Belgium and achieve her financial goals once there. Both the crime boss and her erstwhile boyfriend sell Lorna out and she is forced to flee for her safety. The film ends with a classic road movie gesture: the protagonist on the move again. In positive films this would generally be interpreted as symbolic of an optimistic or liberatory vantage point on mobility (or at least a romanticised take on spiritual homelessness), but in this case Lorna's flight is more representative of her inability to gain solid footing in the world. The inherently unequal nature of mobility is central to this chapter: once they arrive, migrants and refugees do not seek mobility but strive for solidity. This is in contrast with the protagonists in many films covered in prior chapters, who strive for flexibility and as Martin O'Shaughnessy has put it, 'struggle to retain mobility in a world of flows' (2007: 173).

It is worth recalling here the idea I forwarded in the introduction: in the context of contemporary Europe, 'positive' and 'negative' voyages are two sides of the same coin.[3] Whereas 'positive' travellers aim to keep their options open (Mazierska and Rascaroli 2006: 1) as they voyage, instability is a bane to migrants who struggle to 'achieve stability according to the ever-shifting demands and exigencies delineated by EU insiders' (Thomas 2014: 446). Building on Bauman's observation that 'there are no tourists without vagabonds' (1998: 93), Aga Skrodzka sums up the extremes of female mobility in contemporary Europe in her analysis of two recent films narrating very different types of voyages by European women, *Bibliothèque Pascal* (Szabolcs Hajdu, 2010, Hungary/Germany/UK/Romania) and *Hanna* (Joe Wright, 2011, UK/Germany/USA):

> The two characters are the polar opposites in how they experience the celebrated freedom of movement (of labour, capital, resources, etc.) that is the hallmark value of the European unification project. The two women traverse the same roads and cross the same 'open' borders within Europe, yet they do not meet, because, as Bauman would argue, the late capitalist 'tourists' and 'vagabonds' never meet in Fortress Europe. They might occupy the same spaces, often in very intimate proximity, yet their economic and political status ensures their symbolic distance. (2014: 110)

With this firmly in mind, Skrodzka points out key differences in the fashion that each journey is filmed: in one, long shots and open vistas predominate and the Western protagonist Hana 'dominates' space; in the other the Eastern Mona's journey is filmed close-up, in claustrophobic darkness (2014: 110–11). Without seeking to refute this insightful assessment of 'bifurcated' (2014: 109) female mobility and the uneven experience of mobility in general, this chapter will nonetheless aim to explore some of the continuities between positive and negative films and voyagers.

Two facets of this connection will be the focus of my investigation: one narrative, the other aesthetic. First, certain narrative aspects of these ostensibly 'negative' films could – to different degrees – in fact be read as problematising the positive/negative distinction. Likewise while on the surface the migrants represented in these films would appear to represent a very different strain of travel from that generally on display in positive films, in the course of this chapter we will encounter a variety of more ambivalent and arguably empowering labels that might be applied to apparently 'negative' voyagers. Secondly,

I have theorised the travelling shot as the single most important element in a road movie. In this chapter I will analyse examples of a 'negative' brand of travelling shots in comparison to the 'positive' variety and also argue that post-voyage films in fact suggest that the trip to Europe for many migrants does not end upon arrival in Brussels or Paris. In short, by looking at both narrative and technical links between 'positive' and 'negative' films, I am interested here in fleshing out how the road movie toolbox is employed to treat a topic that in political, cultural and even ethical terms could portend the end of the road, so to speak, for European open border policy and by extension the road movie boom. The same ostensibly open borders celebrated in so many road films have increasingly become the source of alarm from certain quarters. The January, 2015 Paris terrorist attacks against the satirical publication *Charlie Hebdo* and a kosher supermarket led to calls from the French political right and far right to scale back the Schengen Agreements. More than simply a reaction to those events, this line of thinking is indicative of an ongoing and wider unease caused by border anxieties. Already a proposal had been made by former president Nicolas Sarkozy in the run-up to EU parliamentary elections the previous year in response to concerns that all nations in the open border treaty were not equally well suited to police the ever-growing traffic of migrants and refugees towards Europe (Thomas 2014: 457–8).[4] Such pronouncements, indicative of what Isolina Ballesteros labels the '"Fortress" approach' to official and public discourse' (2015: 12), also present an opportunity for the arts and engaged artist in particular. Filmmakers across Europe have endeavoured to counter the alarmist and often demagogic nature of social, political and media discourse on the subject of immigration (Ballesteros 2015: 12). Even more, they attempt to save migrants from the fate of being ignored. When they are not the object of political grandstanding and media sensationalism, migrants are often invisible in public discourse (as *L'iceberg*, covered in Chapter 3, cleverly points out). Indeed it is safe to say that the authors of the three films considered in this chapter – all of which are based on true stories – see the testimonial power of cinema as a response to such political stances. The films covered here have been selected in part, however, because they are not simply accounts or 'autopsies' (Guha 2015) of migrant voyages. While each film does follow migrants through very harrowing circumstances, they also contest the dominance, as noted by Elizabeth Ezra and Terry Rowden, of 'loss' as fundamental narrative dynamic of transnational cinema (2006: 7). Indeed Mireille Rosello has framed the issue of (im)migration in today's Europe as both a 'global crisis of storytelling' that challenges both the 'refugees' as she names them (referring to, among others, Tania in *Illégal*) and those who attempt to make their stories into films and other works of art. In the process what is created is the space for 'transnational dialogues' (2014: 13), something that all of the road movies under discussion in this book can also be said to be engaging in.

In the context of the films in question, it should be pointed out that the practice of border policy and policing in Europe is complex and borders are already less 'open' in spirit (and certainly in practice) than suggested by conceptions of 'Fortress Europe' as a free space of movement within the confines of a sealed perimeter. The 'fortress' element of that equation refers not simply to an impermeable exterior barrier but a constellation of efforts to limit access Europe's external frontiers, as well as to police and detain migrants from outside the EU already present within those borders (Thomas, 2012a: 177). Even within the territory of 'Fortress Europe', borders and checkpoints are 'ubiquitous' (Balibar 2009: 203). Moreover, the efforts to police and control migrants also extend far beyond the outer limits of the EU to spaces, such as the Sahara, which must be via traversed by migrants en route to Europe (Mezzadro 2004). Before moving on to the individual case studies, a final point of terminology should be clarified. It is precisely for the policy reasons outlined above that I have opted to refer to the protagonists in these films as migrants, whether they are forging a path to Europe as in *Hope*, or already there but living in a state of precariousness and restless motion caused by the fact that the status of 'immigrant' (not to mention potential citizen) is denied them. It is worth citing some other terminology that has been employed in the scholarly debates on migrant cinema. Carrie Tarr (2007) has divided films about migrants into the categories of 'pre border-crossing', 'border-crossing' and 'post border-crossing'. Ballesteros (2015) opts for the term 'immigration cinema' as an umbrella for both 'migrant' and 'diaspora cinema', which she argues should be considered together. My argument in this chapter acknowledges a similar notion of continuity between the experience of migration to and post-settlement existence in Europe. As for the subjects undertaking these voyages, the following discussion will consider a variety of terms from 'adventurers' to *flâneurs* – forwarded by theorists and filmmakers alike that complement and sometimes problematise the sometimes simplistic conception of these characters (and the people they are based on) as migrants defined solely by their suffering and lack of agency. The notion of the migrant partaking in adventure provides another thematic connection to the road movie tradition. As Ballesteros points out, migrant films can often be interpreted as 'adaptations of the outlaw road movie, in which characters are on the road out of necessity rather than choice' (2015: 179). One final question of terminology should be raised here in light of the proliferation of refugees making their way to and through European territory in the second half of 2015. The continent's French-language press has drawn distinctions between 'migrants' and 'refugees', who 'flee their nations to escape a mortal danger' (Jedwab 2015), a formulation that expresses a higher degree of necessity. By these definitions, the protagonists in films covered here would fall into the former category.

THE TRAVELLING SHOT AND MIGRANT FILMS: PANORAMIC PERCEPTION OR 'REFUGEE GAZE'

Before analysing the films individually, I will consider travelling vision, potentially the most important point of comparison between migrant films and the typical road cinema model. Arguably the single crucial component and defining characteristic of road movies is the travelling shot. As I have claimed in previous chapters, the pleasure of viewing space rolling past in travelling shots and montages is often a central part of the experience for characters and viewers of road cinema alike. That space may be 'landscape', that is to say natural, or include vestiges of culture and architecture. It might also involve mobile elements of the local culture that share the roads with travellers such as the plodding peasant caravans in *Il Sorpasso* (see Chapter 1) and so many other European road films. Whatever the scenery involved, viewing in motion becomes an important element in the transformation and representation thereof that often takes place in road films. What Dimitris Eleftheriotis calls 'panoramic perception' (2010: 15–16) often plays a key role in the 'knowledge acquisition' that transpires in road narratives (2010: 78). Road movies generally are concerned with following the growth, transformation, enlightenment and, in a broad sense of the term, education of mobile characters. Road protagonists change their outlooks and their lives in the course of their itineraries. The elements of voyage that render these possible are the encounters with cultures and people found along the route and the experience of travel. This can include interactions between characters, often within the space of a vehicle, but most commonly it involves a discovery of the space traversed. As Chapter 2 outlines, landscape often has an impact on the travelling subject. Landscape has two primary roles in road films. It might signify something crucial related to the heroes' pasts or offer a blank slate in the tradition of the 'Wild West', to be explored and mapped according to the characters' desires and onto which personal transformation is projected. What a particular slice of countryside, mountain range or coastline (or less typically cityscape) represents may be different for different characters and directors, but in many road films the act of viewing landscape in itself becomes a transformative experience. Landscape on the road symbolises something new or rediscovered and represents a change from the mundane and, by extension, a chance to transform one's life. As Eleftheriotis argues, 'the dizzying experiences of mobile vision challenge established and traditional certainties as they push travellers out of the stability of home and into unknown and uncertain territories' (2010: 77).

Stability is, of course, economically and socially relative, and cinematic movement and perception can play very different roles in positive and negative films. Eleftheriotis adds that 'cinematic movements with even pace and clear sense of direction (most obviously tracking and panning shots) constitute assured and confident visual explorations, offering comfortable and spectacular views' (2010: 79). If instability – visual and otherwise – is welcome and inspiring in positive films, it is potentially dangerous and even life-threatening in negative films, in which movement is not an end to itself but a means to reach a desperately desired destination (Ballesteros 2015: 179). If the travelling shot captures the spirit of travel for some, in migrant films it tracks the limited vision, disorientation, misery and bleakness involved in travel through deserts, fields, underground passageways and places of transit. In other words, frame mobility can 'confirm and enhance spatial information placing viewers and/or characters in positions of control or mastery or, alternatively, it can undermine such positions by initiating unclear, contradictory, destabilizing or "catastrophic" spatial explorations' (Eleftheriotis 2010: 82). Therefore, for Eleftheriotis, in what I have referred to as 'positive' films 'the narratives of self-discovery are fleshed with visual explorations of the space travelled' (2010: 101). By contrast, migrants are often granted solely or primarily limited viewpoints and sightlines that only afford them what Loshitzky terms the 'refugee gaze' (2010: 28). Sometimes in migrant voyage films viewers are treated to stunning visuals while the migrants suffer, offering a dramatic and poignant contrast (Ballesteros 2015: 192). However, more commonly road travelling shots are characterised by a certain visual parsimony. If in positive road cinema the act of travel opens the door to exploration and discovery (Mazierska and Rascaroli 2006: 4), in negative voyages the traversal of space serves the primary purpose of 'exposing the ordeals' faced by migrants on the road (Ballesteros 2015: 199). Seeing is obviously less important than survival and sightlines are often reduced or eliminated by the necessity to travel clandestinely. In *Nulle part terre promise* (Emmanuel Finkiel, 2008, France), a group of Kurds headed to the West have a small ventilation grate in place of the window that many travellers gaze out of, while the French voyagers they cross paths with gaze at the world through large windows on trains and in hotels (Gott 2013c). The drearily commonplace non-places that dominant the visual space of migrant voyages – McDonald's arches, highway overpasses and isolated, unmarked borders – could be anywhere in Europe, or beyond. As I will discuss later, the 'refugee gaze' extends to the urban films, in which the heroes have reached their goals but often must creep around the fringes of European capitals, through dark streets and subterranean passageways, maintaining a low profile in order to avoid detection

A related point of distinction between positive and negative voyages is the relationship between the route, that is the voyage itself, and the destination. Both categories often involve circular and open-ended voyages and constant movement. In positive films the road often takes precedence over the destination, which is often mutable or at the very least is proved to be less important than the experience of travel that is involved in reaching it. Positive films that do lead their protagonists to the intended destination tend to end with them back on the road again, not because the travellers are unable to find stable footing but because they have the luxury of remaining mobile and a thirst for new routes and experiences. By contrast, in negative films the migrants often reach their destination but face the likely prospect of more travel because their foothold, like their future, in Europe is uncertain (Ballesteros 2015: 199). In a similar vein, Everett contends that in films focused on economic migrations – as in European road cinema in general – the 'events of the journey take over', rendering the end point 'meaningless' and resulting in an inevitably open-ended structure (2009: 171). However, Everett also acknowledges that for the economic migrants in question, which she contrasts with 'nomads', a category within which she includes the tourist and the *flâneur*, the road is not a place to change one's outlook but simply a means to an end (2009: 171). With the transitory position of negative voyagers in mind, films about migrants who have reached their destination should be seen not as a rupture from voyage films but as a continuation of them. In order to consider these issues, in the following I will examine more closely one film that narrates a migrant voyage and two that follow the lives of migrants who have already arrived in their intended destinations.

Hope: 'Adventure', Optimism and Reality on the Road to Europe

Hope (2014, France) is the first feature from Boris Lojkine, who previously directed two documentary films about Vietnam. Lojkine, a self-described 'French director with a Russian name who speaks Vietnamese' (RFI 2015) attempts to approach migrant voyages from a perspective that remains atypical in European cinema. *Hope* is a fiction film with a strong documentary element, something that aligns it with many films about migration (Ballesteros 2015: 20). The story picks up in southern Algeria in the early stages of the route towards Europe of Hope, a young woman from Nigeria, and the Cameroonian Léonard. The actors are amateurs cast from migrant milieus in Morocco and much of the feel of the film, from dialogue to *mise en scène*, is the result of their input. Although Lojkine does not shy from realist depictions of the travails migrants are faced with, he also grants them a great deal of agency. Those on the road to Europe are not simply migrants or refugees, but also latter-day 'adventurers' (RFI 2015).

Hope is trying to pass for a man as she travels, but the ruse is uncovered in the opening scene. The ensuing narrative will reveal how perilous the road to Europe can be for all migrants, but for women in particular. Hope and Léonard become linked after she is raped and left by the roadside by soldiers who have stopped the truck that the group is travelling in. The other migrants move on, but Léonard objects that a woman cannot be left alone in the desert and returns to help her. This gesture of fundamental humanity is the starting point for their shared narrative, which follows their trek to the Mediterranean coast. Hope and Léonard must face many of the usual dangers and stumbling blocks that confront migrants in films about clandestine trajectories towards destinations in Europe. Migrants may struggle with natural perils (deserts and water), often must pause to perform labour (whether menial or perilous) in order to pay their onward passage, are ruthlessly tracked down by police, soldiers and border guards, and often fall prey to unscrupulous smugglers who scam them or leave them stranded short of their desired or promised destination. Lojkine, however, opts to focus on an element of the migrant experience that has been largely absent from cinematic representations. Alongside the police, the most significant threat to Hope and Léonard is posed by those who run a series of migrant 'ghettos' along the way. These groups are divided up along national lines and represent parallel structures of authority that exert 'taxes', prostitute women, and have their tentacles in a gamut of illegal activities from smuggling to counterfeiting. It is one of these organisations that will ultimately be responsible for Hope's passage by boat to Spain.

Lojkine suggests that the while *Hope* is a journey film, the itinerary of the migrants most closely resembles an obstacle course (Sotinel 2015). While on the surface such pauses at the expense of forward motion would seem to distinguish *Hope* from more conventional road movies, this focus on the obstacles to voyage represents only a slight change in perspective from the classic road structure. Whether planned or unanticipated, pauses and stopovers are practically ubiquitous elements of the road movie formula, and the waypoints of the voyage are a crucial extension of the road itself, particularly in a European context of border policing (Gott, 2015b: 300). The voyage of Hope and Léonard is paused indefinitely after the latter is forced to pay a bribe to one Cameroonian ghetto 'chairman', as the leaders are known, in order to allow the Nigerian 'outsider' Hope to stay with him. They will try to replenish their travel funds by selling her body first to other residents of the ghetto and then in the nearby town, where the money is better. However, the boss catches wind of the activity and shakes down Léonard for everything that Hope has earned, leaving the pair without the means to continue their voyage. They finally manage to leave after robbing a French man who paid to sleep with Hope. While this criminal act seems out of place in films about migrants, it is indicative of the connection between migrant and outlaw films suggested by Ballesteros (2015: 179). In the latter it is entirely common for a desperate traveller to hold up a bank, saloon or petrol station in order to make onward motion possible. Their progress will only be incremental, however, for they will soon find themselves yet again waiting with scores of other migrants in the Gourougou forest outside the Spanish territory of Melilla and then in a ghetto in Nador.

Nonethless, *Hope* is a film in which forward movement – fuelled at key moments by the 'hope' invoked ambivalently by the title – generally trumps the obstacles that line the route towards Europe. It is significant that although we initially meet the heroes of Lojkine's film during a pause in their voyage, they will resume forward progress and Hope ultimately remains in motion at the end. If her future prospects in Europe – and indeed whether or not she will make it to Europe – remain unclear, the voyage and by extension the destination are unquestionably central to the film. This separates *Hope* from 'stop-over' films such as Sissako's *Heremakono* and *Morgen*, by Romanian director Marian Crişan (and co-produced by France with Romania and Hungary), both of which turn their attention away from plodding, difficult treks in order to focus on pauses in the respective voyages rather than the voyages themselves (Gott 2015b). Scholarly examinations of European road cinema have drawn attention to these and a number of similar films that depict stalled voyages and focus on 'socio-cultural tension that cannot find release in the transformative experience of the journey' (Rascaroli 2013: 22).[5]

What sets *Hope* aside from the ostensibly post-journey films discussed later in this chapter is its focus on a representation of the voyage itself. What marks it as distinctive from the 'positive' films discussed in previous chapters is the fashion in which that process of travel is represented. A combination of non-place locales, limited sightlines and single-minded focus on the destination at the expense of the space being traversed leads to a very different engagement with the travelling shot. In the remaining discussion of the film I will examine contrasts and comparisons of the travelling shots and montages in *Hope* with those in positive films explored in prior chapters. I will also consider the continuity between *Hope* and the post-journey films addressed later in this chapter.

I have already forwarded the idea that road movies are defined by travelling shots. *Hope* contains several travelling shots and sequences that are typical of representations of the limited 'panoramic perception' involved in 'negative' road travel. The first example is a shaky one-minute shot on the back of an open truck bed near the beginning of the film. Following the furtive glances between Hope and Léonard, who did not yet know each other, the shot focuses on the group of travellers, leaving the landscape only visible in fragments. The migrants sway back and forth almost rhythmically as they are jostled by the movements of the truck over uneven roads. The only sound is the noise of the truck moving over rough terrain, in stark contrast to the music-propelled travelling shot so common in positive films. Soon after, when they are walking together after her abandonment by the rest of the group, Hope and Léonard approach a precipice. The handheld camera follows their unsteady course up a rocky, difficult slope, the frame completely submerged by the dark land mass behind them. When they arrive at the summit, earth makes way for the comparatively brighter pre-dawn sky that fills a corner of the frame. Here they

Figure 5.1 In the background, Hope struggles to keep up in *Hope* (Boris Lojkine, 2014).

have reached a milestone of sorts, or at least conquered one obstacle, and one might expect the camera to espouse their vantage point as they look out over the route ahead and enjoy for a brief moment the vista. Instead, we see only a corner of the horizon as they gaze towards the path before them. The next shot is again of the unsteady, hand-held variety accompanied by the sounds of feet on the uneven, rocky terrain. In it Léonard is tracked backwards as he plods along. He remains at medium close-up distance, at the side of the frame, with Hope weaving more slowly behind him, slightly out of focus (Figure 5.1). At one point she topples and we wait to see if he will turn to remark her absence. After he does, the shot continues as the camera follows him back to her side. This nearly ninety second take serves two purposes that are important in the context of my argument. First, in marked contrast to smoother mechanical tracking shots – the travelling shots so central to many road films – the haptic quality of this shot combined with the unadulterated sound of travel offers some insight into the difficulty of the terrain and the experience of trekking through it. As the migrants trudge over rocks, so too does the unsteady camera. Similarly, it also reinforces the idea that the voyage to Europe will not be exclusively defined by forward progress; for the second instance in the initial ten minutes of narrative Léonard has backtracked. Secondly, as in the scene at the top of a hill, the expectations of what visual parts of a voyage spectators are privy to are defied. The camera remains close to the migrants and denies us the anticipated reverse shot that allows us to share their mobile vision. These elements combine to demonstrate what a 'negative' travelling shot looks and sounds like: shaky, not necessarily tracking forward motion, relying on natural sounds and offering limited mobile vision. The latter can often be interpreted as a representation of a lack of clear direction: the travellers in this film often do not know where they are headed and must rely on *passeurs* for navigation. Again, this represents a twist on a rather conventional road trope: protagonists are often 'lost', but seldom are the stakes and the dangers so high.

The sole conventional motorised travelling shot in the film occurs immediately after the robbery of a French man helps the pair secure enough money to continue on the road after a lengthy pause. For twenty seconds the camera tracks the daytime Algerian landscape as the bus advances along a desolate road, with diegetic music in Arabic playing discretely in the background from a radio. The brevity of this generally common road movie shot exemplifies the distinctive approach that Lojkine and cinematographer Elin Kirschfink take to filming the road from a migrant perspective. The travelling montage continues with a longer two-shot that frames the characters in their seats while allowing a sliver of passing landscape to remain visible behind them. As is often the case in road movies, this two-shot serves to exhibit character development and the shifting relationships that take place in the course of travel. Hope and Léonard are silent and introspective, as if both are considering the ethical implications of the knifepoint robbery that made this segment of their travels possible. She glances at him, perhaps sizing him up and wondering what type of person he is. Ultimately, however, after a long period of waiting, she seals their bond as a travelling duo – if not yet a couple – by laying her head on his shoulder. As with other rare pleasant moments on the migrant road to Europe, their communion in motion is ephemeral. The montage is marked as a 'negative' road sequence by the next cut, a dramatic shift from the brightly lit forward momentum of the bus to a night-time river crossing with a group of migrants. When someone inquires if the other side is Morocco they are ordered to be quiet. 'Silence' is an oft-repeated refrain in *Hope* and this instance underscores the contrast between normal travel by those with proper documentation and ample money and the darker side of voyages to Europe. The final portion of this travelling montage is not accompanied by music – indeed noise equates to danger of discovery – and there are no road signs in sight.

Another variation on the travelling montage takes place at the end of the film. Like the river crossing, the final passage by Hope and Léonard to Europe begins under cover of darkness. The camera initially follows the boat from land after it embarks and eventually disappears into the night. When we rejoin the group, the camera is in the boat and the tiny vessel is in motion towards Spain, but the focus remains on the travelling pair, who are filmed at close distance. In an inversion of the bus scene, Léonard is now resting his head on Hope's shoulder as he bleeds from a wound he received while saving her from the chairman of the last ghetto they passed through (who planned to place her in a prostitution ring in Europe). The importance, but also the difficulty and scarcity of vision in migrant voyages is again highlighted in this final shot. It is daylight when some of the passengers catch a first glimpse of the coast, exclaiming 'Spain!' when land comes into view. Hope implores Léonard to look, but by then he has already died in her arms, leaving her to grieve as the other migrants celebrate their proximity to Europe. If Hope is focused on Léonard and does not look out, the others – despite their joy at the sight of the coast – also lack a clear line of sight. The camera lurches up and down with the boat as it navigates the choppy waters, rendering mobile vision distinctly more difficult than in the more steady bus, a larger boat such as a ferry and in other, non-clandestine modes of transit.

Beyond the preoccupation with the destination and their frequent reliance on modes of travel that are less conducive to mobile vision, the other primary reason that vision for migrants is generally limited to the 'refugee gaze' is their preoccupation with avoiding detection. In a harbinger of things to come for those who do make it to Europe (as in the following films), Hope and Léonard find themselves in transit and/or in waiting mode in several urban spaces en route to the continent. In the first one, a guide advises them to walk quickly and stay close to the wall in order to avoid being spotted by the police, who would further impede their progress by sending them back to Tinzaouten, in the far south of Algeria along the borders with Mali and Niger. Later they must navigate the dark streets of modern Nador and narrow passageways of the older part of town, where the camera follows claustrophobically close behind them as they seek out the local ghetto. This camera technique can be contrasted with more touristic tracking shots in positive movies that venture into urban spaces such as *Le corniaud* (Chapter 1).

The only panoramic vista that spectators share with the heroes is during a particularly optimistic segment of the film after Hope and Léonard have grown closer, avoided arrest and registered significant progress towards their goal. In this case, when they arrive at a precipice in the forest of Gourougou, overlooking the Mediterranean and Melilla, we share their momentary enjoyment and renewed elan as they gaze over what they imagine is the ending point of their trek. As the destination nears, viewers and characters alike are finally granted a view of the 'open landscape and seductive horizons' (Laderman 2002: 14) often associated with road cinema. However, befitting Lojkine's focus on obstacles, not to mention his attention to the harsh realities of migrant travel, each moment of pleasance, repose or optimism quickly gives way to reality. In this case, reality is imposed through recourse to fantasy. As they admire the view, a young Ivorian appears out of the blue and inquires if they 'came for Europe'. He promises that his guide services are free and proceeds to recite a litany of myths about a European promised land, to which he has added a decidedly fabulous twist. Over there, he proclaims, food falls from the skies and 'mosquitos drink Coca-Cola'. The reference to the unrealistic fantasies that nourish so many migrant voyages suggests that their momentary joy at the sight of an enclave of Europe is a product of no more than false hope, and even if they were to make it the voyagers' future prospects are uncertain at best. This is reinforced when Hope reveals the next morning to Léonard that she is pregnant and cannot possibly successfully climb over the fence into Melilla. This option closed to them, they are left to seek another ghetto where they can find a way to buy forward passage by sea.

Added to the Ivorian's fables, the testimonials by the other migrants who have congregated in the forest before trying to cross into Melilla further demonstrate the pre-eminence of the destination in 'negative' road films. The Gourougou migrants pass the time before their final push that they hope will take them over the border by telling stories about prior attempts. They entreat the first-timers to aim for a single-minded focus on the goal, to ignore the police, to sprint, to put everything they have into the last desperate leg in order to reach Europe, despite the physical toll that fences and barbed wires will take on their hands and feet. Hope and Léonard, like the migrants camped in the forest, do not enjoy the luxury of discovering places along the way and must focus on doing what it takes to reach their goal. During one of their extended stops, while waiting to continue onward, they call on a photographer to get pictures taken for fake passports. In addition to these eminently practical snap-shots he offers them a portrait in front of a large painted image of the Eiffel tower at night, a moment that recalls a similar scene in Abderrahmane Sissako's *Heremakono*.[6] Léonard insists that he cannot afford such an indulgence, but he and Hope pose nonetheless. Paris, an idealised and symbolic end point for all migrant voyages to Europe, remains the object of unrelenting focus during the voyage because it represents a new beginning. The reality of post-migration life in Europe is the subject of the next two films to be discussed. *Illégal* and *Marussia* pick up at some point after where *Hope* and open-ended migrant narratives often end. As I will argue, the ostensible 'post-voyage' narrative frequently retains a close connection to migrant voyages. While the global nature of cities such as London and Paris (Guha 2015: 6) allows migrants to blend in better and mitigates – if not eliminates – the need to remain hidden, it remains uncommon in migrant cinema for the clandestine migrant subject to enjoy panoramic perception while moving through the urban spaces that are the illusory ending points for their voyages.

THE END OF THE ROAD? MIGRANTS IN POST-VOYAGE FILMS

David Laderman's reading of *La Promesse/The Promise*, the 1996 film by Jean-Pierre and Luc Dardenne, within the generic parameters of road movies provides a starting point for my analysis of post-voyage films. Although migrants are not the main protagonists in this film, they play a central role and arguably take control of the narrative after the titular promise is made. Indeed we first encounter them at the apparent end point of their voyage, when the father–son pair Roger and Igor, who run an illicit operation in the (post) industrial city of Seraign that involves housing migrants, under the table construction work and trade in forged identity documents, pick up a new group of Eastern Europeans and Africans who have been smuggled into Belgium in an auto carrier. This suggestive layering of automobility, trafficking and traffic in the most literal sense offers an insightful glance into the interwoven web that links the rather small time illicit operations overseen by Roger to a wider network of transit – legal and illegal, visible and invisible – that moves people and goods into and through Europe. The auto carrier loaded with automobiles hiding human commodities exemplify what Vicente Rodríguez Ortega calls the 'business-bound dynamic' that furnishes the fundamental logic structuring the 'multi-layered set of socio-economic structures that organizes' the voyages of migrant 'bodies-in-motion' (2011: 4). Indeed mobility in the broadest sense is critical to the project of European unification and is fundamentally based on the principle of 'free movement of goods, people, services and capital', as well as the recognition that all citizens of the EU have the right to reside wherever they desire within the limits of the Union (Verstraete 2010: 4). With this context in mind, Laderman situates *La Promesse* within what he labels 'traffic' in the wider oeuvre of the Dardenne brothers:

> Throughout the Dardenne brothers' oeuvre since *La Promesse*, traffic functions as a key trope of congestion and corruption, not to mention a palpable extension of the globalised economy. Both the noun and verb denotations of 'traffic' are germane here: the flow, or lack thereof, of vehicles through postmodern urban and suburban matrixes; but also the illegal trading of commodities—including human 'souls'. (2013: 174)

What interests us the most here is Laderman's contention that what distinguishes *La Promesse* from 'most other recent French-language road movies is its articulation of motion in terms of confinement' (2013: 175). Most road films use horizontal movement to explore the world, thus making 'the traversal of space necessary for internal revelations and socio-political commentary' (2013: 175). However, the Dardennes employ 'a kind of hyperrealist claustrophobia to dramatise persistent but arrested motion. Rather than coding liberation through long distances, *La Promesse* situates mobility in a distinctly repressive setting and enclosed *mise-en-scène*' (2013: 175). The crucial point here is that, for Laderman, the road movie need not necessarily involve a classic point A to point B voyage. More broadly, motion is unmistakeably a fundamental element in the Dardenne brothers' oeuvre even though the narratives do not centre on voyages. In the case of their film *Lorna's Silence*, as with *Illégal* and *Marussia*, films that to different degrees can be situated in the Dardennes' lineage, the element that I am comparing to a 'road movie' is situated after the initial destination has been attained. The narrative connection to voyage films is that the heroes have already travelled to Europe and remain in constant motion in the search for stability and lodging or as they fight to avoid deportation.

ILLÉGAL: THE BORDERS AFTER THE VOYAGE

Illégal, a 2010 film by Belgian director Olivier Masset-Depasse and co-production of Belgium, France and Luxembourg, was one of three Belgian films selected for the *La quinzaine des réalisateurs* at Cannes in 2011 (Bouli Lanner's road movie *Les géants* was also in the group). Like *Hope*, *Illégal* retains a certain documentary element. The film was inspired by the director's realisation that he lived near a detention centre for illegal migrants. The result is the product of an investigation he undertook with a journalist from the Belgian daily *Le Soir* and a human-rights lawyer working for *la Ligue des droits de l'homme*. It follows Tania, a Russian woman who has lived and worked clandestinely near Brussels for eight years with her son Ivan. Although she was a French teacher in Russia, Tania works as a cleaner in Belgium. This choice by Masset-Depasse highlights the imbalance in the way that many Eastern migrants view the West versus how the West tends to view them. Despite the fact that this type of labour is essential to the functioning of Western societies and economies in a globalised economy, European policies and discourses on migration are based on the fundamental undesirability and disavowal of these migrants and their role in European cities (Guha 2015: 6). The distinction between Europeans and outsiders is both underscored and, in a circular logic, reinforced by the maintenance of an expanding series of 'administrative detention centres or facilities, holding areas, deportation centres or removal centres' (Thomas 2014: 461) much like the one in which Tania finds herself enclosed. *Illégal* aims to render visible the struggle of migrants and asylum seekers detained in such centres. Masset-Depasse also cast a Belgian actress (Anne Coesens) who had to learn to speak Russian for the role, a gesture that effectively puts a Westerner in the shoes of a migrant, if only temporarily.

Illégal offers an illustration of Etienne Balibar's contention that contemporary European borders are no longer situated at the frontier but have been dispersed and are now found within the nations of Europe, 'wherever the movement of information, people and things is happening and is controlled – for example, in cosmopolitan cities' (2004: 1). While Tania has long since successfully navigated the crossing of any official hard borders along her road to Belgium, the scene in which she is stopped by police and detained as she and

Ivan exit a bus furnishes a reminder that her voyage never truly ended. Her discovery by the police is an example of the constant potential transformation of soft borders into hard borders within the cities of Western Europe, border checks that take place anywhere that the 'illegal' presence suggested by the title may be found. Tania and Ivan are stopped not because they attempt to cross an official frontier but because she was overheard speaking Russian. In other words, she is identified linguistically as a 'foreigner'. This is remarkable given both the prevalence of foreign-born residents in Brussels (see Chapter 3) and Belgium's own internal linguistic diversity, and it is tempting to read into the scene a critique by Masset-Depasse of his nation's tendency to demarcate – indeed to 'police' – identities along linguistic divides. Conversing in Russian also went against Tania's normal practice of always speaking French with her son instead of their native tongue, a stance motivated by her desire to avoid detection and to help Ivan integrate into Belgian society. The fact that she and Ivan have gone out of their way to conform to what is considered 'good citizenship' – she works, speaks French well and sends her son to school – is demonstrated in the film's opening scene that takes place before an ellipsis fast forwards the primary narrative eight years into the future. Despite these efforts, Tania is detained, Ivan escapes and will live with a family friend, and the rest of the narrative recounts her struggle to avoid deportation. Inside the detention centre Tania will encounter a global population of 'illegal' migrants on par with the diversity of the population of Brussels. There she befriends a Chilean and her daughter and a Malian woman named Aïssa who has been waging a violent physical resistance against her impending deportation.

Illégal does something similar to the Dardenne brothers' *La Promesse* but traces a very different, if not unrelated, type of story, of which migrants are the main players. If the circulation of goods Laderman refers to is not immediately evident, trafficking, trade in false papers and the black market in housing for undocumented migrants all lurk menacingly below the surface of Tania's life. Rather than focus on the dark criminal network that makes the illicit movement of people possible (despite the visit of a local mafia type who Tania appears to largely keep at bay), the film turns its critical focus to the sometimes equally shadowy yet official apparatus that polices Europe's internal and external frontiers. While Tania has long since crossed any physical border she would be required to clear in order to make it to Belgium, the film frames her daily struggle to avoid detection by the police who have made the city a site of border checks and against the system of laws and agreements that seeks to detain and deport her. Because Tania has not admitted her identity or her origins, and burned off her fingerprints in a painful self-operation shown in a flashback, she can only be traced by her accent and profile to the 'East'. As already mentioned, this grouping triggers a series of negative associations and border anxieties in Western European cultures (Skrodzka 2011).

In order to protect her son and avoid deportation she resists all attempts by the police and her appointed lawyer to induce her to reveal her identity. She finally relents when threatened with prosecution and claims the name of her Belorussian friend Zina in order to request political asylum. Due to the vagaries of EU law Zina would theoretically be more likely to be granted asylum due to Europe's classification of her nation as a dictatorship, but the authorities find that the real Zina had already filed for asylum in Poland (unbeknownst to Tania). Under European law, this would mean Tania, under the name Zina, would be returned to the nation where she filed that claim in order for it to be processed. The constant movement undertaken by Tania, then, is not just about the 'articulation of motion in terms of confinement', but as part of a struggle for immobility, against her forced deportation and in the hopes of attaining a solid footing in Belgium. In this light, the airplanes that make numerous appearances in the film take on a dark symbolism even before the authorities attempt twice to send Tania 'back' to Poland on commercial flights. In one shot the plane is shown overhead, framed by the detention centre wall that symbolises Tania's confinement. Flight is not a mode of conveyance common in road movies and, as demonstrated in Chapter 1, air travel has been presented in European films as an efficient yet rather drab alternative to a road trip. Airplanes are nonetheless a pre-eminent symbol of facile and inexpensive mobility in contemporary Europe. Low-cost air travel made possible by deregulation of the airline industry has made 'borderless' travel within Europe increasingly affordable and common for those with the right passports (Rodríguez Ortega 2011; Gott 2015b). Two brief examples of this will suffice to demonstrate the point: Ryanair, the largest low-cost carrier in Europe, links twenty-seven European nations on routes with an average one-way fare of €45. In 1986 Ryanair transported 82,000 passengers, a figure that climbed to 79 million in 2012 (Ryanair 2014). The tagline for EasyJet, which carried almost 65 million passengers in 2014 (EasyJet 2014), 'Europe by EasyJet', and accompanying marketing campaign comprising still images of locales across the continent, reinforces the notion that low-cost mobility plays a role in 'positive' mobility (for tourism, cultural purposes, Erasmus study, work, etc.) and in European identity construction. A more recent campaign, 'An Easier Way Around Europe' trumps the ready mobility offered by the carrier between a variety of iconic cities such as Paris and Rome, Berlin and Barcelona, etc. Both of these take campaigns touting the ease of 'positive' mobility take on a dark irony when one juxtaposes the difficult voyage originally undertaken with the ease of the deportation voyage that migrants must undertake if they are not granted residency in Europe.[7]

While neither *Illégal* nor *Marussia* narrate voyages, they nonetheless both employ travelling shots to trace the seemingly ceaseless motion they undertake. It is essential to my argument that *Illégal* quite literally, to borrow from

Laderman, articulates 'motion in terms of confinement' and 'persistent but arrested motion'. After she is detained by the police, Tania is shown in transit no fewer than eight times, moving incessantly from the headquarters to her detention centre and back repeatedly as her identity is investigated and her expulsion case moves forward. Her voyage to 'Fortress Europe', which she hoped was complete eight years earlier, in fact has no foreseeable end except one that involves her forcible repatriation. In the first of these scenes, her initial approach to the centre, Tania's vantage point is limited to confined spaces. This can be compared to the limited mobile vision enjoyed by the migrants in *Hope*, and it says a great deal about the precariousness of migrants in Europe that even after eight years in Belgium Tania still does not enjoy the vantage points of Western tourists and *flâneurs*. This sense of restricted visual possibility is extended to the viewer through Tommaso Fiorilli's cinematography. The only time we see something from Tania's perspective is during two long shots on the exterior of the centre where she is headed as the police van circles it on the way to the secure entrance. Both travelling shots highlight the system of fences that surrounds the facility and encloses the spaces where the detainees are allowed to venture outside, quite literally tying her sole remaining form of mobility to the 'distinctively repressive setting' pointed out by Laderman in *La Promesse*. The first, filmed with a shaky mobile camera, cuts from a wider angle to briefly focus more closely on a children's play area with an empty, unused slide – an image symbolic of her missing son – shot through the fence. The fence pattern is repeated after the van passes through the gate and arrives inside the compound. There the detainees are framed through the smaller diamond-shaped grates of a security corridor as they walk into the building.

The unsteady camera that often lingers close to subjects is reminiscent of early Dardenne brothers' films and further cultivates the claustrophobic and enclosed feel that Laderman finds in *La Promesse*, and extends the experience of limited vision to the spectator. As the van moves, Tania is framed in a close-up that is partially obstructed by the detainee sitting in front of her and by the back of the driver's seat. The camera, still shaky, will move on to briefly show her fellow passengers gazing uneasily out towards their new transitory home. In two very brief shots it will pull back to frame all of the passengers together from the vantage point of the front seat area. As in the initial travelling shot in *Hope*, in which swaying migrants are precariously framed with a jouncy camera, here the unsteady frame and lurching vehicle render it difficult to fully grasp the setting. The only shots of the moving vehicle that offer a wider sense of perspective are those taken from the vantage points of the guard tower and presumably aligned with the point of view of those surveilling the migrants.

A second scene, in which Tania is on her way to the airport where she is to be loaded upon a commercial flight in order to be deported, exemplifies how 'arrested' motion can be captured via travelling shots. The sequence opens with

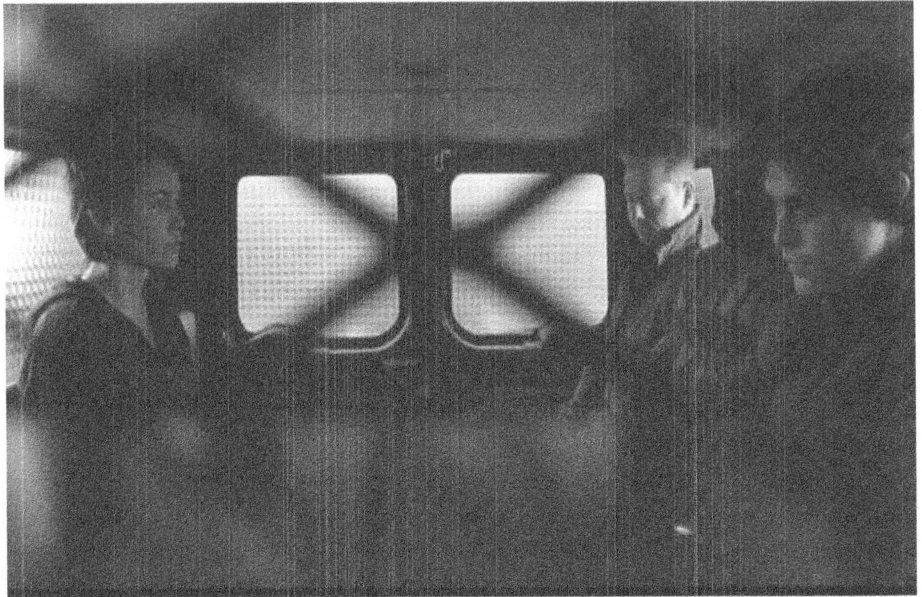

Figure 5.2   Tania travels in her mobile prison in *Illégal* (Olivier Masset-Depasse, 2010).

a shaky close-up of her cuffed hands, accompanied by the sounds of a vehicle in motion. As in her arrival scene, the *mise en scène* highlights her enclosure and limited vision. The camera moves up to frame Tania's face in a close-up set against windows rendered semi-opaque by a covering. We, like Tania, cannot see clearly out the window just as those on the outside cannot see who is being transported inside. The resemblance to the sealed and windowless lorries that so many migrants rely on to reach Europe (in the aforementioned *Nulle part terre promise*, for example) is striking and points to a continuity between the voyage to Europe and the itineraries of migrants who have already arrived. The next shot reframes Tania through the recurring diamond shape of the grates that divide the front and back of the vehicle (Figure 5.2). Across from her we see her fellow passengers: two guards and her Malian friend Aïssa, whose struggle to physically resist deportation has led to repeated beatings at the hands of police but has managed to keep her in Belgium. Aïssa is even more restricted than Tania, her mouth gagged and her body restrained by wraps around her arms and legs. The camera cuts to a close-up of her forcibly covered face and then back to Tania before again taking the latter's vantage point as she looks through the front grates at another scene of enclosure: a fence topped by barbed wire, with the ever-symbolic plane taxiing behind it. The camera cuts back to Tania then counters to her perspective, through which we see first an exterior shot that momentarily pans left to follow the van before a brief establishing shot of the airport setting. As in countless travelling montages, traffic races past the static camera. On a basic level this sequence bears an undoubtedly close resemblance to travelling montages in positive road films: the camera alternates amongst various point-of-view shots and shots framing passengers together and also mixes in exterior shots to show the vehicle and situate it within the surrounding spaces. Yet in this case the protagonists are unwilling participants in the voyage, and though they may know on a fundamental level that they are headed to the airport, they must strain to see the specific space they are passing through. The wide vistas, often shot in Scope, of positive films are replaced with limited and unsteady vantage points. The role of the negative travelling shot, then, is to impart on the spectator – instead of the spirit of travel – the shared disorientation involved in travel when movement is forced.

The deliberate forward motion in this sequence also works to create tension about Tania's fate. The anticipation that builds with each shot of Tania's worried face revolves around the question of how she will react when the police attempt to deport her, as both she and we know will be their next step. Aïssa has told her that they cannot deport her, only 'try' to deport her; intense physical resistance will lead to the mission being aborted. That approach works this time for Tania, and she finds herself back in the van to return to the centre. The second time, the police manage to overpower her and she is loaded onto the plane. Once on board, however, she breaks her longstanding silence and calls for help from her fellow passengers, who verbally revolt against the deportation and chastise the officers for mistreating Tania in plain sight. She is once again spared deportation when the captain orders the police off the plane because of the upheaval caused by their presence. The disturbance is filmed by passengers on their mobile phones and the outcry generated by media accounts of her ordeal (combined with the recent publicity about Aïssa's suicide inside the centre) leads to what her state-appointed lawyer promises will be a positive outcome in the form of asylum. Perhaps because of her mistrust of the lawyer and the government, perhaps because her asylum would be granted not to Tania but to 'Zina', whose name she used, Tania opts to flee from the hospital and again finds herself on the move. We last see her staggering to find her son, an outcome reminiscent of the final scene in the Dardenne brothers' *Lorna's Silence*, in which the protagonist is on the run in the forest with her (presumably fictive) unborn child. If the reunion with Ivan provides an emotional respite for Tania and marks a happy ending, spectators know that given their precarious place in Europe it can only be provisional and more undesired movement is likely in their future.

MARUSSIA: BETWEEN MIGRANT AND TOURIST

The final case study is a quintessentially border-crossing endeavour from production to narrative. *Marussia* (Eva Pervolovici, 2013, France/Russia) was directed by a Romanian based in Paris who studied cinema in Edinburgh and produced by a Croatian who set up shop in the French capital after studying there. The two protagonists and virtually all secondary characters are Russian and both their native tongue and French are widely used in dialogues. The debut feature by Pervolovici, *Marussia* was well-received on the film festival circuit and during its theatrical run in Paris. Like *Hope* and *Illégal*, Pervolovici's film is based on a true story, in this case one inspired by the director's encounter in Paris with Larisa Shteynman and her young daughter Marie-Isabelle, the latter of whom plays the title character based on herself in the film. Unlike the previous two films, however, *Marussia* brings a playful eye to the topic, eschewing a documentary-style approach for an often more whimsical rendering of migrant life in Paris.

Marussia espouses a child's perspective and employs small doses of fantasy together with sometimes dreamy visuals in order to blur the boundaries between the worlds of positive and negative travel. The itinerary that mother and child forge across Paris, from its picturesque centre to its peripheral housing projects and dark back streets, plays with distinctions between 'nomads' and 'migrants' (Everett 2009) and 'vagabonds' and 'tourists' (Bauman 1996, 1998). I have already discussed in the context of *Hope* the distinction forwarded by Everett between migrants and nomads, a category within which she includes the tourist and the *flâneur*. Everett's conception of a nomad is not restricted to privileged travellers such as those we find in positive films. Indeed she includes in her list of cinematic nomads who exhibit postmodern characteristics (in Deleuze and Guatteri's sense of the term, which she sums up as 'alternate, oppositional, and essentially mobile', 2009: 171) the drifters in films such as *Sans toit ni loi* and *Western* (see introduction). Implicit in this stance is the notion of choice: Mona in Varda's film and Nino in Poirier's are certainly not tourists in the conventional sense but they are, arguably, on the road because they resist stability and fixity. Bauman's classification is a useful addition to the discussion because he lays out a more vivid contrast between tourists who voyage because mobility is desirable and 'vagabonds', who are on the road 'because they have no other bearable choice' (Bauman 1998: 93). *Marussia* is unique within the context of migrant narratives because it bridges both of Bauman's categories, not to mention Everett's more permeable labels, by telling the story of migrants whose displacements are simultaneously the product of free choice and the source of suffering. Despite the fact that the itinerary of Marussia and her mother has little in common – in purely material terms – with typical tourist travel, issues and obstacles that commonly present themselves to 'negative' voyagers are entirely absent. Borders, checkpoints, police checks or deportation are never shown and hardly evoked.

As in *Illégal* the details of Lucia's trip to Western Europe or the motivations behind it are never elucidated. Lucia has been in France with Marussia for an untold amount of time. An opening voice-over by the child characterises their life as a constant back-and-forth between France and Russia, but the length of their current stay is not revealed. Also unexplained is how they managed to get to France and the specifics of Lucia's past. She claims to have been a journalist for *Vogue* in Russia and her interlocutors are surprised by her dubious claim to be seeking political asylum because a former lover, a powerful and rich Russian, was murdered. Despite the practical connection she shares with the protagonists of *Illégal* and other related films such as *Lorna's Silence* – they each have sought the necessary documents to stay in the West through various means – her outlooks and ambitions could not be more different. While Tania irresolutely seeks out solidity in European society, Lucia demonstrates more ambivalence. Although she claims to aspire to 'tranquillity and stability', she also has a clear aversion to being tied down and to gaining that stability in a fashion that would require her to sacrifice her freedom to a man or through any variety of menial work. While Tania and countless migrants both real and cinematic toil away doing the menial work that is often considered the purview of immigrants, Lucia has more glamorous ambitions. When she is offered helpto find a position as a babysitter she claims to have other 'projects' and to be waiting for something 'wonderful to happen to us here'. At other times Lucia poses as a journalist and suggests that she has insights and connections into the world of stage acting. In *Illégal*, the more grounded quest and drudging realities of Tania are filmed in sparse, realist style. However, in *Marussia*, as critic Jean-Michel Frodon opines, the protagonists and the director seem to share a 'ludic and fundamental energy' (Frodon 2015). Marussia's naïvety and her mother's seemingly irrepressible, if obtuse, optimism are conveyed in Pervolovici's sometimes whimsical style. The result is a very different kind of movie about migrants, one that eschews the typical tropes and stereotypes and embraces an optimism that as Frodon puts it is 'without foolishness or blindness' and yet does not exclude the real (Frodon 2015). In the following analysis I will consider both the optimistic and the realist elements of the mother–daughter duo's incessant traversal of Paris in their attempt to evade homelessness. Over the course of the film Lucia and Marussia find shelter or sleep in approximately ten provisional abodes – including apartments and hotel rooms where they are offered hospitality, phone booths, two different centres for the homeless and even a movie theatre – and are in constant movement between those sites, both on foot and (less commonly) in public transit. This would seem to qualify them as 'vagabonds' according to Bauman's nomenclature. However, not only is this trajectory explained by Lucia's choices, but their itinerary also includes a significant dose of tourism. The tourist element comes in when they walk playfully past a vantage point on the Eiffel Tower or pause on a nearby bridge in the middle of the Seine to enjoy the views, vistas that migrants such as those in *Hope* can only dream of. One ride on the metro clearly demonstrates the different mobile vision that Lucia and Marussia enjoy. As they travel on the elevated portion of line 6 towards the aforementioned bridge, both mother and daughter enjoy glimpses of the streets below and unmistakably Parisian rooftops above. This version of Paris, the 'Paris that inhabits imaginations around the world' (Rearick 2011: 1), is not only tangibly absent from other migrant films, in which it represents a dream but not a real presence, but largely missing from road cinema in general.

Pervolovici conceived of *Marussia* as a road movie in an urban setting and the film involves both physical and symbolic quests and its own particular brand of travelling shots, two of which I will analyse in the following. It is not, however, a typical road movie – even of the urban variety[8] – but a would-be road movie that in keeping with the whimsical approach by Pervolovici is fuelled by optimism and dreams rather than actual petrol. Lucia thirsts for the adventure and the new beginnings so common in positive road cinema but lacks the means of conveyance and must generally make do with imagination and substitutes for vehicles. The first such ersatz road movie vehicle is the first thing we see, and indeed hear, in the film. As the credits roll against a black background we hear an unidentifiable sound evocative of transit noises. The voice over from Marussia identifies the source of the sound as a 'magic ball'. When the sound is joined by an image, we see that the source is much more pedestrian: two pieces of a metal clothing rack that Lucia and Marussia are dragging behind them in the middle of a narrow street in central Paris. The opening recalls the numerous road movies that begin with the sound of yet unseen travel. This apparatus, which Marussia identifies as a 'magic ball' and states can be used to travel and 'sounds like butterflies' wings' exemplifies both the fantasy element of the film and the stark reality of their situation: the cheap, wobbly rack is just the sort one would use in a provisional living arrangement. After briefly tracking the duo as they walk along the narrow street, which is unidentified but clearly in a nice district of central Paris (it was filmed on the exclusive Île Saint-Louis), a frontal tracking shot displays the rather morose expressions on both faces before Marussia drops her part of the rack and proclaims she is tired. When the pair reach their intended destination in what appears to be a suburban housing block (actually filmed in the more central yet still slightly peripheral 13th arrondissement), a voice in Russian refuses them entry via the buzzer system and warns Lucia that her belongings will only be returned if she hands over the identity documents she apparently took from the woman who was hosting them. The camera then cuts to the mother and daughter sorting through their affairs in the courtyard; they can only manage to carry just a small part of it in their suitcase and backpack so difficult choices must be made. Lucia's choice to find room for some stylish boots and a selection of novels, including *Madame Bovary*, says a great deal about the impractical disposition that sets her apart from Tania and other cinematic post-migrants. This is reinforced later when she trifles away money offered her to pay for a hotel on a nice restaurant dinner and a black rabbit that Marussia eyed in a pet shop window. They set off on what will be an interminable voyage through Paris, leaving a pile of clothing and other goods behind and dragging their suitcases, which have replaced the slightly more permanent clothes rack. In just a matter of minutes reality has seemingly vanquished the 'magic ball' and Lucia is faced with problems related to the two items most associated with migration: identity documents and baggage. Yet unlike in *Hope* and *Illégal*, films in which the protagonists are preoccupied by identity cards, Lucia's lack of valid documentation will not pose any problems.

If the initial sequence leads us to read Marussia's fantasies as simply an escapist reflex against a harsh reality, the vision of Pervolovici and the cinematography of Alfredo Altamirano intercede in a way that suggests a largely positive side to the fantasy. The opening scene also bears a resemblance to the credit sequences of two of Krzysztof Kieślowski's final films, *Bleu/Blue* and *Blanc/White* from the 'Three Colours' trilogy, which open with mechanical noises that project the protagonists, respectively, along in a car and a luggage trunk along an airport conveyor belt. More than simply an artistic homage, this affinity reminds us that in 2013 Europe is just as much 'a question of space' (Galt 2006: 1) and mobility as it was in the 1990s when the trilogy was filmed. As for Marussia's 'magic ball', it will become a recurring image that is also evocative of the imagery in the Polish director's later work. Repeated visions of spheres and bubbles shown from Marussia's perspective (sometimes in dreams, at others of unexplained provenance) are similar to what Joseph Kickasola calls the 'liminal images' in Kieślowski's work. The Polish director's liminal style 'hinges on his careful use of visual abstraction' that is employed to explore the limits between categories such as rational and non-rational, concrete and abstract, and physical and metaphysical (Kickasola 2004: 38, 41). *La double vie de Véronique* (1991, France/Poland) opens with an abstract, unidentifiable image that we soon learn is from the vantage point of a young girl. That child's translucent marble, which creates an image that is inverted and abstract, will form a recurring motif in the film (Kickasola 2004: 75).

The spheres and bubbles in *Marussia* evoke the 'magic ball' referenced by the protagonist in the opening voice-over and refract reality in a fashion that adds another dimension to an otherwise realist film about migrants trying to get by and find solid footing in Paris. As they watch a stage production with Claudio, one of the men that Lucia courts over the course of the film, Marussia is shot through a large 'bubble' that is apparently part of the set while in a voice-over she describes taking the 'magic ball' from her pocket, climbing into it and flying away. In another scene at a laundry she dreams of the performance as she watches the bubbles in a washing machine. Her concurrent voice-over suggests that we view the duo as 'adventurers' in their own right, although in a much more whimsical sense than the term can be applied to migrants in *Hope*: 'in adventures, you always have to carry everything you will need . . . a toothbrush and wings'. The fruit of her imagination evokes simultaneously fantastic (wings) and banal (toothbrush) sides of a mobile lifestyle. The abstract bubbles and lights blur distinctions between her memory and the sound of water to link to the next scene, which cuts to a Seine-side perch where they pass time waiting for news about another temporary lodging situation. The incursion of whimsical imagery creates an unusual contrast with the setting that is rendered rather drab and even morose by the grey winter skies.

As in *Illégal*, in which Tania's time in Belgium is at the risk of ending abruptly with a deportation flight, Lucia's and Marussia's adventure in Paris appears set to come to an end at the airport. Troubled by the effects that their nomadic lifestyle might have on the child, members of a Russian church where Lucia has turned up on occasion when in need of assistance pool their money to purchase them tickets back to Russia. Lucia puts up some resistance but eventually relents, and the pair appears ready to leave until a ticket agent at Orly notices that Marussia has stashed her rabbit in her checked bag. A cut to an airplane taking off seems to indicate that Lucia's argument against the airline policy that animals require a ticket has been resolved and that mother and daughter are on their way. The next scene, however, reveals that they abandoned the return plan and are back in Paris, with the rabbit. Lucia, it seems, has opted for the excitement of the unknown over a return to her native land, reinforcing Pervolovici's conception of the film as a 'road movie within a city' (Pervolovici 2013). In true road movie fashion, the end of the narrative does not correspond to the end of the voyage, and Lucia and daughter will ride off into their Parisian equivalent of a road movie sunset. An optimistic reading of the film is reinforced by this final scene. In keeping with Lucia's quest for excitement and adventure at the cost of stability and often shelter, their first move when they return from Orly is to visit the Palais de Tokyo. There, in the plaza facing the Seine and the Eiffel Tower, which remains off screen (but surely present for viewers familiar with Paris), Marussia finds a discarded pair of roller blades. They will share them, each taking one to awkwardly but happily scoot about on as the film closes to the background of upbeat music. The image provides a bookend for the opening scene, the shared rollerblades recalling Marussia's imagined travelling apparatus. If the final scene exudes a certain hopefulness and sense of possibility, it also quite fittingly demonstrates the heroes' handicap as migrants from the East struggling to keep up with the flows of Western society.

CONCLUSION

The potential 'end of the road' that this chapter's title alludes to has at least two interpretations. Most literally, the ultimate goals (whether geographic or other) of each voyage prove elusive and migrant subjects are compelled to remain in motion. Symbolically speaking, one might also wonder if negative voyages – the dark side of European open borders – might portend the expiration of the European road movie 'boom'. In this chapter I have argued that films that narrate migrant voyages to Europe and ostensibly post-voyage films featuring migrant protagonists share numerous formal qualities with more evident examples of road movie category. The common, if not preponderant, preference in European road movies for slower modes of conveyance such as walking or public transit demands a new (and broader) conception of the travelling shot as a tracking shot that captures at any speed, and depending on the film's positive or negative outlook, either the spirit or the disorientation involved in travel, particularly when movement is forced. Just like the films analysed in previous chapters, *Hope*, *Illégal* and *Marussia* are all structured around travelling shots and travelling montages. Unlike the previous films, however, the migrants in these films do not enjoy the same level of mobile vision as protagonists in positive road movies, and travelling shots and montages in migrant films look and sound different from those in more 'typical' road cinema. The approach in these films offers insight into the migrant experience. If travelling shots in 'positive' films provide a shared experience of discovery and escape, in these films 'negative' iterations of travelling shots provide a window on what the road is like for migrants, whether they are en route or already provisionally settled in Europe. Yet before we settle on a clear distinction between 'positive' and 'negative' approaches to cinematic mobility, the agency and freedom to determine one's own mobility shown in varying degrees by the protagonists of these films must be considered. Despite their travails – effectively the 'road event' in its most extreme and perilous incarnations – the 'adventurers' in *Hope* and Tania in *Illégal* stubbornly maintain their forward motion and manage to end the film on the move towards their respective desired goals. Despite their heroic efforts, the best example of a film that problematises conceptions of 'negative' voyages is furnished by *Marussia*. As I aimed to demonstrate, the infusion of whimsy into the migrant experience calls into question ready-made binaries between those who Bauman (1998) has labelled 'vagabonds' and 'tourists'. If Marussia and Lucia cannot be said to be liberated by Europe's open border policies, neither can they be described as imprisoned or shut outside. Indeed the film is the result of the types of mobility – of students, of cinematic production – encouraged by EU policies. If *Hope* and *Illégal* are testimonials, *Marussia* also testifies: in this case to the potential of actual mobility to incubate cinematic mobility that in turn might engender more complex and multifaceted representations of contemporary Europe. In this sense, 'negative' road films might hold a liberatory potential very similar to that of 'positive' films. Put differently, these 'negative' road films retain enough of the spirit of adventure that is the essence of the road cinema template to demonstrate that the European road remains open to travellers of many different stripes. In the conclusion I will revisit this question of the symbolic and indeed practical or juridical 'end' of European open roads in the context of a brief consideration of recent direct confrontations between the two apparent extremes of European mobility.

NOTES

1. Films about migrant land voyages produced or co-produced in or involving travel through French speaking nations *Frontières* (Mostefa Djadjam, 2001, Algeria/France), *Eden à l'Ouest/Eden is West* (Costa-Gavras, 2009, France/Greece/ Italy), *Heremakono/Waiting for Happiness* (Abderrahmane Sissako, 2002, France/ Mauritania), the hybrid documentary *Indignados* (Tony Gatlif, 2012, France), *Nulle part terre promise/Nowhere Promised Land* (Emmanuel Finkiel, 2008, France) and *Welcome* (Philippe Lioret, 2009). *Harragas* (Merzak Allouache, 2009 Algeria/France) and *La Pirogue* (Moussa Touré, 2013, France/Senegal/Germany) follow sea crossings to Europe and the documentary *La Forteresse/The Fortress* (Fernard Melgar, 2008, Swizerland), *L'envahisseur/The Invader* (Nicolas Provost, 2011, Belgium), *Le Havre* (Aki Kaurismäki, 2011, Finland/France/Germany) and *Le silence de Lorna/Lorna's Silence* (Jean-Pierre and Luc Dardenne, 2006, Belgium/ France/Italy/Germany) address the fate of migrants who have recently arrived in Europe.
2. The voyagers in *La Pirogue* are all men while the groups in *Frontières* and *Harragas* contain more men than women. *Indignados* is an exception in its framing of a voyage across Europe by a female migrant from Africa.
3. The term 'negative' requires some unpacking, given the fact that negative is of course subjective and what is negative to some can be positive to others. The cinematic voyages of migrants are often defined in aspirational terms, as in the tagline used to market *In This World*, a 2002 road movie-docudrama about the voyage of two boys from Pakistan to England: 'The journey to freedom has no borders' (see Ballesteros 2015: 199) and the title of the 2014 film *Hope*. Thus while the narratives involve positive aspirations – and the protagonists will doubtlessly be viewed by many spectators with a great deal of sympathy and their presence welcomed by some elements of the population – these films take on their 'negative' characteristics vis-à-vis the political logic of Fortress Europe and the structural/generic logic of the road movie. In other words, these migrants and their voyages are defined by what they do not have: namely passports that allow access to Europe, but also access to their own vehicle or more broadly the free will to choose a mode of conveyance and a route. They also, as I will discuss in more depth later, are not generally granted the same privileged (and often pleasurable) vantage point, or what Eleftheriotis calls 'mobile vision' (2010: 15).
4. The concept that some Eastern European nations in particular are not equipped to meet European standards of border policing is evidenced by the fact that Bulgaria and Romania, two nations that joined the EU in 2007, have as of 2015 still not been admitted into the Schengen Agreements.
5. Rascaroli's analysis hones in on three road films that for various reasons do not

fulfil the expectation of mobility: are *Loin/Far* (André Téchiné, 2001, France), *Depuis qu'Otar est parti . . ./Since Otar Left* (Julie Bertucelli, 2003, France/Belgium/Georgia) and *Welcome* (Philippe Lioret, 2009, France).

6. See Loshitzky (2010: 32) for a discussion of migrant imaginaries of Western Europe.
7. This contrast is also evident in Swiss director Fernand Melgar's 2011 documentary film *Vol spécial*, which follows the stories of asylum seekers as they await their imminent deportation, often on so-called 'special flights' that are chartered by the Swiss government.
8. David Laderman (2002: 14) includes in his corpus of American road movies some films that replace border crossings and open spaces with 'confined urban settings'.

CONCLUSION

In the first four chapters of this book I characterised road films as a cinematic gesture that in narrative and production terms transcends boundaries and avoids containment. If European road films generally retain some national specificity and have something profound to say about the place that the protagonists call home, they are by their very definition defined by the traversal of frontiers both figurative and literal. Contemporary French-language road cinema traces a web of interconnections and constant border-crossings that transcend national spaces and linguistic categories. Some of these demonstrate that language is more important than national identity in European cinematic production, as is the case with the French–Belgian space of cooperation and co-production that involves a constant back and forth of actors, directors, crews and films. Yet 'French-language Europe' is also an imperfect designation because in contemporary Europe films are apt to be multilingual. In the course of their voyages protagonists are often forced into contact with other languages: Swedish, Arabic, Spanish and Inuktitut to name just a few. While this tendency is not limited to road cinema, travelling films are particularly well suited to explore interactions between various spaces, places and cultures. The films I have covered employ travelling shots to film identities as fundamentally malleable and places as inherently unbounded, to return to Doreen Massey's (1994) assertion that I cited in the introduction. Road cinema therefore compels viewers and academics who study it to rethink categories of national or linguistic containment. 'French-language Europe' cannot be mapped exclusively along the lines of French-speaking nations, regions or zones. Rather, it is a fluid sphere of cinematic inspiration and production. It would also be inaccurate to label it as exclusively European. The films I consider are 'based' in Europe in various ways, with different places on the continent serving as starting points and funding sources. Yet many of them explore links between Europe and places on its fringes: Turkey, Armenia, Morocco and even the Arctic, demonstrating Randall Halle's contention that 'Europe is not bound by clear borders' (2014: 12). At its full potential, the road cinema of French-language Europe offers a compelling conception of a continent that while not entirely borderless is characterised by fluid boundaries both within and on its frontiers. Directors who wish to map these contours continue to find inspiration in road cinema, as demonstrated by a list of recent films that I was unable to find time or space to address. Titles such as *Elle s'en va/On my Way* (Emmanuelle Bercot, 2013, France), *Je m'appelle Hmmm . . ./ My Name is Hmmm . . .* (Agnès Troublé, 2013, France), *La marche* (Nabil Ben Yadir, 2013, France/Belgium), *La tendresse/Tenderness* (Marion Hänsel, 2013, Belgium/France/Germany), *Boys Like Us* (Patric Chiha, 2014, France/ Austria), *Floride* (Philippe Le Guay, France, 2015), *Je suis mort mais j'ai des amis* (Guillaume and Stéphane Malandrin, 2015, France/Belgium), *Valley of Love* (Guillaume Nicloux, 2015, France/Belgium) and *Voyage en Chine* (Zoltan Mayer, 2015, France) collectively suggest that road cinema retains its attraction to those who fund and make films in French-language Europe.

All of this said, road cinema, especially at this moment, cannot simply be summed up by what I have labelled 'positive' voyages, even if we take into account the representations of 'negative' treks that I aimed to problematise in Chapter 5. The wider European trend towards 'porosity of borders and the permeability of cultures' (Wagstaff 2007: 162) that I have highlighted as the fundamental current in road cinema is increasingly menaced by the spectre of closed, or at least newly policed, borders within the EU and Schengen Zone. The refugee crisis of late 2015 and concomitant media debates and political quarrels have thrust into the light the stark contrasts between positive and negative uses of the road and images thereof. The first fourteen years of the twenty-first century comprised a halcyon era of sorts for (cinematic) European mobilities. Despite a wave of films by francophone directors about migrants from Africa, the Maghreb and stateless Kurds that began to appear in 2008, European road cinema was skewed to the generally positive representations of mobility explored in the previous chapters. That is not to say that European road cinema has not considered the implications of stalled mobility, as in films like *Welcome, Nulle part terre promise* and *Morgen*.[1] However, the influx of primarily Syrian (but also Afghani, Eritrean and other) refugees and the Paris terrorist attacks and subsequent border closures in November 2015 have further imperilled the very open border principles that made travel so inviting – as a theme and in practice – to so many contemporary directors. Refugees and tourists have been crossing paths in growing numbers on the Greek island of Lesvos, leading to the worries about the tourism sector there. This merits further attention because of the essential role of tourism in the propagation of the European myth of unity-in-diversity (Verstraete 2010: 43). It should also be recalled that tourism within Europe, as discussed in Chapter 2, is increasingly overlapping with other, generally less-maligned mobility practices, from travel for education or work to cultural voyages and 'visiting friends and relatives', or 'VFR tourism' (Gott 2015a). Indeed mobility in its various forms – however limited to those with the correct passport – has been critical to the project of European unification, fundamentally based on the principle of 'free movement of goods, people, services and capital' as well as on the recognition that all citizens of the EU have the right to reside wherever they desire within the limits of the Union (Verstraete 2010: 4). Perhaps it is easier to reconcile within road cinema these other types of travel with migrant and refugee treks. Can 'positive' and 'negative' travellers share the same generic and discursive spaces within a conception of European road cinema? The unquestioned freedom of movement central to contemporary Europe, heralded in films analysed in the previous pages such as *Lisbon Story* (Chapter 1) and viewed more critically but still largely viewed as an opportunity in *Le grand voyage* (Chapter 2), is directly threatened by the current crisis. Due to the refugee influx, voyagers of all stripes had their mobility paused in Budapest in September 2015 when the Keleti train station was closed for two days and international rail links suspended. Days later border controls were temporarily reinstated along some of the borders of Germany, Austria and Slovakia.

If it is beyond our purview to consider here with any adequate attention the moral and political dimensions of this crisis playing out on the roads, in the stations and at the reopened border posts of Europe, it does seem constructive to ask what these developments might portend for European road cinema. I have already suggested that migrant films and indeed European anxieties over the issue of migration might lead to the end of the road for ready mobility and by extension the road movie boom. Certainly cinematic production has not yet had time to fully account for the latest developments. Already films such as *Hope* and *Illégal* (Chapter 5) have offered some insight through their tales based on true stories and extensive research into the migrant experience. Before following its protagonist on an eventful journey to Paris, *Eden à l'Ouest*/*Eden is West* (Costa-Gavras, 2009, France/Greece/Italy) seems to foresee current events in its consideration of what happens when migrants and tourists collide on a beach resort and tourists are asked to help uncover the illegal bodies in their midst. In a similar vein but using a very different setting, the boat 'road movie' *Fidelio, l'odyssée d'Alice* (Lucie Borleteau, 2014, France) evokes clandestine migration without explicitly portraying it. As the titular protagonist crisscrosses the world on a cargo vessel her co-workers tell of migrant stowaways who had spent weeks on-board because no European nations would take them. Another notable contribution to our understanding of the fates of refugees and migrants who travel to Europe is Fernand Melgar's acclaimed film *La forteresse/The Fortress* (2008, Switzerland), which documents life inside a facility where asylum seekers bide time and plead their case during an extended 'pause' in their voyage. The centre where they reside is the ultimate 'non-place' along the symbolic road to a new life in Europe. As with Tania in *Illégal*, these migrants' time in Europe is at constant risk of coming to term with a deportation order. Melgar's 2011 follow-up documentary film *Vol spécial* follows the stories of asylum seekers as they await their imminent deportation, often on so-called 'special flights' that are chartered by the Swiss government. While neither film is an obvious example of road cinema, both draw on certain elements and expectations of road cinema, but ultimately focus on states of what Rascaroli identifies in an analysis of different films as 'strain and discomfort, for which little or no relief is found through motion' (2013: 21).

We cannot predict what directions European road cinema after 2015 will take. Perhaps screens will be dominated by darker representations of suffering on the road or stalled voyages will become ever more present in representations of mobility. However, given the above recent examples of filmmakers who desire to offer more nuanced responses to media images of migration, one can expect to see the current refugee drama represented in some significant fashion on the big screen. What is less certain is if the flow of positive films that have mapped Europe and indeed at least some of the places beyond its official borders as a largely connected space with interwoven yet distinctive cultures will abate. Also unclear is how positive and negative voyagers might intersect and interact within the representational confines of road cinema. Given that cinematic travel has been an effective way of problematising monolithic, closed constructions of national and cultural identities, it seems clear that road movies will have a role to play in forthcoming debates.

NOTE

1. See Loshitzky (2010) and Gott and Schilt (2013), particularly Laura Rascaroli's chapter, and Ballesteros 2015.

WORKS CITED

Amago, S. (2007), '*Todo sobre* Barcelona: Refiguring Spanish identities in recent European cinema', *Hispanic Research Journal*, 8: 1, 11–25.

AMSFWB (Audiovisual and Multimedia Service of the Fédération Wallonie-Bruxelles) (nd), 'Bilan', <http://www.audiovisuel.cfwb.be/index.php?id=6225> (last accessed 16 March 2013).

Anonymous (1966), '*Le Corniaud*', *Monthly Film Bulletin*, January, p. 92.

Anonymous (2012), *Le Moniteur du film en Belgique*, November–December.

Archer, N. (2013), *The French Road Movie: Space, Mobility, Identity*, New York: Berghahn.

Atkinson, M. (2014), '*Il Sorpasso*', *Sight & Sound*, July.

Augé, M. (1992), *Non-lieux: introduction à une anthropologie de la surmodernité*. Paris: Seuil.

Balibar, E. (2004), *We, the People of Europe? Reflections on Transnational Citizenship*, Princeton: Princeton University Press.

Balibar, É. (2009), 'Europe as borderland', *Society and Space*, 27, 190–215.

Ballesteros, I. (2015), *Immigration Cinema in the New Europe*, Bristol: Intellect Press.

Bauman, Z. (1996), 'From pilgrim to tourist – or a short history of identity', in S. Hall and P. du Gay (eds), *Questions of Cultural Identity*, London: Sage, pp. 18–36.

Bauman, Z. (1998), *Globalization: The Human Consequences*, New York: Columbia University Press.

Bauman, Z. (2000), *Liquid Modernity*, Cambridge, MA: Polity Press.

Berghahn, D. (2011), 'Queering the family of nation: Reassessing fantasies of purity, celebrating hybridity in diasporic cinema', *Transnational Cinemas*, 2: 2, 129–46.

Berghahn, D. (2013), *Far-Flung Families in Film: The Diasporic Family in Contemporary European Cinema*, Edinburgh: Edinburgh University Press.

Boer, I. E. (2006), *Uncertain Territories: Boundaries in Cultural Analysis*, Amsterdam: Rodopi.

Burgess, J. (2014), 'Sex and the Italian driver', <http://www.criterion.com/current/posts/3154-sex-and-the-italian-driver> (last accessed 2 June 2014).

Christie, I. (1994), *The Last Machine: Early Cinema and the Birth of the Modern World*, London: BBC Educational Developments.

Cohan, S. and Hark, I. R. (eds) (1997), *The Road Movie Book*, New York: Routledge.

Conley, T. (2007), *Cartographic Cinema*, Minneapolis: University of Minnesota Press.

Corrigan, T. (1991), *A Cinema Without Walls: Movies and Culture After Vietnam*, New Brunswick, NJ: Rutgers University Press.

Council of Europe (COE, 2014), 'The Santiago de Compostela pilgrim routes', <http://www.coe.int/t/dg4/cultureheritage/culture/routes/compostella_en.asp> (last accessed 15 March 2015).

Craeybeckx, J., Meynen, A. and Witte, E. (2000), *Political History of Belgium: From 1830 Onwards*, Brussels: VUB Press.

Criterion Collection (nd), 'Road trips', <http://www.criterion.com/explore/189-road-trips> (last accessed 9 September 2015).

Crisan, C. (2012), 'Transnational experiences of Eastern European women and feminist practices after 1989', in G. Tibe Bonifacio (ed.), *Feminism and Migration: Cross-Cultural Engagements*, Dordrecht and New York: Springer, pp. 165–86.

De Certeau, M. (1984), *The Practice of Everyday Life*, Berkeley: University of California Press.

De Wenden, C. (2011), 'Les flux migratoires légaux et illégaux', *CERISCOPE Frontières*, <http://ceriscope.sciences-po.fr/content/part4/les-flux-migratoires-legaux-et-illegaux> (last accessed 9 September 2015).

Debray, R. (1998), *La République expliquée à ma fille*, Paris: Seuil.

Deleuze, G. and Guattari, F. (1987), *A Thousand Plateaus: Capitalism and Schizophrenia*, trans. B. Massumi, Minneapolis: University of Minnesota Press.

Delorme, S. (2011), 'La France dans tous ses états', *Cahiers du Cinéma*, March, 5.

Deprez, K. and Vos, L. (1998), 'Introduction', in *Nationalism in Belgium: Shifting Identities, 1780–1995*, New York: St. Martin's Press, pp. 1–22.

Durmelat, S. and Swamy, V. (eds) (2012), *Screening Integration: Recasting Maghrebi Immigration in Contemporary France*, Lincoln: University of Nebraska Press.

EasyJet (2014), Annual report: 'Making travel easy and affordable', <http://2014annualreport.easyjet.com> (last accessed 9 November 2015).

Eder, K. (2006), 'Europe's borders: the narrative construction of the boundaries of Europe', *European Journal of Social Theory*, 9: 2, 255–71.

Eleftheriotis, D. (2010), *Cinematic Journeys: Film and Movement*, Edinburgh: Edinburgh University Press.

Elsaesser, T. (2005), *European Cinema: Face to Face with Hollywood*, Amsterdam: Amsterdam University Press.

Everett, W. (2009), 'Lost in transition? The European road movie, or a genre "adrift in the cosmos"', *Literature/Film Quarterly*, 37: 3, 165–75.

Ezra, E. and Rowden, T. (2006), 'General introduction: What is transnational cinema?', in E. Ezra and T. Rowden (eds), *Transnational Cinema: The Film Reader*, London and New York: Routledge, pp. 1–12.

Frodon, J.-M. (2015), '"Marussia": une aventure à Paris', Slate.fr, 21 January, <http://blog.slate.fr/projection-publique/2015/01/21/marussia-deva-pervolovici/> (last accessed 2 November 2015).

Frois, E. (2006), 'Guédiguian sur les traces de ses ancêtres', *Le Figaro*, 28 June.

Galt, R. (2006), *The New European Cinema Redrawing the Map*, New York: Columbia University Press.

Geist, K. (1988), *The Cinema of Wim Wenders: From Paris, France to 'Paris, Texas'*, Ann Arbor: UMI Research Press.

Georgescu, L. (2012), 'The road movies of the new Romanian cinema', *Studies in Eastern European Cinema*, 3: 1, 23–40.

Gilroy, P. (1993), *The Black Atlantic: Modernity and Double Consciousness*, Cambridge, MA: Harvard University Press.

Gott, M. (2012), 'Borderless possibilities, hesitant voyagers: Mapping identity in three post-1989 Czech road movies', *Studies in Eastern European Cinema*, 3: 1, 7–22.

Gott, M. (2013a), '"Bouger pour voir les immeubles": *Jeunesse dorée* (2001), *L'année suivante* (2006) and the Creative Mobility of Women's *Banlieue* Cinema', *Modern & Contemporary France* 21: 4, 453–72.

Gott, M. (2013b), 'Traveling beyond the national: Mobile citizenship, flexible identities, and layered Republicanism in the French return road movie', *Contemporary French Civilization* 38: 1, 73–93.

Gott, M. (2013c), 'Under Eastern eyes: Displacement, placelessness and the exilic optic in Emmanuel Finkiel's *Nulle part, terre promise* (2008)', in M. Gott, and T. Schilt (eds), *Open Roads, Closed Borders: The Contemporary French-Language Road Movie*, Bristol: Intellect Press, pp. 137–54.

Gott, M. (2015a), 'After the wall: Touring the European border space in post-1989 French-language cinema', *Transnational Cinemas*, 6: 2, 165–83.

Gott, M. (2015b), 'The slow road to Europe: The politics and aesthetics of stalled mobility in *Heremakono* and *Morgen*', in T. de Luca and N. Barradas Jorge (eds), *Slow Cinema*, Edinburgh: Edinburgh University Press, pp. 299–311.

Gott, M. and Schilt, T. (eds) (2013), *Open Roads, Closed Borders: The Contemporary French-language Road Movie*, Bristol: Intellect Press.

Gott, M. and Schilt, T. (2015), 'Crossing borders and queering identities in French-language European road cinema', *Studies in European Cinema*, 12: 3, 1–15.

Grandena, F. (2013), 'The constant tourist: Passing intimacy and touristic nomadism in *Drôle de Félix*', in M. Gott, and T. Schilt (eds), *Open Roads, Closed Borders: The Contemporary French-Language Road Movie*, Bristol: Intellect Press, pp. 39–54.

Grillo, R. (2007), 'European identity in a transnational era', in M. Demossier (ed.), *The European Puzzle: The Political Structuring of Cultural Identities at a Time of Transition*, New York: Berghahn.

Guha, M. (2015), *From Empire to the World Migrant London and Paris in the Cinema*, Edinburgh: Edinburgh University Press.

Halle, R. (2014), *The Europeanization of Cinema: Interzones and Imaginative Communities*, Champaign: University of Illinois Press.

Hargreaves, A. (2007), *Multi-Ethnic France*, New York: Routledge.

Hayward, S. (2005), *French National Cinema*, 2nd edn, London and New York: Routledge.

Hée, A. (2007), 'L'identité dans tous ses états', Critikat.com, 4 December.

Higbee, W. (2007), 'Re-presenting the urban periphery: Maghrebi-French filmmaking and the banlieue film', *Cineaste* 33, 38–43.

Higbee, W. (2012), '"*Et si on allait en Algérie?*" Home, displacement, and the myth of return in recent journey films by Maghrebi-French and North African émigré directors', in S. Durmelat and V. Swamy (eds), *Screening Integration: Recasting Maghrebi Immigration in Contemporary France*, Lincoln: University of Nebraska Press.

Higbee, W. (2013), *Post-Beur Cinema: North African Émigré and Maghrebi-French Filmmaking in France since 2000*, Edinburgh: Edinburgh University Press.

Higson, A. (2006), 'The limiting imagination of national cinema', in E. Ezra and T. Rowden (eds), *Transnational Cinema: The Film Reader*, London and New York: Routledge, pp. 15–25.

Hjort, M. and Petrie, D. J. (eds) (2007), *The Cinema of Small Nations*, Edinburgh: Edinburgh University Press.

Iordanova, D. (2010), 'Migration and cinematic process in post-cold war Europe', in D. Berghahn and C. Sternberg (eds), *European Cinema in Motion*, Basingstoke: Palgrave Macmillan, pp. 50–75.

Jaafar, A. (2005), 'Le grand voyage', *Sight and Sound*, November, pp. 66–7.

Jedwab, L. (2015), 'Migrant, exilé, réfugié: les mots pour le dire', Le Monde.fr, *Le Monde*, 4 September.

Johnston, C. (2010), *French Minority Cinema*, Amsterdam and New York: Rodopi.

Kalinowska, I. (2002), 'Exile and Polish cinema: From Mickiewicz and Slowacji to Kieslowski', in D. Radulescu (ed.), *Realms of Exile*, Lanham: Lexington Books, pp. 107–21.

Kickasola, J. (2004), *The Films of Krzysztof Kieslowski: The Liminal Image*, New York: Continuum.

Kopp, K. (2014), '"If your car is stolen, it will soon be in Poland": Criminal representations of Poland and the Poles in German fictional film of the 1990s', in E. Mazierska, L. Kristensen and E. Näripea (eds), *Postcolonial Approaches to Eastern European Cinema: Portraying Neighbours On-Screen*, London and New York: I. B. Tauris.

Laborde, C. (2001), 'The culture(s) of the Republic: Nationalism and multiculturalism in French republican thought', *Political Theory* 29: 5, 716–35.

Laderman, D. (2002), *Driving Visions: Exploring the Road Movie*, Austin: University of Texas Press.

Laderman, D. (2013), 'Traffic in souls: The perils and promises of mobility in *La Promesse*', in M. Gott and T. Schilt (eds), *Open Roads and Closed Borders: The Contemporary French-language Road Movie*, Bristol: Intellect Press, pp. 173–86.

Lefort, G. (1999), 'Un acteur français', Libération, 17 March, <http://www.libera tion.fr/portrait/1999/03/17/un-acteur-francais_267736> (last accessed 20 October 2012).

Loshitzky, Y. (2010), *Screening Strangers: Migration and Diaspora in Contemporary European Cinema*, Bloomington: Indiana University Press.

McGonagle, J. (2007a), 'The end of an era: Marseilles at the millennium in Robert Guédiguian's *La Ville est tranquille* (2001)', *Studies in French Cinema*, 7: 3, 231–41.

McGonagle, J. (2007b), 'Gently does it: Ethnicity and cultural identity in Olivier Ducastel and Jacques Martineau's *Drôle de Félix* (2000)', *Studies in European Cinema*, 4: 1, 21–33.

Malcolm, D. (2002), 'Wim Wenders: *Kings of the Road*', <http://www.theguardian. com/culture/2000/oct/26/artsfeatures1> (last accessed 3 August 2015).

Massey, D. (1994), *Space, Place, and Gender*, Minneapolis: University of Minnesota Press.

Mazierska, E. (2013), 'Tourism and travelling in Jean-Luc Godard's *Allemagne 90 neuf zero* and *Eloge de l'amour*', in M. Gott and T. Schilt (eds), *Open Roads, Closed Borders: The Contemporary French-Language Road Movie*, Bristol: Intellect Press, pp. 119–36.

Mazierska, E. and Rascaroli, L. (2006), *Crossing New Europe: Postmodern Travel and the European Road Movie*, London: Wallflower Press.

Mezzadra, S. (2004), 'Citizenship in motion', MakeWorlds, 22 February, <http://make worlds.org/node/83> (last accessed 18 March 2014).

Moores, S. (2012), *Media, Place and Mobility*, New York: Palgrave Macmillan.

Morain, J.-B. (2008), 'Eldorado', Les Inrockuptibles, 18 June, <http://www.lesinrocks. com/cinema/films-a-l-affiche/eldorado/> (last accessed 16 March 2013).

Morley, D. (2000), *Home Territories: Media, Mobility and Identity*, London: Routledge.

Moser, W. (2008), 'Le road movie: un genre issu d'une constellation moderne de locomotion et de médiamotion', *Cinémas: revue d'études cinématographiques*, 18: 2–3, 7–30.

Mosley, P. (2002), 'Anxiety, memory and place in Belgian cinema', *Yale French Studies*, 102, 160–75.

Mulcahy, S. (2011), *Europe's Migrant Policies: Illusions of Integration*, New York: Palgrave Macmillan.

Naficy, H. (2001), *An Accented Cinema: Exilic and Diasporic Filmmaking*, Princeton: Princeton University Press.

Nestingen, A. (2013), *The Cinema of Aki Kaurismäki: Contrarian Stories*, London: Wallflower Press.

Noiriel, G. (1996), *The French Melting Pot: Immigration, Citizenship and National Identity*, Minneapolis: University of Minnesota Press.

O'Shaughnessy, M. (2007), *The New Face of Political Cinema: Commitment in French Film since 1995*, London: Berghahn.

O'Shaughnessy, M. (2011), 'French film and the new world of work: From the iron to the glass cage', *Modern and Contemporary France*, 19: 4, 427–42.

O'Shaughnessy, M. (2013), 'Nowhere to run, somewhere to hide: Laurent Cantet's *L'emploi du Temps*', in M. Gott and T.Schilt (eds), *Open Roads and Closed Borders: The Contemporary French-language Road Movie*, Bristol: Intellect Press, pp. 156–70.

Ong, A. (1999), *Flexible Citizenship: The Cultural Logics of Transnationality*, Durham, NC: Duke University Press.

Orgeron, D. (2007), *Road Movies: From Muybridge and Méliès to Lynch and Kiarostami*, New York: Palgrave Macmillan.

Ostria, V. (2007), '*Aaltra* Benoît Delépine & Gustave Kervern', Les Inrockuptibles, 14 June, <http://www.lesinrocks.com/cinema/films-a-l-affiche/aaltra/> (last accessed 9 September 2015).

Peden, S. (2013), 'Crossing over: On becoming European in Aki Kaurismäki's cinema', in R. Merivirta, K. Ahonen, H. Mulari and R. Mähkä, *Frontiers of Screen History: Imagining European Borders in Cinema, 1945–2010*, Bristol: Intellect.

Pervolovici, E. (2013), 'Director's notes', KinoElectron, Paris.

Petek, P. (2010), 'Highways, byways and dead ends: Towards a non-Eurocentric cosmopolitanism through Yugonostalgia and Slovenian cinema', *New Review of Film and Television Studies*, 8, 218–32.

Porton, R. (2014), '*Il Sorpasso*', *Cineaste*, 1 June, p. 70.

Portuges, C. (2009), 'French women directors negotiating transnational identities', *Yale French Studies*, 115, 47–63.

Provencher, D. (2013), 'Ludovic-Mohamed Zahed's performance of universal French citizenship and good Muslim brotherhood', *French Cultural Studies*, 24, 279–92.

Raissiguier, C. (2010), *Reinventing the Republic: Gender, Migration, and Citizenship in France*, Stanford: Stanford University Press.

Ramis, S. (2012), *El Camino de Santiago*, London: Aurum Press.

Rascaroli, L. (2003), 'New voyages to Italy: Postmodern travellers and the Italian road film', *Screen*, 44: 1, 71–91.

Rascaroli, L. (2006), 'The place of the heart: Scaling spaces in Robert Guédiguian's cinema', *Studies in French Cinema*, 6: 2, 95–105.

Rascaroli, L. (2013), 'On the eve of the journey: Tangiers, Tblisi, Calais', in M. Gott and T. Schilt (eds), *Open Roads and Closed Borders: The Contemporary French-language Road Movie*, Bristol: Intellect Press, pp. 19–38.

Rearick, C. (2011), *Paris Dreams, Paris Memories: The City and Its Mystique*, Stanford: Stanford University Press.

Regnier, I. (2008), 'La Belgique, ses grands espaces, ses virées en Chevrolet', *Le Monde*, 18 June.

Renault, G. (2005), '*Tenja*, trajet identitaire', *Libération*, 2 February.

RFI (Radio France International) (2015), 'Boris Lojkine: sortie du DVD de «Hope»',

<http://www.rfi.fr/emission/20150606-cinema-lojkine-hope-sortie-dvd> (last accessed 9 September 2015).

Robertson, P. (1997), 'Home and away: Friends of Dorothy on the road in Oz', in S. Cohan and I. R. Hark (eds), *The Road Movie Book*, London and New York: Routledge, pp. 271–86.

Roddick, N. (2008), 'The road goes on forever', *Sight and Sound*, January, <http://old.bfi.org.uk/sightandsound/feature/49421> (last accessed 24 November 2015).

Rodríguez Ortega, V. (2011), 'Digital technology, aesthetic imperfection and political film-making: Illegal bodies in motion', *Transnational Cinemas*, 2: 1, 3–19.

Rollet, B. (2015), *Jacqueline Audry: la femme à la caméra*, Rennes: Presses universitaires de Rennes.

Romney, J. (2003), 'Last exit to Helsinki', *Film Comment*, 39: 2, 43–7.

Rosello, M. (1996), 'The "Rachid System" in Serge Meynard's *L'OEil au beur(re) noir*', in D. Sherzer (ed.), *Cinema, Colonialism, Postcolonialism: Perspectives from the French and Francophone Worlds*, Austin: University of Texas Press, 147–72.

Rosello, M. (1998), *Declining the Stereotype*, Hanover: University Press of New England.

Rosello, M. (2011), 'Ismaël Ferroukhi's babelized road movie', *Thamyris/Intersecting*, 23, 257–76.

Rosello, M. (2014). 'Olivier Masset-Depasse's *Illégal*: How to narrate silence and horror', *Substance*, 43: 1, 13–25.

Ross, K. (1996), *Fast Cars, Clean Bodies: Decolonization and the Reordering of French Culture*, Cambridge, MA: MIT Press.

Ross, K. (2002), *May '68 and Its Afterlives*, Chicago: University of Chicago Press.

Ryanair (2014). 'History of Ryanair', <http://www.ryanair.com/en/about> (last accessed 15 March).

Schilt, T. (2007), 'Hybrid strains in Olivier Ducastel and Jacques Martineau's *Drôle de Félix* (2000)', *Contemporary French and Francophone Studies*, 11: 3, 361–8.

Skrodzka, A. (2011), 'Clandestine human and cinematic passages in the united Europe: The Polish plumber and Kieślowski's hairdresser', *Studies in Eastern European Cinema*, 2: 1, 75–90.

Skrodzka-Bates, A. (2014), 'Cinematic fairy tales of mobility in post-wall Europe: Reflecting on race, gender, and affect', in M. Gott and T. Herzog (eds), *East, West and Centre: Re-framing Contemporary European Cinema*, Edinburgh: Edinburgh University Press, pp. 109–24.

Sotinel, T. (2015), 'Amours errantes', *M le magazine du Monde*, 23 January.

Spaas, L. (2000), *The Francophone Film: A Struggle for Identity*, Manchester: Manchester University Press.

Springer Berman, S. and Pulcini, R. (2006), *Wanderlust* (Documentary Film), IFC Films.

Swamy, V. (2006), 'Gallic dreams? The family, PaCS and kinship relations in millennial France', *Studies in French Cinema*, 6: 1, 53–64.

Tarr, C. (2005), '*Reframing Difference: Beur and Banlieue Filmmaking in France*', Manchester: Manchester University Press.

Tarr, C. (2007), 'Maghrebi-French (*Beur*) cinema in context', *Cineaste*, Winter, 32–7.

Tarr, C. and Rollet, B. (2001), *Cinema and the Second Sex: Women's Filmmaking in France in the 1980s and 1990s*, London: Bloomsbury.

Thomas, D. (2012a), *Africa and France: Postcolonial Cultures, Migration, and Racism*, Bloomington: Indiana University Press.

Thomas, D. (2012b), 'Sarkozy's law: The institutionalization of xenophobia in the new Europe', in A. Pusca (ed.), *Roma in Europe: Migration, Education, Representation*, New York: International Debate Education Association, pp. 17–24.

Thomas, D. (2014), 'Fortress Europe: Identity, race and surveillance', *International Journal of Francophone Studies*, 17: 3–4, 445–67.

Tribalat, M. (1995), *Faire France: une grande enquête sur les immigrés et leurs enfants*, Paris: Editions La Découverte.

Turel, M. (2012), 'Thierry Dubois et la Nationale 7 en dessins', Le Parisien, <http://en-voiture.blog.leparisien.fr/archive/2012/05/22/thierry-dubois-et-la-nationale-7-en-dessin.htm> (last accessed 3 August 2015).

Urry, J. (1990), *The Tourist Gaze: Leisure and Travel in Contemporary Societies*, London: Sage Publications.

Urry, J. (1995), *Consuming Places*, London, New York: Routledge.

Urry, J. (2007), *Mobilities*, Cambridge, MA: Polity Press.

Van de Craen, P. (2002), 'What, if anything, is a Belgian?', *Yale French Studies*, 102, 24–33

Vander Taelen, L. (2009), 'Les ghettos de Bruxelles', *Le Soir*, 6 October.

Vandezande, V. (2011), 'Do feelings of discrimination explain the riots in Brussels? A comparison of Moroccan and Turkish groups in Brussels and Antwerp', *Brussels Studies*, 47: 7, <https://lirias.kuleuven.be/handle/123456789/305412> (last accessed 16 March 2013).

Van Heuckelom, K. (2014), 'Changing sides. East/west travesties in Lionel Baier's *Comme des voleurs (à l'est)*', in M. Gott and T. Herzog (eds), *East, West and Centre: Re-framing Contemporary European Cinema*, Edinburgh: Edinburgh University Press, pp. 37–50.

Van Hoeij, B. (2010), *10 Réalisateurs, 10 Ans de Cinéma Belge Francophone – Les Années 2000*, Brussels: Ministère de la Communauté Française de Belgique Service général de l'Audiovisuel et des Multimédias.

Vavasseur, P. (2014), 'La route, c'est le miroir de notre société', *Le Parisien*, 9 April.

Verstraete, G. (2010), *Tracking Europe: Mobility, Diaspora, and the Politics of Location*, Durham, NC: Duke University Press.

Viard, J. (2006), *Éloge de la mobilité*, Paris: Editions de L'Aube.

Viard, J. (2011), *Nouveau portrait de la France: La société des modes de vie*, Paris: Editions de L'Aube.

Vincendeau, G. (2000), *Stars and Stardom in French Cinema*, London: Bloomsbury.

Vincendeau, G. (2005), *La haine*, Urbana and Chicago: University of Illinois Press.

Vivier, H. (2007), 'Car tel est notre bon plaisir: un regard belge sur la "Sérénissime République de la France . . ."', in K. E. Bitar and R. Fadel (eds), *Regards sur la France*, Paris: Seuil, pp. 248–55.

Wagstaff, P. (2007), 'Remapping regionalism', in M. Demossier (ed.), *The European Puzzle: The Political Structuring of Cultural Identities at a Time of Transition*, New York: Berghahn.

Ward, S. (2012), '"Danger zones": The British "road movie" and the liminal landscape', in H. Andrews and L. Roberts (eds), *Liminal Landscapes: Travel, Experience and Spaces In-between*, New York: Routledge, pp. 185–99.

Weil, P. (2005), *La république et sa diversité: Immigration, intégration, discrimination*, Paris: Seuil.

Wieviorka, M. (1999), 'Le Multiculturalisme, Solution ou Formulation d'un problème?', in P. Dewitte (ed.), *Immigration et intégration, l'état des savoirs*, Paris: La Découverte, pp. 418–25.

Williams, J. S. (2013), *Space and Being in Contemporary French Cinema*, Manchester: Manchester University Press.

Windisch, U. (2004), 'Beyond multiculturalism', in T. Judt and D. Lacorn (eds), *Language, Nation, and State: Identity Politics in a Multilingual Age*, New York: Palgrave Macmillan, pp. 161–84.

Wood, J. (2007), *100 Road Movies*, London: British Film Institute.
Yuval-Davis, N. (1999), 'The "multi-layered citizen"', *International Feminist Journal of Politics*, 1: 1, 119–36.

INDEX

EU Authorised Representative:

Easy Access System Europe Mustamäe tee 50, 10621 Tallinn, Estonia

gpsr.requests@easproject.com

Printed and bound by CPI Group (UK) Ltd, Croydon, CR0 4YY

22/05/2026

02116342-0004